THE VOLUMES OF TRUTH
By YAHUSHUA-YAHUWAH
Through His Servant, Timothy

Heed the sound of this Trumpet,
For this is indeed The Trumpet Call of God!

VOLUMES ONE THROUGH SIX

THE VOLUMES OF TRUTH
By YAHUSHUA-YAHUWAH
Through His Servant, Timothy
Copyright © 2004-2018. All Rights Reserved.
ISBN 978-0-359-12035-2

Thus says The Lord
To everyone who hears or
Looks upon the words of this Book:

If anyone adds to these words,
I will add to them the punishments
Written in this Book.

And if anyone takes anything
Away from the words in the Book
Of this prophecy, I will take away
Their share in The Tree of Life
And The Holy City, as it is written.

For as I am, so shall I be;
As I have spoken, so I speak;
And that which was written by
My prophets of old remains standing,
Even to this day.

I AM THE LORD.

TABLE OF CONTENTS
VOLUME ONE

TABLE OF CONTENTS
VOLUME ONE

TABLE OF CONTENTS
VOLUME ONE

TABLE OF CONTENTS
VOLUME TWO

TABLE OF CONTENTS
VOLUME TWO

TABLE OF CONTENTS
VOLUME TWO

TABLE OF CONTENTS
VOLUME THREE

TABLE OF CONTENTS
VOLUME THREE

TABLE OF CONTENTS
VOLUME THREE

TABLE OF CONTENTS
VOLUME FOUR

TABLE OF CONTENTS
VOLUME FOUR

TABLE OF CONTENTS
VOLUME FOUR

TABLE OF CONTENTS
VOLUME FIVE

TABLE OF CONTENTS
VOLUME FIVE

TABLE OF CONTENTS
VOLUME FIVE

TABLE OF CONTENTS
VOLUME SIX

TABLE OF CONTENTS
VOLUME SIX

TABLE OF CONTENTS
VOLUME SIX

VOLUME ONE

8/31/04 **From The Lord, Our God and Savior**
The Word of The Lord Spoken to Timothy
For Timothy, and For All Those Who Have Ears to Hear
Chosen By God

Thus says The Lord to His servant: Many things you must overcome in the years ahead; many things will I show you, many things will I teach you. And though you feel weak and helpless, as a young child struggling to gain his feet, I will strengthen you, for I am with you. For the years draw short, Timothy, and soon all things must come to pass. Therefore be steadfast, My son; strengthen your faith, and I shall make you an immovable stone for My name. For I am your God, and you are one of My chosen sons of the Gentiles, for the Gentiles, living in their midst... *Grafted into The Vine, of the branch of Levi, adopted son of Abraham, says The Lord.*

10/6/04 **From The Lord, Our God and Savior**
The Word of The Lord Spoken to Timothy
For All Those Who Have Ears to Hear
Honor Not the Day of the Dead... Honor God

This question was asked of The Lord: Lord, is celebrating Halloween OK?

[The Lord answered] In regards to the day in which your land celebrates "the Day of the Dead," those who hear not, speak not, think not nor pray, for all their thoughts have perished with them, I say this: To honor this day is to honor nothing, and is contemptible. And to honor death and darkness is to cast your lot with satan; it is to partake in the works of demons... *I am The Light and The Life! Honor Me!*
So again, I say to you, do not do it! In no way make for yourself images of the dead. Do not buy or sell such things, nor decorate your house; carve no image, nor adorn yourself or your children with these symbols. Rather celebrate autumn and its splendor, and give thanks; offer up praises to The Lord your God, for all creation declares My name.
Beloved, I created autumn so all may partake of My brushstrokes, and know I am God, and give Me glory. For My splendor is written in the leaves of the trees. It is carried upon the wind, as it moves through the tall grasses. It soars high above on the wings of eagles, yet remains as near as the fragile flower at your feet. Behold, everywhere you look, the hand of God is clearly seen.

Therefore, be separate from the world and its evil ways;
Stand apart from the corrupt traditions of men,
And delight no more in those things I hate...

For as it is written:
The highway of the upright is to depart from evil;
And he who watches his step preserves his life...

Says The Lord.

10/7/04 **From The Lord, Our God and Savior**
The Word of The Lord Spoken to Timothy
For Timothy and His Wife
And For All Those Who Have Ears to Hear
Christmas

This question was asked of The Lord: Lord, what is your will for us regarding Christmas this year?

[The Lord answered] Timothy and Beloved, I tell you this: Let your hearts guide you, for on them have I written many things, and will continue to do so. Yea, even greater things will I reveal to you in the days to come. Then shall you be changed, from that which is perishable to that which is imperishable, your innermost desire realized.

As for this holiday called Christmas, you must forsake it. For on this day, The Son of Man did not come into the world by way of water and blood; neither shall My people worship Me in this way. Yet of Messiah's birth, you may indeed remember it with your family, for it was the beginning of your salvation. For where there was once only darkness, behold, a great light has appeared! Therefore, blessed are those who worship with gratitude, giving thanks for the birth of My Son. Even more blessed are those who worship and give thanks for His death and resurrection.

Yet woe to those who associate the name of The Son of God with pagan practices and idolatrous traditions! YOU HAVE SURELY TAKEN THE NAME OF THE LORD IN VAIN!

Woe to all who celebrate this holiday called Christmas, for you do dishonor Me by all you say and do! For this season of so-called giving is detestable in My sight! ABOMINATION! IDOLATRY! Woe to all who ignore My warnings and break My Commandments! YOU ARE ALL SLAVES! You have made mammon your master, materialism has bound you in chains, for you want no part with Me as I truly am! Behold, from you My spirit is far removed, for you have surely made yourselves enemies of God! I tell you the truth, the day is coming and is already here, when the quality of each man's work shall be tried and the faith of every self-proclaimed believer tested! For the Day of The Lord shall surely declare it!

Know you not, that to imitate The Messiah is righteousness?! My people, you were to walk in His ways! Yet you have made of Him a mockery! How long shall you cleave to the harlot?! How long shall you walk in her ways?! My people, come out of her, and touch no more the unclean thing!

For I tell you the truth, to replace Christ,
Or to associate His name with sin, is to
Partake in that which is called antichrist!...

And to honor The Messiah with pagan customs and
Filthy traditions is to take the name of The Lord in vain!...

DESECRATION! BLASPHEMY!

I know many in this world celebrate this holiday in ignorance of its origins, yet it is an abomination to Me, pagan practices and idolatrous traditions which I loathe in My zeal!

7

Therefore, woe to those who willfully walk in ignorance! And woe, even three times woe, to those who knowingly place their stamp of approval on these things, doing so in The Messiah's name; yours shall be a most bitter place, your discipline severe! Woe to all who knowingly lead others into rebellion against The Lord, for the mouth of Sheol is open and ready to receive you! Beloved ones, worship Me as I am and not as you would have Me be! Obey MY voice! Depart from every form of evil and tear down every whitewashed wall of abomination! CHURCHES OF MEN, STOP TWISTING THE SCRIPTURES TO UPHOLD YOUR OWN WAY! Be separate from this world, and no more endorse those things I hate! Again, I say, be separate and come out from among them, and repent! Return to Me, in spirit and in truth, and in the day I stretch out My hand against the inhabitants of the earth, you shall surely be gone from this place, says The Lord.

So then, My beloved servants, share your gifts: *Lift up the poor and help the needy, give drink to the thirsty and feed the hungry, share My love and wash each other's feet.* Yet no longer be a friend of this world, and no more walk in the ways of the churches of men, for they have not known Me.

Be set apart! Rejoice and give thanks!...

Honor The Messiah in spirit and in truth,
And walk closely in His example;
Testify of Him, from His birth to His passion;
Glorify His name in all the earth!...

For HE is the true gift, says The Lord.

This question was asked of The Lord: Lord, what do you say about the modern Christmas?

[The Lord answered] Though you ask of Me once again, Timothy, concerning this holiday which I hate, this season which the people in your land, even in many lands, mistakenly refer to as Christmas, I will not press down upon you the many cups filled to overflowing with My indignation. For you haven't the paper or strength of hand to write it. I AM THE LORD.

10/16/04 **From The Lord, Our God and Savior**
The Word of The Lord Spoken to Timothy
For All Those Who Have Ears to Hear
**Wisdom Regarding Those Who Killed The Messiah,
   Who Is Called Christ**

Thus says The Lord: Those who say the Jews killed The Messiah
speak rightly. For I know all the works of men, and in that day
did I harden their hearts to accomplish My purpose. For in the
days of Abraham, even unto Moses, did I establish My people as
the chosen to give sacrifice for the cleansing of sin... *Behold, I
gave unto them My Only Begotten Son, The Lamb without spot
or blemish, that all written by the prophets should be fulfilled in
The Son of Man.*
Yet to those who cry, *"But the Romans crucified The Christ, not
the Jews,"* I say this: You lack understanding, and do not know that
which was foretold by the prophets and written in the Scriptures
of Truth. For the Romans did indeed crucify Him, and His blood
is on their hands, even as it was on the hammer which drove the
nails. Yet I ask you, are the Romans liken unto the hammer, or he
who forged the hammer? Whose guilt is greater, he who holds the
hammer, or he who had placed the hammer in his hand? Most
assuredly, I say to you, both are guilty! But woe to those who
forged the hammer and placed it in his hand! Theirs is the greater
sin! For they denied The Holy and Innocent One, reviling Him,
and instead asked for the murderer to be set free! THEY KILLED
THE AUTHOR OF LIFE!

Yet those of greater wisdom know all are guilty, for all have sinned and fall short of the Glory of God; there is none righteous, no, not one. And for this reason YahuShua The Messiah was sent to die for all men, thereby freeing mankind from the chains which held him captive, loosing him from the bonds which bound him to the punishment of sin, which is death.

So then as The Messiah was crucified,
And died, and is risen, so too must you
Crucify your life of old...

Who you were must perish,
Along with your sinful ways,
Then shall you truly be born again...

Revived and restored in The Image of God.

10/17/04 **From The Lord, Our God and Savior**
The Word of The Lord Spoken to Timothy
For Timothy, and For All Those Who Have Ears to Hear
Humility and The Word of God

Thus says The Lord to His servant: I have bestowed upon you many gifts, and that which was given the twelve shall be yours also. So then, you shall go out and you shall come in. And like the twelve, I shall be with you, and you shall speak on My behalf. Yes, you shall surely testify and give Me glory in the sight and hearing of men; yea, even greater things shall you do. Behold, even as the prophets of old, you shall go out and you shall come in. For I shall rise up within you, and you shall write My words and give a shout, and blow the Trumpet.

> *Thus it is not by some new wisdom*
> *You shall write, but the wisdom of old,*
> *That which was and is and has always been,*
> *The same and unchanging,*
> *The Everlasting Word of God...*
>
> *Established...*
>
> *Even before the foundation of the world...*
>
> *For I AM, and My Word the same.*

Therefore, as blades of grass are beset with dew in the cool of the night, even till the morning, so shall I beset you with My words; each word a glistening drop from Heaven, every letter a shining jewel. Through you shall I set all these crooked paths straight, preparing My way before Me. Indeed, I shall reveal Myself to many, and by this Word, which I shall cause you to write, shall they begin to see Me as I truly am.

Yet take care, Timothy, lest your mind betray you, and you unwittingly take My words to yourself. For though I have indeed appointed you a prophet, setting you over nations and over kingdoms, to root out and to pull down, to destroy and to throw down, to build and to plant, never forget your station: *You are a servant, of both God and man.* Behold, you shall be for Me a mouthpiece, through whom I shall make My plans known, for I do not change. Therefore, do not cease from humbling yourself before Me. I am your strength.

10/20/04 **From The Lord, Our God and Savior**
The Word of The Lord Spoken to Timothy
For His Wife, and For All Those Who Have Ears to Hear
God Is The Fosterer and Protector of Those
   Tossed Away in Bitter Ignorance

Timothy asked this question of The Lord, for his wife: Lord, should My wife write a letter about abortion to her friends and family?

[The Lord answered] Write these words, Timothy, to your wife: Beloved, your aims are both admirable and righteous, and in this you do honor Me. For these things weigh heavily upon My heart also; behold, the cup of the wrath of My fury has come to the full on account of that which I see!

Thus to these nations and peoples who murder My precious created ones, My very gifts to men and women, I say this: You also will I abort! Behold, I shall tear you in pieces and cut your lives short! For as it is written: *It would be better for you if a millstone were hung around your neck, and you were drowned in the depths of the sea, than to suffer My wrath over these little ones!* Therefore, I call all those whose guilt rises to heaven, to repent with all their heart, to repent in sackcloth and ashes.

So then shine forth, O child of Zion, stand firm. Defend the helpless, speak on the behalf of those who have no speech, uphold the cause of those who are yet unseen. For it is I who formed them, it is I who caused them to be.

For I tell you the truth, these little ones know The Kingdom of Heaven already, and will return with The King at the time appointed. For The Kingdom of God belongs to all such as these, says The Lord.

Blessed be the name of The One
Who is, and was, and is forevermore,
The Fosterer and Protector of those
Tossed away in bitter ignorance!

Timothy asked this question of The Lord, for his wife: Lord, what should My wife include in the letter?

[*The Lord answered*] Beloved, do all you have conceived in your heart to do, and make The Commandment known, saying, *"YOU SHALL NOT KILL!"* Include also the words of The Son of Man concerning the little ones, and how I made them pure and blameless, gifts from God. For I tell you the truth, the day is coming quickly, whether they believe or believe not, when all must stand in judgment and give an account. For LIFE IS, before its very conception, says The Lord.

10/24/04 **From The Lord, Our God and Savior**
The Word of The Lord Spoken to Timothy
For Timothy, and For All Those Who Have Ears to Hear
Belong to The Church Without Walls

Thus says The Lord: When those who call of themselves Christian, ask you, *"To which church do you belong?"* You shall answer them: *"I belong to no church named of men. I belong to The Lord, YahuShua HaMashiach, whom you call Jesus and Christ. And together with all those who remain in His love[1] and obey His voice[2] is The Church in which I dwell."*

1. John 15:10
2. John 3:36

16

10/28/04 From The Lord, Our God and Savior
The Word of The Lord Spoken to Timothy
For All Those Who Have Ears to Hear
Sex

Thus says The Lord: When lying together, remember the decrees of God concerning these things of sex and intimacy: You shall not lie with another outside of marriage; even sex before marriage, called fornication, is adultery. Do not think of others while lying with your spouse; this is adultery of the heart. You shall not lie with your wife during her monthly shedding of blood. You shall not behold sexual sin with your eyes, nor partake of any form of pornography, for to do so is to sin with them; this too is adultery. You shall perform no unnatural acts, nor shall you partake in sodomy[1]. And no man or woman, in all creation, shall lie with another of their same gender! This is abomination in the eyes of The Most High God and filled with blasphemy!

For I gave unto man woman,
From his side did I form her,
And he who was one became two...

And behold, the two became one again
In marriage, two of one flesh,
Man and woman...

And I saw that it was very good.

1. *Genesis 19:4-5*

17

10/29/04 **From The Lord, Our God and Savior**
The Word of The Lord Spoken to Timothy
For Timothy, and For All Those Who Have Ears to Hear
What's In a Name

Thus says The Lord to His servant: Timothy, both your earthly father and his namesake are no more. For even your earthly father shall be given a new name, if he so chooses, in the Day of Reckoning. Therefore, from this day onward you shall be called Timothy, he who honors God. And all who walk this path with you should refer to you as such. For you shall number your steps before Me, seeking always to do that which is right and good in My eyes. I AM THE LORD.

Yet those who withstand you and persecute you on account of My words, all these hypocrites who have come out to fight against you and slander your name, shall all be made to fall at your feet in the day I send you. Then they will know, I AM THE LORD, and I Myself have loved you. For in that day you shall go out and you shall come in, and bring glory to My name.

Yet you ask, *"What's in a name? It has no power."* Timothy, you speak in ignorance. For The Name, the name above all names, is YAHUWAH. And there is only one name under Heaven by which you must be saved. And oh how blessed are those who put their trust in Him.

Behold, My name has weight and power!...

And in the day I cause My name to resound
In all the earth, My enemies shall fear
And the multitudes shall tremble!
Lo, many shall be cut to the heart in that day!...

Yet blessed is the man whose name
Is written in The Book of Life;
For he shall inherit everlasting life,
And his name shall endure forever...

Says The Lord.

10/31/04 From YahuShua HaMashiach, Our Lord and Savior
The Word of The Lord Spoken to Timothy
For All Those Who Have Ears to Hear
And He Shall Be Called I AM

I am The I AM...

I am The Lord Your God.
I am Immanu El.
I am The Lord Your Righteousness.
I am The Anointed One.
I am The Messiah.
I am The Only God and Savior.
I am The Holy One of Israel.
I am The Glorious One on High.
I am The Star Out of Jacob.
I am The Everlasting Light of the World.
I am The One Who Is and Was and Is to Come.
I am The Almighty.
I am The One Who Reigns Forever.
I am The Kingdom.
I am The Power.
I am The Glory.
I am The Only Lord of Hosts.
I am The Source of Life.
I am The Creator.
I am The Maker of All Things.
I am He by Whom All Things Consist.
I am The Breath of Life.
I am Eternal Life.
I am The Passover.
I am Your Sacrifice.

I am The Lamb of God.
I am Your Ransom.
I am The Firstfruits of Those Who Have Fallen Asleep.
I am The Firstborn from the Dead.
I am He Who Died and Is Alive Forevermore.
I am The Resurrection and The Life.
I am He Who Ascended on High.
I am He Who Led Captivity Captive.
I am The Bestower of Gifts.
I am Your Salvation.
I am The Horn of Salvation.
I am God's Salvation, YahuShua.
I am The Loving Mercy of God.
I am The Gift.
I am The Redeemer.
I am The Mediator.
I am Your Advocate.
I am Your High Priest.
I am The Keeper of My Saints.
I am The Lover of Souls.
I am The Song of Your Heart.
I am Your Tears of Joy.
I am The Nectar of Life.
I am He Who Loved You Before
    the Foundation of the World.
I am He Through Whom You Were Made.
I am Your Father.
I am Your Protector.
I am Your Rearguard.
I am Your Strength.
I am The Guardian of Your Soul.
I am The Author;
I am also The Finisher.

I am The Wisdom.
I am The Word of God.
I am The Answer You Search For.
I am The Truth You Seek.
I am The Only Truth, The Truth Absolute.
I am The Faithful and True Witness.
I am The Sower;
I am also The Reaper.
I am The Dayspring.
I am The Water of Life;
I am also Your Bread, The Very Manna from Heaven.
I am The Savior.
I am The Risen One.
I am The Bright and Morning Star.
I am The Fulfillment of The Law.
I am The Goal at Which The Torah Aims.
I am The Fulfillment of All Things.
I am The Reward.
I am Holy.
I am The Mercy Seat;
I am also Wrath and Justice.
I am He Who Searches the Hearts and Minds.
I am The Righteous Judge.
I am The Son of Man.
I am The Cornerstone.
I am The Rock.
I am The Tree;
I am also The Branch.
I am The Son of David.
I am The Shepherd.
I am The Gate for My Sheep.
I am The Master.
I am The Good Teacher.

I am The Voice of Truth.

I am The Day Star Who Arises in the Hearts of Men.

I am Your Heart's Desire.

I am The Beloved.

I am The Bridegroom.

I am The Love That Never Fades.

I am The Holy Presence.

I am the Spirit.

I am the Helper.

I am The Counselor.

I am The Inspiration.

I am The Still Small Voice.

I am The Hope.

I am The Healer.

I am The Sanctuary.

I am The Firstborn Over All Creation.

I am He Who Sits at The Right Hand of God.

I am The Face of God.

I am The Image of The Invisible God.

I am The Son of God.

I am The One Who Has the Seven-fold Spirit of God.

I am The Holder of the Book of Life.

I am The One Who Has the Key of David.

I am He Who Opens Doors No One Can Shut.

I am The One Who Holds the Keys of Death and Sheol.

I am The Authority.

I am The Mighty and Strong One.

I am The Strong One of Jacob.

I am The Lion of the Tribe of Judah.

I am The Warrior of God Who Needs No Weapon.

I am The One with the Double-Edged
    Sword in His Mouth.

I am He Who Sits on the White Horse.

I am He Who Is Coming on the Clouds.
I am He Who Will Shine from the East unto the West.
I am He Who Holds the Seven Stars in His Right Hand.
I am He Whose Eyes Are Like Flames of Fire.
I am He Who Wears the Golden Sash.
I am He Who Holds the Iron Scepter.
I am King of Kings.
I am Lord of Lords.
I am The First and The Last.
I am Lord Over Heaven and Earth.
I am The In All, Be All, of Existence.
I am The Meaning of Life.
I am The True Vine.
I am The Fountain of Living Waters.
I am The Restoration of All Things.
I am The Prince of Peace.
I am The Amen.

I am The Way.
I am The Truth.
I am The Life.

I am YahuShua HaMashiach.
I am for you, and you for Me.

I am The All in All.

I AM.

11/15/04 **From The Lord, Our God and Savior**
The Word of The Lord Spoken to Timothy
For All Those Who Have Ears to Hear
(Regarding the state of the dead)
Death and Awakening

Thus says The Lord: All people sleep in death, both those who have done good and those who have done evil. In no way are they among the living, nor are they aware. They know nothing at all, for all their thoughts have perished with them. All remain at rest, until the day I call them to awake; some to the first, the resurrection of life, and many more to the second, the resurrection of judgment. Blessed and holy are those who take part in the first resurrection. For over them the second death has no power, as it is written.

You have heard it said:
To be absent from the body
Is to be present with The Lord...

This saying is true...

For all those who die in Messiah will
Indeed look upon Him at the Last Day,
Yet it will be to them as the blink of an eye...

For the dead know not the passage of time,
Nor do they know they have fallen asleep...

Thus there is indeed life after death,
Yet during death there is most certainly not.

For I tell you the truth, if there is life during death, as it is commonly taught amongst the people, then none truly die. And if all have the victory over death, then all are like The Messiah; thereby making The New Covenant useless and the resurrection of no effect. This teaching is false, denying both the sacrifice of The Messiah and the Word of God. For if none truly die, then The Messiah is no longer the firstfruits of those who have fallen asleep. And if He is not the first to be freed from death and the grave, then The Messiah did not die. And if The Messiah did not die, then the power of sin has the victory and the grave has become your final resting place, leaving you with no hope of salvation.

Yet the Scriptures do not lie. The wages of sin is death; from the beginning, I declared it! And yet the churches continue to stand divided against themselves, corrupting My Word as they fall in line with satan, deceiving and being deceived, preaching, *"You will not surely die[1]*,"* teaching that which runs contrary to the Scriptures.

Therefore, hear the Word of The Lord, O foolish and deceived generation: If as you say, there is no death and all continue on as living spirits, whether it be in Heaven or in hell or in some other place, then you also say there is no God and no Savior who was sent to save you from the penalty of sin, which is death.

Where then does that leave you? You are lost, a people without hope, multitudes of deceived people waiting for their own inevitable destruction, a creation wrought in vain! Yet The Messiah did indeed pay the penalty for your sins, even unto death... *He is risen, The Firstborn from the dead; by which you are also delivered from death, if you so choose to receive of His life, if you so choose to embrace Him as He truly is!*

For He alone will stretch out His hand
In that day, and lift His beloved from
The grave in which all must sleep,
Save those who remain awake
At His coming, as it is written...

And behold, the time is indeed coming,
When all who are in the grave will hear
His voice and come out...

Those who have done good,
To the resurrection of life...

And those who have done evil,
To the resurrection of judgment...

I AM THE LORD.

1. Genesis 3:4

11/17/04 **From YahuShua HaMashiach, Our Lord and Savior**
The Word of The Lord Spoken to Timothy
For All Those Who Have Ears to Hear
Regarding the Celebration of Christmas

Thus says The Lord: Most assuredly, I say to you, any and all rituals which are rooted in paganism are an abomination in the eyes of God! And all who place My name upon them, or do them by permission in My name, have surely taken the name of The Lord in vain!

I know many say they celebrate this holiday in loving memory of My earthly birth, yet on this day I did not come into the world by way of water and blood. For that day and hour remains unknown to you, nor do you understand. For you cast off knowledge, and refuse to honor the appointed times which The Father commanded you to keep holy and remember. Thus My people are indeed destroyed for lack of knowledge, as it is written.

How long shall you mar My image before the people?!
How long shall My name be blasphemed
Because of you, O churches of men?!...

How long shall you commit adultery with the
Harlot and revel in the idolatries of the pagan?!
How long shall you remain married to this world
And all its fornications against God?!...

Again I tell you, ALL religions, religious rituals
And celebrations, rooted deeply in paganism,
Are an abomination in the eyes of The Most High God!

Well did My servant Sha'ul (also known as Paul) prophesy of you, saying: *In the latter days some will depart from the faith, giving heed to deceiving spirits and doctrines of demons, speaking lies in hypocrisy, having their consciences seared as with a hot iron.* And well did he prophesy of this generation, saying: *Men will be lovers of themselves, lovers of money, boasters, proud blasphemers, disobedient to parents, unthankful, unholy, unloving, unforgiving, slanderers, without self-control, brutal, despisers of good, traitors, headstrong, haughty, lovers of pleasure rather than lovers of God, having a form of godliness but denying the power thereof.*

Therefore, woe to all who celebrate this detestable holiday of men! Woe, I say to you! And three times woe, to all who do so in MY name! Hypocrites! Workers of idolatry! You are a perverse people who do always take the name of The Lord in vain! Yet I hear you saying, *"But we only seek to honor You, Lord, in any and all ways."* Yet I ask you, how can we be one if your heart belongs to another? And how does reveling in those things I hate honor Me? I tell you the truth, all who love this world more than Me are not worthy of Me! And all who honor the ways of the harlot dishonor Me and shall share in her judgment! And ALL, who revel in the ways of the pagan, have cast their lot with satan! Or have you never read these Scriptures: *You can not drink the cup of The Lord and the cup of demons; you can not partake of The Lord's table and of the table of demons?!*

Indeed, what do all these things have to do with Me? Why do you decorate the tree? Is it not beautiful as it is? And why do you decorate your house? A household, which seeks to honor Me, has no need of worldly decorations. For in humility, set apart, shall you shine forth.

And why do you give worldly gifts in My name? Am I not The Gift, He who ascended on high, He who led captivity captive and gave gifts to men? Therefore receive of Me, of all I offer, and be separate. For in following My ways do you give gifts to Me and to each other, even to all those around you, for the gifts I bring endure forever.

Therefore, again I ask you, what matter these things of the world and men, which shall soon pass away? Yet you say, *"All these things are a metaphor and a testament to You, Lord."* Yet I tell you, anything which comes from sin *is sin*; do not do it! Tear down all these whitewashed walls of abomination, and do only as The Word of God instructs! For the season of giving is each and every day, and the season of love is every day, every hour, every minute, every moment of your life lived in Me. So then, share My gifts and withhold not; lift up the poor in spirit and feed the hungry, help the needy and comfort the sick, doing so in My name. Yet do not do as the pagans do, for this is sin. Be completely separate and shun these perverse holidays of men; stop breaking My Commandments!

You wish to celebrate My name and My earthly birth, do so; yea, bring glory to My name by your obedience, set apart. You wish to enjoy festivals with your family, do so; I have given you seven. And in these seven is wisdom and understanding, the very mind of God, revelation beyond words, the will of God made manifest. Yet no more do as the pagans and false teachers would have you do. Cast off this holiday; throw away your tree and lights, rid your house of all decorations, turn away from these filthy traditions. Honor Me as I truly am, obey the Scriptures, and turn away from the commandments of men.

Know this: The Salvation Day of Men is four-fold...

It was ordained before the foundation
Of the world, fulfilled at My birth,
Finished at My death on the cross,
And solidified eternally upon My resurrection...

I AM THE LORD.

11/19/04 **From The Lord, Our God and Savior**
The Word of The Lord Spoken to Timothy
For Timothy and His Wife
And For All Those Who Have Ears to Hear
Duty

Behold, the Spirit of The Lord is upon you. For it is written, and behold, the time has come: *In those days I will pour out My spirit, and My sons and daughters will dream dreams and prophesy.* Therefore give heed to My spirit, and also receive, for that which is revealed is of utmost importance. For I have spoken, and shall continue to speak, and that which I give you shall be written in a book, says The Lord.

Thus I shall speak to you, Timothy, and you shall write My words, and you together with your wife shall place them in My Book. For I have called you to be a prophet, as in the days of old; and you, Beloved, shall be his scribe. Thus you shall receive of the Truth and blow this Trumpet, you shall dream dreams and prophesy. For you are two of one flesh. Therefore as one you shall serve Me, and together you shall accomplish My will.
As Baruch served Jeremiah, so shall you, Beloved, serve your husband, handling all affairs unique to your office. And as I called Jeremiah, so have I called you, Timothy. From your birth, I set you apart for My purpose; yea, before your formation in the womb, I appointed you a prophet. And in like manner have I set you over nations and over kingdoms, to root out and to pull down, to destroy and to throw down, to build and to plant.

Therefore, Beloved, listen to your husband with all attentiveness and humility, for he is the head. You together are of one body, yet Timothy is the head. For he is your husband, and he speaks for Me... *Yet I am The Head of all, even over all creation, known and unknown, Lord of Heaven and Earth.* And though he must be separated from you during the time appointed, he will not be alone, I will be with him. And he too shall come to know My dwelling place, going out and coming in, walking always in the fullness of My spirit. And this is the means by which he shall perform My will, accomplishing even all I command him. I AM THE LORD.

Timothy, I have made you a watchman for My people,
A witness, of the number, My mouthpiece,
And through you shall I make My plans known...

You shall proclaim My words aloud,
Reprove, rebuke and exhort,
And convict this generation of its evil ways;
You shall dream dreams, see visions and prophesy,
Until the day I send you into the midst of the battle...

Fear not, for greater is He who dwells within you
Than he who is in the world...

I AM THE LORD.

12/11/04 **From The Lord, Our God and Savior**
The Word of The Lord Spoken to Timothy
For All Those Who Have Ears to Hear
I Shall Correct and Discipline All Those I Love

Thus says The Lord: My children, struggle not against the principles of another, nor rebuke them with your own words, nor correct them by your own understanding. Let go of your personal notions of right and wrong, and strive to love others in spite of yourselves, and have compassion for those with whom you disagree. Do not judge them, nor shun them in your heart. Rather love those who speak against you, because you obey My Word; bless those who curse you, and pray for those who mistreat you, as it is written.

Yet have no part with them, nor give them a platform from which to proliferate their sinful ways; remain separate. For they do rebel against their God. Their argument is with Me, though it may seem as though you have become the object of their scorn. For they do always fight against Me, in an effort to justify their sins.

For I have written The Law in the hearts of all men; all are able to discern right from wrong. Thus they *choose* to rebel; they remain in their sins. For I have indeed written it, even on tablets of stone and within the heart of man, and within the pages of My Book it is made plain. Thus they are without excuse.

For I am God alone, The Righteous One. I alone am holy, just and good; I alone have divided right from wrong; I alone have established The Law and define what is sin. Behold, I expose the darkness and bring all hidden things into the light. For I alone sit as Judge, The Only Faithful and True Witness.

Therefore let it be known to you, O peoples of the earth, and to all who dwell within the churches of men: I must bring My hand against you, I must correct and discipline all those I love. For you have gone astray; behold, from Me you are far removed. And with great malice you do always persecute those I send to you, rejecting the Word given them on account of your pride, persecuting them in word and by deed, stoning some and killing others.

Therefore in My jealousy I shall speak, and in the fire of My wrath I shall rebuke you! Behold, My wrath shall come forth and My judgment shall not sleep! For I am coming down to correct, to discipline and to punish, to pour out judgment upon the whole of this wicked generation! Yet those who repent in sincerity and in truth will be delivered, and those who turn from their evil ways will be shown mercy. For I do not change, says The Lord.

Thus says The Lord: O you blind leaders of the blind, dumb people who attempt to speak to the deaf, you are lost. You fear I am coming to destroy you. I am not coming to destroy you, but to humble you, that you might be delivered from all this evil which encompasses you round about; I am coming to destroy that which stands against Me, to tear down all man has made!

> *Therefore, again I say to you, I shall surely*
> *Correct and discipline all those I love,*
> *And upon this most wicked generation*
> *Shall I pour out judgment...*

> *Yet as it is written, I will do nothing until I have*
> *Revealed My plans to My servants, the prophets...*

> *For I am The Lord, and I do not change.*

12/13/04 **From YahuShua HaMashiach, Our Lord and Savior**
The Word of The Lord Spoken to Timothy
For a Brother in Christ
And For All Those Who Have Ears to Hear
Know That Which Has Been Poured Out - The Word of God

Thus says The Lord: How is it you have not recognized that which comes from The Father? For that which is of the devil is made plain and surrounds you on every side. Therefore the things of God become that much more precious, even as you, My son, are most precious in My sight... *Like a gemstone shining in the midst of all this darkness, easily found by the eyes of God, so shall you be in the day you surrender your life, the day you give up this fight and return to Me.*

Do you not understand that I have saved you? No, not by your own works, but by My life, which I willingly gave up for you. Therefore, turn to Me wholly and in truth. And no more let the doctrines of men in the churches steal from your trust; nor let their traditions pollute your faith anymore. Be set apart from the ways of this world, and depart from the churches of men. For I alone am your faith, I alone am your completion. Therefore listen, and you will also know, for by the Spirit of God are all things revealed to the chosen. Search your heart, My son, and you will find Me; embrace My words, and you will begin to know Me.

For indeed, there are many gifts of the Spirit which I bestow upon all those who love Me, many gifts given to those who are willing to give up everything and follow Me. Thus Timothy is just one among many who hear My voice, one voice in a great chorus growing ever louder, of the number I am sending.

Yet to him did I say, *"Write that which I speak, and place it in a book"*; also commanding him to share that which the Spirit causes him to understand. For the latter is that which My people call inspired of God or inspired in the Spirit; and the former, that which the prophets hear, the voice of The Living God.

Therefore listen to Timothy, for he speaks for Me, he hears My voice. Behold, he has sat in My presence and strives to obey all I ask of him. Do not say then, nor conceive any notion within your heart, that he may be deceived by the devil. Or have you never read these Scriptures: *Every kingdom divided against itself will surely be brought to ruin, and every house divided against itself will collapse. If satan also is divided against himself, how then will his kingdom stand?*

Do men gather grapes of thorns, or figs of thistles?...

For a good tree brings forth good fruit,
But a corrupt tree brings forth evil fruit;
Neither can a corrupt tree bring forth good fruit...

And every tree that does not bring forth
Good fruit is hewn down and cast into the fire...

Thus by their fruits you shall know them.

And was I speaking only of the false prophets, or of the true also? Is it not also implied that I speak of their message? And what of all these self-appointed scholars, teachers, pastors, preachers, ministers and priests, who have set themselves up as an authority? What fruit do they bear according to the Scriptures?

Come out from among them! No longer embrace their corrupt doctrines, nor take part in their filthy traditions! Stand apart from those who mix the holy with the profane, depart from that which is covered in purple and scarlet, and no more practice that which is an abomination in the eyes of God! For it is the humble, penitent man who hears God, one who is willing to give up his life in this world for My sake.

Therefore take My words to heart, and understand: Any man who shares My Word with others is My servant. And any man who hears My voice, in whose hand I have placed the Trumpet, is My prophet. Even all those I send are My apostles. And any who heed these words, and also do them, shall be called a friend of God.

Beloved, this Word, even every Volume to every Letter, is the Word of My glory which I have put forth once again; a testament of My love and sacrifice, the announcement of My coming, a proclamation of truth, revelation of who I really am - *the Trumpet Call of God, so all those called and chosen may hear and come to Me in their proper time and season.*

Behold, it is also a strong correction for all those who have taken to themselves MY name and MY Word, to pollute it, a plumb line for this wicked generation. For this Word is a waving banner, an ensign to all nations! - *A trumpet of alarm and war, the sound of recompense and judgment, which shall soon fall upon every nation!*

For I AM WHO I AM!
The Only Begotten of The Father,
The One True God and Savior, The Mashiach!...

YAHUSHUA-YAHUWAH!

12/23/04 **From The Lord, Our God and Savior**
The Word of The Lord Spoken to Timothy
For All Those Who Have Ears to Hear
Run From the Forest and Loose All That Binds You

Timothy, write as I speak. For the time has come, and is already upon you, when the children of God must be cleansed and set apart for My glory, says The Lord. Yet today the sanctified will be lashed, and the wicked uplifted. And tomorrow evil shall come in, allowed only for a short season, that My people may be tested and the multitudes divided, a sifting of the wheat for the harvest; some to the first, while many others left to the second, with all tares burned in the fire; those on My right to everlasting life, and those on My left to everlasting punishment. Even so, amen.

For Salvation had come and has remained in the midst of you, even from the beginning, freely offered to all people since the time of Immanu El on earth. Yet the people refuse to see, nor will they listen; their eyes are blinded, their ears deaf. For the nations have no love for the Truth, for they barter for falsehoods and set up their exchange upon lies. They are lost, wandering aimlessly in a forest without hope, amongst many tall trees of abomination, with darkness and deceit on every side.
Yet those who have received eyes to see, see the way ahead clearly and without obstruction, and follow it. And those who have received ears to hear, hear the Truth and obey it. For the way of the upright is well lit, it is not at all hidden, though the men of this world cease not from trying to cover it.

Yet the more they strive to push it down, hide it by force and cover it over, the greater will it shine forth... *Bursting forth from its hold, filling the entire earth, devouring all darkness in its path and transforming all things in its wake!*

Behold, the time has come! The Day is very near!...

The Thief shall enter the house
And steal away all who are not tied down,
Fastened, or shackled to the house...

And all those in whom He sees of Himself
Shall surely be gone from this place!...

Says The Lord.

12/25/04 **From YahuShua HaMashiach, Our Lord and Savior**
The Word of The Lord Spoken to Timothy
For a Brother in Christ, and For All Those Who Have Ears to Hear
Seek The Lord and He Will Open The Way

Thus says The Lord: It is written: *Ask, and it will be given you; seek, and you shall find; knock, and it will be opened to you.* My son, I am The Answer you search for, I am The Truth you seek. Therefore, he who abides in Me shall reside in the presence of The Almighty, and shall be given knowledge and receive understanding. Thus those who remain void of the Spirit must continually seek Me, and they too shall find Me, for I have written all in My Book. Yet those who read the Word of The Lord must also believe it, or how shall they know Me? For those who truly know Me seek to abide in My love. Yet how can one remain in My love, if they do not obey My teaching? For My grace descends upon all who repent in sincerity and in truth, and My spirit dwells within those who keep The Commandments and testify to My glory. Therefore, My son, receive of Me; then will that which you seek become clear. For your heart's true desire can not be found in the world... *Seek God!*

Again I say to you, search not in the world,
For there you will not find Me;
Nor seek Me in the churches of men,
For there you will not find Me...

For I tell you the truth,
The Kingdom of God is within you...

And that which is most needful, is it not written for you?

Therefore, do not place your trust in any man, nor lean upon man's invention, for the things of this world deceive you. Beloved, turn away from those who teach as doctrine the commandments of men, and stand apart from all this modern ideology, for it is poison. Close your eyes to all these images on the screen, shut your ears to the noise of this world, and separate yourself from all these mocking voices. For the evil one is, at present, the lord of the air; indeed, every corrupt seed planted within the heart of man is of the evil one.

From the beginning he was a liar, and from the beginning he planted seeds of wickedness in My garden, for it is written: *There is no truth in him. When he tells a lie, he is only doing what is natural to him, because he is a liar; indeed, he is the father of all lies.* Therefore, embrace only that which is good and comes down from your Father in Heaven. For God is love, and that which He sends is Spirit and Truth. And by these things shall you be led, even as you in like manner lead those around you, if you so choose to obey My voice and walk in My ways.

Yet remember this: Those who boast of their own works are prideful, and seek after the praises of men. Yet those who boast of The Lord's works, for your sake, are humble, and seek to honor Me; in these pride is far removed. For those who give Me glory honor Me, and those who give thanks without ceasing offer up perfect praise. To the likes of these listen closely, for their desire is righteous and their love true. Behold, they seek The Kingdom of Heaven and My righteousness, and salvation has become their companion.

Therefore, My son, do not worry because you do not have all the answers, nor be upset because you do not fully understand. For The Lord your God is Truth, even as I am The Truth. For all knowledge resides within The Father, even as I am in The Father and He is in Me. Thus I am also The Answer.

My son, trust in Me, and you shall be set free;
For it is the humble, penitent man who shall see God;
Behold, he shall look upon My face,
As I restore him in My image...

For I am the image of The Invisible God,
The perfect reflection of The Father,
The face of The Majesty from on high,
Immanu El...

Therefore open your heart to Me,
And I shall create you anew...

Says The Lord.

12/29/04 **From The Lord, Our God and Savior**
The Word of The Lord Spoken to Timothy
For All Those Who Have Ears to Hear
The Signs of the Coming of The Son of Man

Thus says The Lord: Many great signs have been given to this generation, yet all have went greatly ignored by the multitude. Yet those who are Mine have clearly seen. For those who truly know Me rejoice in the Truth and embrace My correction, and strive always to walk in My ways, glorifying My name without ceasing. For they shine like the sun at noonday, even in the height of summer.

Yet understand this,
These signs are but the first of many,
And shall continue, increasing by measure
Until the time be fulfilled...

Then shall The Son of Man appear,
Clothed in the brightness of His glory,
A brilliance which has no equal;
Even the blind shall see!

Behold, I called to the sea, saying, *"Rise up! Churn, and bring forth a terrible wind! Go ashore, increase in height and make a great noise! Blow like the voice of The Almighty and release a great deluge upon men! Move all things from their places, break apart and destroy! Cause this people to flee in fear, that they may now call upon My name!"*

And still those who dwelt near the shore did not call upon My name in sincerity, nor in truth, nor did they repent of their evil deeds. Behold, three more times did I call the sea to rise up and come ashore, causing that which had lessened to regain strength and return once again. And still the people did not awake, their eyes remained shut, their hearts hard and unyielding.

Indeed, the multitudes refuse to give Me glory! And oh how quickly they do always return to their sin, as they seek to fortify their rebellion against God. Therefore the seas shall become angry, the earth shall rumble and quake, and the waves shall continue to crash before the Great and Terrible Day of The Lord! Behold, even the powers of heaven shall be shaken, and the world shall seek to become one, as it is written.

Yet I tell you, there is a sign greater than these. For all creation obeys My voice; from the deepest depths to the highest peaks, to the rocks which lay upon the ground; from the multitudes of insects to the animals of the field and those which fly above; from the waters of the sea to every living creature which dwells within them, great and small; from the winds of heaven to the stars above, all creation obeys the voice of The Almighty.

Yet with man it is not so. For the heart of man remains hard and unyielding, and oh how he sets his ways in stone. For in his arrogance, he refuses to listen to the Word of God, nor will he accept My correction. And because of his pride he remains unwilling to heed the call of The Most High. Yet I tell you the truth, that which is made of stone shall break! And that which refuses to be broken shall be crushed beneath the weight of The Cornerstone!

Yet that which is laid atop it shall be broken and refashioned, made new. Thus a heart made new in The Lord is the greatest sign of all.

For the whole earth is set under My authority, obeying My will without question. Whether upon the land or in the sea, or in the heavens above, all things obey the voice of The Living God, save man. For to him alone did I give the will to choose. And what is life without love? And what is love without the free will to choose love? I tell you the truth, a gift commanded is no gift at all! Yet a gift accepted is where you shall find life, love and salvation.

Behold, all shall be moved from their places, that the eyes of the prideful might be opened and the ears of the arrogant unstopped, that all might repent and return to Me! Therefore watch! For the time has come for the will of God to be made manifest, for the earth to tremble and quake, to spew its fervent heat! Now is the time for signs in the heavens above and in the earth beneath, for the judgments of God to be poured out, for the wrath of God to fall from Heaven!

Therefore, come out from among them,
And take refuge in Me...

For I am your only shelter,
Your only sanctuary from the storm...

Says The Holy One of Israel.

12/30/04 **From The Lord, Our God and Savior**
The Word of The Lord Spoken to Timothy
For Timothy, and For All Those Who Have Ears to Hear
(Regarding the Indonesian tsunami)
Make Way For The Coming of The Lord

Thus says The Lord to His servant: Timothy, hear My words and write, receive My words and have understanding. For My words are truth, a gift for those who give heed, a blessing for those who walk in them, bringing peace to the hearts of all who believe.
My son, I know your pain, I feel your anguish. Yet you need not shed tears over these little ones who were swept away, for they have returned home. They dwell in the bosom of their Father, once again. Therefore do not be troubled, be at peace. Trust in My will, though you do not yet fully understand.

Indeed, many shall fall asleep
On account of My quaking footsteps...

For the Day draws near when I shall tread
The grapes in the winepress of the wrath of My fury,
When I shall shake the heavens and the earth,
When all at rest shall be moved from their places...

For the peoples of the earth rest in things they should not;
They lie down in perverse traditions, and give themselves
To the abominations of the pagan and the heathen;
They put their faith in things that can not save.

47

Behold, they worship the works of their own hands, as they deny their Creator! They trust in that which is worthless, and in vain they bow down to lifeless statues and pray to graven images! FALSE GODS ABOUND! Yes, they pay homage to idols which can not grant life, neither can they take it away! There is no healing power in them, worthless images which neither speak nor hear! All is vanity and vexation of spirit, doctrines of demons! For all the religions of man are utterly useless!

Yet the people cry, *"Disaster! Death and mourning!"* Yet I say, do not mourn for the dead, for they only sleep. They abide in darkness for but an instant, for the dead know nothing at all; they know not the passage of time, nor of the seasons. They have closed their eyes to this life, yet they shall surely open them again; behold, all shall look upon the face of The Lord their Redeemer, The One who died yet is alive forevermore. Amen.

Now look upon those left, look at these who have escaped disaster and death. Their hearts have begun to change, as they cry, *"Have compassion!"* saying within themselves, *"What is this life of mine filled with all manner of material things and devices, all manner of comforts and pleasures?! None of it matters! Only LIFE is important!"* And so they cry and lament. Again, I say to you, wail not for those who have passed away, as though you had no hope, nor for the little ones, for they have returned home. For most assuredly, I say to you, by no means does death have the last word.

Therefore, thus says The Lord to the peoples of the earth: Wail for yourselves! Wail loudly for those whose hearts have become like stone! Wail for those who have eyes yet refuse to see, for those who have ears yet refuse to hear! Wail! For they know not The Kingdom of God, nor do they seek Him; they have forgotten the place from whence they came, and want no part with Him through whom they were made.

Therefore, wake up and pay attention!
Awaken out of this sleep, be shaken out
Of this slumber, and call upon My name!...

Seek out My will that you may know it;
Heed the sound of this Trumpet and prepare!...

For My Kingdom comes, and My will
Shall be done on earth as in Heaven...

Says The Lord God.

1/2/05 **From The Lord, Our God and Savior**
The Word of The Lord Spoken to Timothy
For All Those Who Have Ears to Hear
To Whom Does The Kingdom of Heaven Belong?

Thus says The Lord God: Let the truth be known regarding the innocent, My most precious gifts, My beloved little ones. When one of these little ones pass from your sight, grieve not, for they have returned home. Rather grieve for yourselves. For a precious gemstone has been taken; behold, a treasure which has no equal has been hidden before its time. For The Kingdom of Heaven belongs to all such as these. Thus these who have come forth from The Kingdom, who remain without blemish, whose lives were cut short, return to Him from whom they came. For the little ones need not sleep in death. For the penalty of sin is death, yet they remain in their innocence... *And oh how blessed are the pure in heart, for they shall surely behold My face.*

Therefore, thus says The Lord to all who have harmed or killed the little ones, and to all who stand in agreement: It would be better for you if a millstone were hung around your neck, and you were drowned in the depths of the sea, than to suffer My wrath over these little ones! FOR I HAVE SEEN IT! You have mistreated and abused them, you have murdered My gifts! And in so doing have you ripped *yourselves* from The Kingdom of Heaven!... *You are cast out! And shall remain outside the gates, unless you repent wholly and in truth, striving always to make your repentance full!*

I tell you the truth, all upon the earth
Who have gained maturity have become
So very poor and desolate...

For once you were wealthy,
Rich beyond words, for then you knew
The Kingdom of Heaven as a child...

Yet now you are grown, your light quickly fading,
As the ways of this world pull you down to the pit...

Therefore return to Me, humble and penitent,
Come to Me as a child, for by no other
Means shall you pass through...

Says The Lord.

1/3/05 **From YahuShua HaMashiach, Our Lord and Savior**
The Word of The Lord Spoken to Timothy
For All Those Who Have Ears to Hear
To He Who Has Understanding, Let Him Hear
 The Truth of the Inheritance of Sin and Salvation

Hear the Word of The Lord, all those who seek to know wisdom and receive understanding, all those who love the Truth, for thus says The Lord: I have spoken, and behold, I speak once again, that all who love the little ones may be encouraged and have peace; and so this most wicked generation may know My anger and tremble in fear.

I ask you, what is a child's inheritance on earth and in Heaven, if the years of their life be few in number and they remain in their innocence? Assuredly, I say to you, they will inherit The Kingdom of Heaven, for The Father holds the pure of heart in the palm of His right hand. For like the firefly which alights upon the tall grass, so are these little ones, precious lights shining among men.

Therefore, woe to those who catch them and shut them away! Woe to any who do them harm! AND WOE, EVEN THREE TIMES WOE, TO ALL WHO EXTINGUISH THEIR LIGHT! For behold, I am coming quickly with a shout, with the voice of the archangel and with the trumpet call of God, to remove the light, to take from the earth My own, and this world shall be plunged into darkness! For judgment shall fall from Heaven, covering the face of the earth like a flood! Behold, as a terrible deluge, punishment from on high shall break out against them and wash them away, until every last trace of evil and wickedness is utterly destroyed!

And though the little ones may suffer at the hands of men in this world, I tell you the truth, all arrive at The Father's house in a moment, in the twinkling of an eye, where healing is complete and every tear is wiped away, the ways of the world and men forgotten... *Only love abides, as they look upon the face of their Father forever.*

Yet the scholars cry, *"What of the inheritance of sin, and those born with the burden of sin upon them?"*

Listen and have understanding, humble yourselves that you may gain wisdom, and hear the Word of The Lord: All people are born as babes from their mother's womb, into a world of sin. So then, all born by way of water and blood are born *into* sin, not *of* sin.
For how can one who comes from The Kingdom of Heaven, created by the hand of God, have sin upon them? Therefore, you do greatly err. For these little ones do not yet know the ways of the world and men; they have not yet eaten from the tree of the knowledge of good and evil. They remain in their innocence.
Therefore, I ask you, who has blemished My fireflies? Who has tarnished their light? What has corrupted My gifts?! MEN AND THE WORKS OF EVIL IN THIS WORLD!

Thus these little ones, even these young ones
Corrupted by men, need not repent,
For The Son of Man died for them also...

For their cleansing is of that covenant
Which has remained unspoken and constant,
In the loving mercy of God, from the beginning...

Says The Lord.

1/13/05 **From The Lord, Our God and Savior**
The Word of The Lord Spoken to Timothy
For All Those Who Have Ears to Hear
Be Baptized in The Living Waters of Spirit and Truth

Thus says The Lord, concerning baptism: Let My beloved first be baptized in spirit and in truth, filled with the knowledge of The Holy, nourished by the Word of Truth. Let them come to Me in sincere repentance, and receive forgiveness of sins in The Messiah's name... *All burdens lifted, immersed and purified in the Spirit of God.* For The Holy One of Israel is He who baptizes with the Holy Spirit and with fire, and He knows His own.

Therefore, hear and understand: The Water of Life is not of the earth. Rather The Water of Life is that which flows from the body of Messiah. For in Him alone shall one know salvation and receive everlasting life. Therefore be baptized in the knowledge and wisdom of The Beloved. Listen to Him and walk in His ways, and you shall surely be accepted.

Tell Me, is the water of the earth able to take away your sins, or cleanse you of your transgressions? Can a river lead you to salvation or a stream call you to repentance? In what waters have you heard The Word of God speak?

Thus baptism by water can not save you. Rather salvation comes by the hearing of The Gospel, and through the confession of the mouth that YahuShua, called Jesus, is Lord; believing HE IS WHO HE IS, The Risen One - The Only Way, The Only Truth, The Only Life. For only by true repentance, in accord with the heart's desire to be in union with The Messiah, shall one be set free.

So then, go forth and be baptized in the waters of the earth, if you so desire. Yet remember this: Baptism in and of itself is nothing, unless the heart of the one being immersed has truly been converted.

> *Thus baptism is for a testimony,*
> *An exercise in faith for the*
> *One who is saved already;*
> *Or a mere dampening of the clothes*
> *Of the one who came forth in pretense...*
>
> *For I am The Lord...*
>
> *I search the hearts and minds,*
> *And I know whether or not one has*
> *Truly been converted in their heart.*

1/20/05 **From The Lord, Our God and Savior**
The Word of The Lord Spoken to Timothy
For All Those Who Have Ears to Hear
God Eternal

Behold, the judgments of God shall fall from Heaven; the sun, the moon and the stars shall not give their light; the foundations of the earth shall be shaken, and every high place shall be broken down. For The Lord comes as a thief to steal away His elect, and the judgments of God as a multitude of thunder, to shake the heavens and the earth!

Yet the multitudes say, *"What is the said interpretation of The Lord's judgment? These things are much too terrifying to be true!"*

Thus says The Lord: Behold all creation! Is it not beyond the comprehension of men? Can any man number the galaxies in the heavens or count the stars thereof? And what of the love of The Father, fulfilled through The Son? Is it not also beyond comprehension?

Come together and reason, O sons of men. Look upon the works of My hands, and see with new eyes and restored vision, that you may behold the Truth. For all the works of man are here for but a moment, then quickly pass away. And that which remains, shall it not become fuel for the fire in the Day of The Lord's Anger? And the knowledge of man, is it not foolishness in My eyes, coming to nothing before the light of My Glory?

Therefore fear The Lord your God, and accept the truth of who I am. For the fear of The Lord is the beginning of wisdom, and the knowledge of The Holy One is understanding. For I am God alone.

Therefore, O sons of men, hear the Word of My mouth and listen closely to My speech: If the mighty works of God are broken down into mere parables, and the Word of My power is counted only as figures of speech, or metaphors in need of interpretation, then you are lost, forever consumed by talk and confusion. Yet I say to you, let that which is a parable remain a parable; and let that which is a figure of speech be understood by those who have received the love of the Truth; and let that which is an account strike fear into the hearts of all men. For I do not change.

Behold, My Word is truth! And that which requires understanding shall be given to those of a contrite heart and a humble spirit. For those who love Me obey My Commandments, and those who remember My Sabbaths honor Me and shall know Wisdom. Therefore, consider these things carefully. For I have indeed prepared a place for those who seek Me, for those who long to know Me as I truly am, a place for all those accepted in The Beloved, in whom My spirit dwells, The Kingdom without end.

Therefore hear the Word of The Lord, O peoples of the earth, for the Day of The Lord is at hand: Behold, I shall stir up the multitudes, and show wonders in the heavens above and in the earth beneath! There shall be blood and fire and pillars of smoke, and the foundations of the world shall be shaken! For I shall reveal My Glory; behold, every eye shall see! Then all the inhabitants of the earth will know, I AM THE LORD! For as it was in the days of My servant, Moses, when I stretched out My hand against Egypt, with many mighty signs and wonders, so shall it be in the Great and Terrible Day of The Lord!

Yet understand this, O most arrogant generation, My judgment on Egypt was but a mere drop of rain, a single crack of thunder, compared with that which I have prepared for this sleeping generation!

Therefore awake, all you sleepers,
For the time of your slumber has ended;
Awake, and prepare to meet your God!...

Repent, and turn aside from
All this wickedness you have chosen!
Turn your back on all these abominations
You uphold, and embrace The Salvation of God!...

For I AM, and you are in life because of Me;
In Me alone is everlasting life;
Beloved, I AM HE!...

There is no other, a just God and a Savior;
There is none besides Me,
God Eternal.

1/29/05 **From The Lord, Our God and Savior**
The Word of The Lord Spoken to Timothy
For Timothy, and For All Those Who Have Ears to Hear
Clothed With the Presence of God

Thus says The Lord to His servant: Timothy, lift up your head toward Heaven and embrace the prophet's reward. For you have been chosen to stand up in the face of adversity and speak; to persevere through much persecution, to endure contemptible speech on every side, as you strike down all these abominations in My name.

> *Fear not, for The Lord is your Shepherd;*
> *He will be your confidence and*
> *Keep you safe from harm...*
>
> *Behold, in the day I send you,*
> *My presence shall overshadow you,*
> *With the glory of The Holy One of Israel*
> *Shining through you in His strength.*

Yes, this work is indeed difficult, service wrought with much heartache and pain, evil on every side. For many shall come forth from their hiding places to bar your way, in an attempt to halt your steps and squelch your spirit, even to take away your life. Yet fear not, Timothy. For The Shepherd has complete authority, even over all these ravaging wolves. Behold, He shall scatter them before you in that day! And when it is finished, He shall strike them, and their hearts shall fail them for fear!

From the resentful hearer to the outspoken mocker, both those near and those afar off, even to those unseen, ALL shall be made to shudder, ALL shall tremble in fear! For The King shall appear suddenly out of His place, coming forth in power and great glory, and He shall lay all His enemies waste, until every ravaging wolf lies down in death and every brute beast is utterly destroyed! Behold, He shall strike them down in the power of His might, and divide them asunder with the sword of His mouth, and burn up the residue with unquenchable fire!

My son, even now there are many wolves lurking about, both seen and unseen, who wear the raiment of the sheep they seek to devour. For they are most insidious, ravaging whole flocks from within. Yet you and many more like you shall go out and gather together My lost sheep, and bring them to safety, and they too shall be hidden, even for a time and times and half a time.

For those who have ears to hear will heed the sound of this Trumpet in that day, and come forth to drink. Lo, they shall be immersed in springs of living waters, no more blinded by the filthy veil which once covered their heads. And until that day, you also must drink. You must drink deeply and be fully immersed, reborn and remade, abiding in the Holy Place, going out and coming in, until you are fully clothed with the presence of God...

> And behold, your adornments shall be truth and wisdom; atop your head, you shall wear the helmet of salvation; upon your brow, the seal of The Living God; and around your neck, you shall wear the gemstone...

> In your ears, the voice of YAHUWAH shall resonate; and in your eyes, a flame of fire, the reflection of The Most Holy who goes before you and dwells within you...

Over your shoulder, you shall bear the sash of your office; and upon your chest, the breastplate of strength, whereon is written the name of The Holy One of Israel; and about your waist, the belt of fortitude shall be securely fastened...

In your right hand you shall carry the sword of truth, which is the Word of God, with which you shall strike the nations and cut down your enemies; in your left hand, the shield of faith, by which you shall quell every attack of the evil one...

And behold, My son, look down... Your feet rest solidly upon The Rock and have been anointed with oil, says The Lord God.

2/24/05 **From The Lord, Our God and Savior**
The Word of The Lord Spoken to Timothy
For Timothy, and For All Those Who Have Ears to Hear
Remember the Sabbath and Your God,
 And He Shall Remember You

Thus says The Lord to His servant: Timothy, concerning the Sabbath, the seventh day of each week, Saturday is the day you shall remember and keep holy. Yes, you shall keep it holy and rest. You shall do no work on this day, neither shall your wife or children, nor any guest in your house, save that which is needful for your household. You may also do those things which are good and fruitful in My eyes, according to that which I command you. Yet from doing your own pleasure depart and from your own works rest, on the Sabbath day; walk not in your own way, Timothy, but walk with Me in Mine. Rest in Me, and remember. For in this you honor Me and shall surely be blessed.

Therefore, this is what I command you: You shall be prepared for the Sabbath by sunset on the sixth day, ceasing from all your works as I have commanded you. You shall remember and honor the Sabbath; from sunset to sunset, you shall rest and be at peace. For the time is coming when none shall have peace, when no one will be able to work. Yet you, Timothy, shall work. In the midst of deep darkness you shall serve, and in you shall I shine bright, for I have set you up as a lampstand for My people. And in the day I send you, you shall become a beacon.

Therefore, Timothy, cherish the Sabbath. Pray and give worship, offer up thanksgiving in My name. Be refreshed and washed in The Word, renewed in the presence of God. And when others draw near, speak to them also; yea, testify of My Passion on the Sabbath day.

Share My Word and My love and blow this Trumpet, for My Kingdom comes. Yes even on the Sabbath, and in the Day of The Lord, shall you walk in the office for which you are called. For I am also The Lord of the Sabbath; behold, I am Lord over all the earth! Then shall the New Day come, and if you are able to receive it, it is the seventh, The Sabbath of The Lord, wherein the whole world shall rest from its evil ways.

Indeed, many things shall be put to rest
In The Lord's Day, even death and the grave;
Destruction shall have no place,
And evil shall be far removed...

For as it is written:
They shall not hurt nor destroy in all
My Holy Mountain, for the earth shall be
Full of the knowledge of The Lord
As the waters cover the sea...

Therefore, beloved ones, pray always
That you are counted worthy to
Enter My rest, that you may abide
In the presence of The Lord, forever.

Thus those who remember the Sabbath honor Me, and those who rest on the Sabbath rest in Me, as they look to the Day. For I had set the seventh day apart, and sanctified it, from the beginning. Thus it has been a sign between Me and My people, even to this day, and so shall it remain forever.

For as I spoke to the children of Israel, saying, *"Surely My Sabbaths you shall keep, for it is a sign between Me and you throughout your generations, that you may know that I am The Lord who sanctifies you,"* so also do I speak to you, even to all who are grafted in. For those who obey My Commandments remain in My love, and those who remember My Sabbaths keep My company, for The Holy One of Israel dwells in the midst of them. For I long for My children to be with Me where I am, I am eager to return them to the Garden, that we may once again walk together in the cool of the day.

Therefore remember the Sabbath, and I shall remember you. Bless the Sabbath, and I shall bless you. Love one another, as I have loved you. Put away your works, look not to the cares of this world, and let go of your worries on the Sabbath day; spare yourselves the weight of all these troubles for just one day. Let all your thoughts dwell upon your God and Savior, and consider; yea, let your mind be filled with wonder and awe over the works of My hands. For even The Lord your God, Creator of Heaven and Earth, rested on the seventh day.

So then bear your cross six days, and let The Lord carry it on the seventh. Rejoice and be merry, for this is My will for you. Then when evening comes, and the sun dips below the horizon, you may once again return to that which you choose to take up, whether it be the plow or the shears. But see that you do not take up your hand in sin, and be wary of those who do. Be separate, and stand apart from those who forsake the Sabbath and push out the hand against My Holy Days. For My Sabbaths are holy, a blessing, a time to reflect on those things I have prepared for those who love Me.

Why, O churches of men, do you forsake My Sabbaths and cast away My Holy Days, as though the devil had laid them upon your doorstep?! For My people are those who keep My Commandments and take pleasure in My Sabbaths. They abide in My love and have the Testimony, and do not cease from doing those things which are pleasing in My sight.

And behold, the Day is coming quickly
When The Rightful King shall rule...

And His Kingdom shall be a Sabbath,
Even one thousand years;
His reign, forever and ever!...

For The Lord has spoken, and so shall it be:

On earth as in Heaven.

3/6/05 **From The Lord, Our God and Savior**
The Word of The Lord Spoken to Timothy
For All Those Who Have Ears to Hear
Watch

Peoples of the earth, hear the Word of The Lord your God: You are lost, drowning in a deep sea of transgression, sinking in the ever-shifting sands of religion and science. You are stuck in the mire of your iniquities, slowly suffocating, as the fruit of your labor comes full circle to take away your life. For by your own works have you destroyed the garden, on account of your greed have you caused much suffering and death, bringing calamity upon your own heads! Thus because of your great iniquity I have drawn back My hand, and for the multitude of your transgressions the judgment of God has come upon you.

Dead generation, foolish children, evil surrounds you on every side! Darkness closes in, yet you remain unmoved! Detestable birds gather and predators come forth to stalk you as prey, yet you see no cause for alarm! Therefore as I live, says The Lord, My flock has become the prey and My children have made themselves meet for the slaughter!

For the peoples of the earth have forsaken Me, days without end; they have altogether gone astray! My created ones have removed themselves far from Me, and My own beloved have not returned to Me, but do always seek their own way! And of the shepherds, they did not go out to search for My flock, but have fed themselves! They did not feed My flock, BUT HAVE FED THEMSELVES!

Therefore hear the Word of The Lord, all you self-appointed shepherds, and give ear, all you wayward flocks, for you have surely broken the yoke and burst the bonds, you have surely forsaken The Lord your God; for thus says The Lord: I am against you! Your houses are fallen, and the foundations upon which you have built yourselves up crumble beneath your feet! All is dust and ashes, rubble piled up in heaps! Oh what a bitter thing this is, unending sadness, anguish and pain; My own beloved have departed from Me, My own children have gone far astray! I gave My Son for them, that they may live and not die, I laid Myself upon the altar, yet they want no part with Me as I truly am! Thus they choose death, and with the grave they have made their agreement.

Therefore, thus says The Lord: Tremble, O heavens! Shake, O earth! Let the seas rage and the mountains crumble before the coming of The Lord! Let the whole earth be bowed down before The Holy One of Israel, for My Kingdom comes!

Behold, The Almighty is coming down to you,
Yes, The Son who wears the full raiment of The Father,
For in Him alone does the fullness of God dwell...

Thus HE shall pluck you from the fire,
HE shall scourge the nations with the Word of His power,
And strike the wicked with the sword of His mouth.

Yes, HE shall tread the grapes in the winepress
Of the wrath of My fury, wiping the wicked
From existence, destroying all things which
Sicken His sheep and cause His flocks to go astray;
Behold, He shall utterly destroy all that offends!

My people, The Mashiach is your help and your shield; YahuShua, whom you call Jesus and Christ, is The Rock of your Salvation, The One who is and was and is to come. For The Father and The Son are One. Therefore embrace Me in My Mercy, and receive of Me in My Great Love.

Thus says The Lord, your Redeemer: I am indeed coming down to shake the heavens and the earth, to move all from its place; to bring forth that which was hidden and to reveal that which was misplaced; to open that which was shut and to shut that which was opened. Therefore prepare, My people, for the time has come; yes, today is the day of salvation! Go forth, beloved ones, and set all these crooked paths straight; regain the line, prepare and watch. For the leaves of the fig tree are upon its branches; summer is near!

Again I say, watch. For The One who ascended is about to descend... *And lo, I am come, in the volume of the Book it is written of Me, to accomplish The Father's will.* For I have heard the cries of the oppressed and the groaning of the poor and the needy, I know the plight of the fatherless and the widow. I have tasted their tears, and the heart of the faithful is not hidden from Me.

Therefore watch and also listen, and be spared, for I am about to give a shout. For all that is written in the Book of The Lord, both the former and the latter, comes to pass through Me. Take heed therefore, for assuredly I say to you, it shall in no wise come to pass as a mere metaphor or as a parable conceived of by men. For the time of arrogant assumptions and prideful assertions is over, the time of corrupt knowledge and polluted sermons is at an end.

Behold, The Power from on high is coming
Forth to reap and to judge the nations,
To sound the trumpet in the four corners,
To cause the name of The Lord
To resound in all the earth...

Bow before The King, therefore;
Humble yourselves before The Holy One of Israel...

Lay yourselves upon the altar and be broken
Atop The Stone, and it shall bear you up;
Yet stand defiant, and you shall be crushed
Beneath the weight of The Mountain...

For I do not change, says The Lord.

3/19/05 **From The Lord, Our God and Savior**
The Word of The Lord Spoken to Timothy
For All Those Who Have Ears to Hear
Purify Your Faith

This question was asked of The Lord: Lord, how do You feel about "prayer rugs" with images of Jesus on them?

[The Lord answered] This is where blasphemy abides and sin abounds, idolatry covered with purple and scarlet. Therefore write My words to all who call of themselves Christian, to all those who emulate the harlot, who have not ceased from practicing those things I hate.

For thus says The Lord: HYPOCRITES! Where are your hearts?! Why do you do these vain and contemptible things?! I tell you the truth, you have surely forgotten Me, nor do you know Me at all! Cease from bringing graven images before Me; your offerings are not accepted! Cease from opening your mouths in vain repetition; your prayers are not heard! Stop teaching detestable doctrine and contemptible tradition! For you have surely blasphemed My name, you have surely caused My people to sin! Day and night you set stones of stumbling at their feet! Year after year, you hew out great blocks of abomination upon which you build your churches, the weight of which you shall bear in the Day of The Lord's Anger!
Churches of men, be ignorant of My ways no longer. Cast from yourselves all these graven images, and no more bring your prayers before Me in this way. Nor pray to those who have fallen asleep; for they are dead, they know nothing at all... *YahuShua is The Only Way, The Only Truth, and The Only Life!*

Again, I say to you, pray no more to those who lie dead in the grave; there is no life in them. For I tell you the truth, you have surely separated yourselves from Me; according to every Commandment you break, according to every jot and tittle you have endeavored to change, are you far removed. For you have become a wholly vain and ignorant people, a people who want no part with Me as I truly am, a wayward flock who ceases not from taking the name of The Lord in vain.

Therefore, purify your faith!
Be cleansed of all this iniquity,
Turn away from all this impropriety!...

Keep The Commandments of God
As they are written, and not as you
Would have them be; remain in My love!...

For The One alone, whom you
Shall call Father, is in Heaven...

And there is but One Mediator
Between God and man, and His
Name is YahuShua HaMashiach!...

Says The Lord.

3/26/05 **From YahuShua HaMashiach, Our Lord and Savior**
The Word of The Lord Spoken to Timothy
For All Those Who Have Ears to Hear
**Judge Not Others, For That By Which You
   Judge Is How You Shall Be Judged**

O you hypocrites, listen to the voice of The Lord your Redeemer, and repent, says The Lord. For your iniquity is shown upon your vesture, as a garment which has been ripped in two. Shall you judge others by that which you are also guilty? There is one Judge, to whom God has committed all authority, and One only - The Son of Man.

It is written: *Whoever is angry with his brother without a cause shall be in danger of the Judgment.* For those who hold onto anger retain malice, and are filled with hate; they shall in no wise escape the Day of The Lord. For it is written also, and remains standing: *If someone says, "I love God," yet hates his brother, he is a liar and shall be found as such on the Day of Reckoning.* Therefore he who seeks to cast a stone at another, let him first cast it at himself.

Thus says The Lord: Sin is sin. All sin is sin. All have sinned and fall short of the Glory of God. Shall then sin judge sin? No. Only The One who is without sin shall be your judge; and behold, He is also The Son of Man.

Yet you continue to pass judgment on others by the likes of what you know to be true of yourselves, accounting to them those same sins for which you are also guilty. Thus you do greatly err. Therefore repent, and seek now The Way of The Lord. For God is love, and His Mercy endures forever.

Therefore come to Me,
Come to Me in spirit and in truth,
And strive to love others as I have loved you...

For where there is an absence of love,
You will find only pain and suffering,
Hate, and ever-increasing sin;
And when it is finished, death...

Says The Lord.

3/28/05 **From The Lord, Our God and Savior**
The Word of The Lord Spoken to Timothy
For All Those Who Have Ears to Hear
Embrace The Cornerstone Wherein Flows
   Springs of Living Water

Thus says The Lord to this generation, the last of these kingdoms of men: Why do you kick your foot against The Stone, and shake your fists at Heaven when faced with The Truth? You are like a lost traveler without a home, and like the beast of the field you have no shelter. Thus your wisdom is wind, and your every ambition a fool's aspiration.

Yet in My love, I laid for you an everlasting foundation upon which you were to stand. And in My mercy I constructed high walls, made with the finest stone, to protect you, even from yourselves, engraven stones touched by the finger of God. Yet you seek to remove the immovable and hide that which can not be hidden, denying that which is self-evident, as you endeavor to scrape off the writing thereof. Shall you deface The Commandments of God to justify your sins, desecrating The Moral Law to allay your guilt?! The Commandments are a lamp and The Law a light, reproof and instruction, a way of life. And shall you now also attempt to hew out The Cornerstone and cast it into the depths of the sea?!

O most foolish and deceived generation,
Can anyone cut out their own heart and live?...

And who is able to walk alone in darkness,
Without a light to guide them?...

Who shall uphold them when they stumble
Or catch them when they fall?
Who will bind up their wounds?...

O ignorant and confused generation,
Deceived peoples, The Stone which you seek
To cast off is LIFE, your only salvation!

Behold, The Stone is The Head of the Corner and shall become a great mountain, breaking the backs of the rebellious and grinding the wicked to powder. For its weight is heavy beyond measure; its placement sure, immovable, everlasting. Therefore come and be broken atop this Stone, and it shall bear you up! Yet cast it off or cover it over, in an attempt to hide it from others, and you also shall be hidden; into the pit will you stumble, into the grave shall you fall, covered over in the day of My punishment. Behold, the Day is at hand, My anger is aroused and the fire is kindled!
Therefore, I ask you, where will you run and where will you hide, when the bitter rains fall from Heaven and judgment ensues like a mighty flood? For I am coming down to extinguish every fiery dart of the evil one, to put an end to all things which cause My people to sin.

For The Salvation of God has come already, and shall return to gather up the light; and behold, He is also coming in power and great glory, to punish the wicked and destroy the evil of heart. For as it is written, so it is and shall be: *The Law will proceed from Me, and I will make My justice rest as a light for all peoples. My righteousness is near, My salvation has gone forth, and My arm shall judge the nations.*

Therefore, lift up your eyes to the heavens,
And look upon the earth beneath...

For the heavens shall vanish away like smoke,
The earth will grow old like a garment,
And those who dwell in it shall
Pass away in like manner...

Yet My Salvation is forever,
And My righteousness shall never be abolished...

Says The Lord.

VOLUME TWO

3/28/05 **From The Lord, Our God and Savior**
The Word of The Lord Spoken to Timothy
For All Those Who Have Ears to Hear
The Wide Path

Thus says The Lord: Peoples of the earth, why do you corrupt and pollute My garden?! You have made it as the dunghill! Thus you have signed your own certificate, and with death you are in agreement. And though you walk as if you will live forever, I tell you the truth, you are already dead. For you have surely crossed the threshold; behold, you have reached the point of no return.

Yet in your arrogance, you continue to forsake your Maker and Him who has given you breath, holding fast to the wide path which leads to destruction. Therefore, judgment waits for you on the horizon; calamity and desolations shall increase by measure, as the sun sets upon this age of men.

Peoples of the earth and all leaders among men, hear the Word of The Lord, for thus says The Lord: Your knowledge is useless, all your achievements are in vain, and shall come to nothing in the Day of The Lord's Anger! For as it is written: *I shall surely punish this world for its evil, and the wicked for their iniquity. I will put an end to the arrogance of the proud, and utterly humiliate the haughtiness of the tyrant, the mighty, and the terrible.*

Therefore, turn from this wicked way you have chosen! Repent, and kiss The Son, that you may live and not die! For I AM HE!... *He who raises the poor from the dust and lifts the needy out of the dunghill, says The Lord.*

4/18/05 **From The Lord, Our God and Savior**
The Word of The Lord Spoken to Timothy
For All Those Who Have Ears to Hear
The Seventh Day

Thus says The Lord: As it is written, a day in The Lord is as a thousand years. And behold, the seventh day is upon you. For The Lord God created the heavens and the earth, and all therein, in six days, and rested on the seventh. And behold, My rest is at the door.

For the sixth day is ending, yet not as the sun sets upon the horizon, but as a woman suffering to bring forth. For she is in great travail, her contractions close together, increasing by measure until the birth is accomplished... *Behold, the bride's Husband shall embrace her and hold her close, and wipe away all her tears. And she shall be comforted as He holds the babe in His right hand; the pain of birth all but forgotten, of which she shall never suffer again, for the old order of things has passed away.*

Behold The New Day!...

A day of rest from pain and sorrow, from sin and death,
A day set apart from every kind of evil...

Holy... The Sabbath...

A day in The Lord lasting one thousand years...

Peace.

4/28/05 **From The Lord, Our God and Savior**
The Word of The Lord Spoken to Timothy
For All Those Who Have Ears to Hear
A Day in The Lord

Thus says The Lord: Again, I say to you, a day in The Lord is as a thousand years. And there is also a time coming, when a day shall be for a year and a week as seven. Yet the length of the Day of The Lord no one knows, for it remains set within the counsel of My own will. Yet for those who escape, there is a day wherein time has no meaning.

And behold, it shall surely happen, in a moment, in the twinkling of an eye, one shall be taken and the other left. For there shall be two in the world - one discontent, yet filled with joyful expectation; and the other content, yet filled with a great emptiness. The discontent shall be taken, their joy fulfilled; the other left in bitter sorrows, lamentation and great weeping. Yet you need not grieve for those who remain. For they need only humble themselves before Me and repent, and they too shall abide at My right hand.

For thus declares The Lord: I shall indeed rob the world of those who are not of the world, I shall surely steal them away - the first election removed and the pure in heart taken. I AM THE LORD... *Yet the world's loss shall become gain for those who receive understanding and repent, for all those who call upon The Name in sincerity and in truth. Behold, in that day many shall see the angels of Heaven ascending and descending upon The Son of Man, says The Lord.*

4/18/05 **From YahuShua HaMashiach, Our Lord and Savior**
The Word of The Lord Spoken to Timothy
For All Those Who Have Ears to Hear
**I Am The Passover and The Lamb,
The New Covenant With Men**

Thus says The Messiah who is called Christ, The Holy One of Israel: I am The Lamb of God without spot or blemish, the blood which was shed and placed upon the doorposts, delivering My people from the power of sin, which is death. I am The Passover. For as it is written in The Law, all things must be purified with blood, and without the shedding of blood there can be no remission. Thus no one goes to The Father, unless they receive of Me. Unless they eat My flesh and drink My blood, they have no life in them. For whosoever eats My flesh and drinks My blood has everlasting life, and I will raise them up at the Last Day. For My flesh is food indeed, and My blood is drink indeed. Thus all who eat My flesh and drink My blood live in Me, and I in them. I am The Living Bread which came down from Heaven! If anyone eats this bread, he will live forever! And the bread that I gave was My flesh, which was given for the life of the world. This I have already told you. Therefore keep the Passover in remembrance of Me and My Passion, according to The New Covenant. For it is accomplished, and was sealed forevermore upon My resurrection. For The Lamb was slain, My people redeemed in all the earth; and behold, I am risen, crowned with glory and honor, forever and ever. Amen.

Therefore, again I say to you, celebrate Passover, yet not as in the days of Moses; nor as the unbelieving in Israel, upon whom the veil remains, for they have yet to look upon Me[1]. For the Passover was a signpost, a shadow of glorious things to come. Read the writing thereof and have understanding, take its meaning to heart. For the Holy Days are revelation, the Plan of the Ages revealed.

Therefore rejoice, My people, for your Redeemer lives!
Death has passed over you!...

Therefore eat, drink, and give thanks
In remembrance of Me, and I shall also
Remember you in the day I gather My own...

Then shall you truly know Me,
Just as I have always known you,
Even from the foundation of the world...

Says He who is, and was, and is to come,
YahuShua, The Salvation of God.

---

1. *Zechariah 12:10*

4/19/05 **From The Lord, Our God and Savior**
The Word of The Lord Spoken to Timothy
For All Those Who Have Ears to Hear
The Holy Spirit

These questions were asked of The Lord: Lord, should we worship the Holy Spirit? Is the Holy Spirit a person?

Thus says The Lord: Beware of the doctrines and traditions of men in the churches. Stumble not over the letter, nor be led astray by perverse interpretations or biased translations, by which the churches of men have marred My Word before the people. Rather study to show yourself approved unto God, a workman that need not be ashamed, rightly dividing the Word of Truth.

For I ask you, where in the Scriptures of Truth is it written to give praise and worship unto the Spirit? For the Spirit is not a person, nor have I called it by name. For to YahuShua alone did I say, *"You are My Son; today I have begotten You."* Therefore worship God, offering up praises in the name of The Son, and give thanks. For those who believe in The Son, and also seek to obey Him, receive of My spirit. For it is My hand upon you, guiding you in the way in which you should walk, My voice speaking softly from within, reminding you of that which I have taught you, restoring you to righteousness and life. Yet the power of God moving upon the face of the earth is My spirit also, My will made manifest in the world and among men.

Therefore, I ask you, how can one pray to that which he prays through? Shall one pray to the hand of God? Rather pray to your Father in Heaven, in The Son's name, and through the Spirit we shall be one.

For all My servants move, speak and hear Me through My spirit, and only through The Son shall My children come to know Me as I truly am... *And oh how blessed are those who know Him, for they love Him and obey His voice, having truly received of Him, even of His spirit, the Spirit of God.*

Indeed holy, holy, holy is The Lord God Almighty...

One God, invisible and visible, The Father and The Son;
And the Spirit called holy, because I am holy...

Therefore, accept My love and receive of My gifts;
For the Spirit is indeed a gift given by The Father,
Received through The Son...

Call it not a person, call it a blessing;
For blessed are those who have the Spirit of God,
For God dwells within them.

4/21/05 **From YahuShua HaMashiach, Our Lord and Savior**
The Word of The Lord Spoken to Timothy
For His Wife, and For All Those Who Have Ears to Hear
Bear Much Fruit, the Harvest Is Near

This question was asked of The Lord, for Timothy's wife: Lord, should she try to remain friends with those who have separated themselves from her because of Your Word?

[*The Lord answered*] Beloved, bear fruit after the kind I have given you, in open and in secret. For what profit is there in sharing with another that which they believe they already have? And how shall one who pushes out the hand receive a gift? Beloved, let the separation stand. For though they say, *"We are full, we are in need of nothing,"* I tell you the truth, they remain void and desolate.
Therefore, turn aside from those who push out the hand and wag the head. Rather seek out the poor, that I may feed them. Fill the bowls of the hungry, and place the cup in the hands of the thirsty; give them your portion. For My bounty is plentiful, given freely to all who hunger and thirst for righteousness. Beloved, tell them that you were once lost, yet now you are found; that you were once naked, yet now you are clothed in fine linens of white, your filthy rags cast off forever; that you were once hungry and very thirsty, starving in a world of empty promises, lies and vain deceits, yet now you are nourished with The Word of Truth.
Behold, I am The Living Bread which came down from Heaven, The Fountain of Living Waters which sustains My people unto everlasting life! My words never pass away, and My promises stand forever!

Therefore eat and be satisfied, drink deeply and be healed, for The Lord's table is a bounty. And those who eat from My plate are always full, and those who drink from My cup shall never go thirsty. For My cup overflows, bearing fruit in every part of your life, bringing forth love and understanding.

Oh My beloved, you were once sick, mortally ill;
Yet now you are healed in Me, now you are
Restored because of Me, My body, My bride...

My precious flower, My pleasant plant, of which
I shall pluck from the earth at the time appointed,
Replanted in the Garden at dawn on the new day...

Therefore come forth, all My people,
And flourish in the light of The Lord,
And bear much fruit in The Beloved!...

Says The Lord.

4/25/05 **From YahuShua HaMashiach, Our Lord and Savior**
The Word of The Lord Spoken to Timothy
For Timothy, and For All Those Who Have Ears to Hear
(Regarding Passover and the Feast of Unleavened Bread)
Do This in Remembrance of Me

Listen and have understanding, for thus says The Lord your Redeemer: Only those who truly believe keep the Passover. To them it is a memorial, a time of reflection and the giving of thanks, a Sabbath.

Therefore, Timothy, do not your own pleasure on the Holy Days or on the Sabbath. Rather do that which pleases The Lord your God. Keep the feasts holy, and cause your life to follow suit; unleaven your heart. Discern what is most needful, and when in doubt, ask.

And concerning the rites and ceremonial symbols of the feasts, consider their meaning and rejoice in their fulfillment, for it is accomplished. Do not agonize over the details, nor stumble over the letter. And concerning that which you partake of for the body, it is of little consequence. Rather feast upon that which sustains your soul. Remember Me and My Passion, as I have shown you; offer up thanksgiving, and consider your salvation and The Loving Mercy of God. For the intent of one's heart speaks volumes more than the offering put forth by their hands.

Yet I tell you the truth, many will there be who enter The Kingdom of Heaven, who did not keep the feasts of The Lord. And many will there be left standing outside the gates, who kept the feasts of The Lord. For those without the gate retain their sin, for they hold fast to malice and have not yet departed from wickedness.

Yet the hearts of the first election are filled with compassion and a sincere desire to walk in My ways, having called upon My name in sincerity and in truth, as they bring forth new works meet for repentance. For where there are righteous works, there are also those who seek to spoil them for the sake of pride and envy. And where there is pure knowledge, there are also those who defile it among women[1]. Take heed, therefore, and remember My teaching: *Beware of the leaven of the Pharisees and the Sadducees.* For their like still exists today; only their names and vesture have changed.

Yet the ignorance of the meek is
No cause for offense, nor shall the error
Of the humble bring forth rebuke...

For I know the heart and
Look upon the innermost intentions...

Therefore keep the feast, not with
The old leaven, nor with the leaven
Of malice and wickedness,
But with the unleavened bread
Of sincerity and truth, as it is written
In accordance with the New Covenant...

Says The Lord.

---

1. "Women" in this context refers to the churches of men.

5/4/05 **From The Lord, Our God and Savior**
The Word of The Lord Spoken to Timothy
For All Those Who Have Ears to Hear
Ensign

Thus says The Lord: Behold, the time draws near, when they will not see The Thief come; when the judgments of God shall fall from Heaven, even upon the face of the whole earth; when the sign shall appear and the heavens shall be set ablaze with brilliant light. For as The Son of Man was lifted up on a tree in the sight of men, so in like manner shall the sign of The Son of Man be. For that which was the beginning and the end shall also be the end which brings forth the new beginning.

Behold, I shall do a new and wondrous thing! I shall lift up a standard and bring forth a sign, in the sight of all nations! I shall pierce the heavens and bathe the earth in glorious light, and every eye shall see! Yes, even those hidden in caves and shelters shall see and come forth; behold, even the blind shall see! For on that day I shall divide the heavens, and divide them again, and all silence shall flee away!

HEAR THE SOUND OF SCORCHING FIRMAMENT! BE AWESTRUCK IN ASTONISHMENT AT THE MULTITUDE OF THUNDER, AND BE HORRIBLY AFRAID! For as the sparks of a crackling fire, so shall the sign of The Son of Man be, plus ten thousand million-fold! Says The Lord...

Look up, therefore, and keep watch, for He is coming quickly; yes, The Word who became flesh, Immanu El. Thus as it is written, so shall it be: He is coming on the clouds and every eye shall see Him, even those who pierced Him, and all the tribes of the earth shall mourn because of Him... Even so, amen.

90

5/14/05 **From The Lord, Our God and Savior**
The Word of The Lord Spoken to Timothy
For All Those Who Have Ears to Hear
It Is Time... Prepare to Meet Your God

Thus says The Lord: My people have turned from Me, they have
altogether forsaken The Lord their God, foolish children married
to a world awash in vanity and sin. Therefore, the time has come.
Behold, the time has come for My name to resound in all the
earth, for all who dwell upon the earth to be humbled, to be
broken without hand. Indeed, now is the time for all who have
ears to hear, to hear and give heed; and for those who refuse, to
forbear and rebel against Me.

It is time for My servants to stand up, to receive My words
and also do them. It is time to blow the trumpet, to sound the
alarm. It is time for My spirit to be poured out, for the hand of
The Almighty to stir up the multitudes, for The Word of God
to separate and divide the people. It is time for My watchmen
to proclaim the acceptable year of The Lord and the day of
vengeance of The Lord their God. For the ears of the first election
are open, and within My prophets I have placed My voice, once
again; I have surely put My words in their mouths. For I am The
Lord, and I do not change.

*Therefore hear the Word of The Lord, for thus says The Holy
One of Israel:* Awaken, O foolish people! Arise from your beds,
and prepare to meet your God! My children, cast away these filthy
veils which cover your heads; yes, even you, My people who dwell
in Israel, hear the Word of your Messiah. For I AM HE, He who
was and is and is to come, YAHUSHUA-YAHUWAH, God in
the flesh, Immanu El, The Lord your Righteousness.

For I had come into the world, yet you would not receive Me. Behold, I am coming again, and still you deny Me. Therefore hear and understand, and gain wisdom. For The Father has proclaimed My glory from the beginning; even before the house of Israel was My glory put on open display. For I am in The Father, and The Father is in Me, of which My works also testify, the works He sent Me to do, even the cross.

And now the time has come, behold, the day is near,
When I shall give you yet another sign,
Even the sign of The Son of Man...

The heavens shall be divided, and divided again,
The glory thereof stretching from the earth to heaven,
And the clouds shall be rolled back like a scroll...

Behold the brilliance, O earth,
Be bowed down and weep, O sons of men,
For The One whom you pierced is about to appear!...

Let every eye be opened therefore,
Let all in the earth see, until the fullness
Of the revelation is made complete.

For all in the earth shall be humbled, and the pride of man shall be broken in that day. For as it is written: *The loftiness of man shall be bowed down and the haughtiness of men shall be brought low, the idols shall be utterly abolished, and The Lord alone shall be exalted in that day.*

And for fear of The Lord, many shall go into the holes of the rocks, and into the caves of the earth, to hide themselves from the terror of The Lord and the glory of His majesty, when He arises to shake the earth mightily!

And behold, a great remnant shall emerge, who will not go into the holes of the rocks or into the caves of the earth, to hide themselves from the terror of The Lord or the glory of His majesty, but will stand fast with hands uplifted, singing praises to The Lord their God.

Yet woe to those who shake their fists at Heaven; their destruction draws near. For the hearts of the ungodly produce only wickedness. Their throats are like open graves, their speech is full of deadly deceit. They are practiced liars, and with their tongues they spew all kinds of threats. And like venomous snakes, they conceal poison behind their lips. For their mouths are full of bitterness, and cursing is always upon their breath. They are quick to do harm, and are not afraid to kill. Their ways bring only destruction, misery and death. For the way of peace is foreign to them, and the fear of The Lord they have not known.

Therefore as it is written of Me, so I am and shall be: My hand shall find all My enemies, My right hand shall overtake those who hate Me! At My appearing I will make them all like a fiery furnace; I shall swallow them up in My anger, and the fire of My wrath shall consume them! I will wipe their descendants from the face of the earth; behold, I shall rid mankind of their posterity! For they intended evil against Me, and devised many schemes, but will be unable to perform them! For My arrows were made ready from the beginning, and when I aim My bow at their faces they shall surely flee! Therefore I shall be exalted in My strength, and My people shall sing Me praises when I put My power on open display! Says The Lord.

5/14/05 **From The Lord, Our God and Savior**
The Word of The Lord Spoken to Timothy
For All Those Who Have Ears to Hear
Woe to the Church Called Roman and Catholic

Thus says The Lord: Beware, O peoples of the church called mother. For she is a harlot, a false way, a deceitful house filled with both great and subtle deceptions. Be wary, rouse yourselves from this heavy sleep, and look upon the fruit of your doings. For you have been greatly misled, caught up in a faith which is dead; there is no life in it! For as it was written by My servant, so in like manner I now plead with you: *Depart from the way of evil, from the man who speaks perverse things, from those who leave the paths of uprightness to walk in the ways of darkness, who rejoice in doing evil and delight in the perversity of the pagan, whose ways are crooked and who are devious in their paths. Be delivered from the adulterous woman, from the seductress who flatters with her words, who forsakes the husband of her youth and forgets the covenant of her God. For her house is sinking down to death, and all her paths lead to the dead.*

Therefore thus says The Lord God, The Holy One of Israel, to all who have ears to hear: This unholy church of men is a harlot! From the beginning she has been a whore! Yet she would have all believe she is a queen, even the true church and mother. Indeed, she has bore many sons and daughters, daughters who yet bear her likeness; and many sons who shall go to perdition, false fathers and priests, who by their own authority take to themselves proselytes, who they then make twice as fit for destruction as themselves! Behold, deception is hidden within deception, as she continues to build up her sins toward heaven.

For I tell you a mystery filled with corruption,
Abuse of power and contemptible ways:

This church of men is like the woman who rides the beast;
She is clothed with purple and scarlet, enticing the
People to commit fornication with her...

Yet to her own, she is a queen who sits upon
My throne and has taken to herself My authority,
Perverting My Word and changing My Commandments
As she appoints kings and princes in her own name,
Each with names of blasphemy upon their heads,
So-called holy fathers who shall go into perdition with her...

And yet to those against her, she is the beast.

Yet I tell you the truth, all are deceived. For her power and authority come from the beast, which atop she sits. For she has many names of blasphemy, and all her works are an abomination before The Lord. She is indeed a harlot, and her adulteries are many. Behold, she is also like the great whore who sits upon many waters, who has corrupted the earth with her fornications.

And like the false prophet she spews perverse and bitter doctrine, leading many into false worship, even to the committing of fornication with the pagan and the heathen by all her filthy traditions! And like the beast, she has shed the blood of My servants throughout her generations, and has not ceased from opening her mouth to speak great things and blasphemies with a practiced and lying tongue, by which she has deceived many.

Therefore, I must take My people out of her! Behold, I shall snatch them from her very breast! For she is also like Babylon, adorning herself with gold and precious stones and pearls, having in her hand a golden cup full of abominations and the filthiness of her fornications.

Thus says The Lord to the deceptive harlot, to the mother of all fornications: Woe, I say to you! Even three times, woe! For the atheist shall have it far better than you, when the wrath of the great and dreadful God has come! For when they seek forgiveness, they shall surely find it. Yet woe to you who blaspheme the Spirit; from you forgiveness has fled away! Behold, destruction waits for you as you continue to tread the wide path!

For you believe yourself to be a glorious vine, yet your roots are full of rottenness, a vine of deceit with many tendrils spreading forth abomination! Behold, you see yourself as a sovereign nation, as the mother church, universal, and yet you willingly go into captivity and hold fast in your rebellion! Therefore, I shall make you a desolation and an astonishment, an object of horror and hissing; I shall strip you bare!

And behold, you shall become an island, a most desolate place amidst the nations. No more shall anyone draw near to you, nor shall any attempt to pass through. For all shall keep their distance for fear of your punishment. Every traveler shall go roundabout, horrified at the smoke of your burning.

For thus says The Lord: I have set you apart for judgment! I have separated you out for death, for sorrow and for famine, until the fire of My wrath consumes you! For you have caused My beloved to depart from Me; you have turned them aside from The Way! You have caused them to trust in fables and to put their hope in lies and false visions, in worthless things! The Truth is not in you, and from The Life you are far removed!

You have pierced My heart with a hot iron! You have battered and bruised Me, and torn My flesh! My sadness fills the heavens like the unending blackness, My tears cover the earth like the oceans, because of you! My anger wells up within Me like a raging fire, on account of all these you have persecuted and murdered throughout your generations!

Indeed, the cup of My indignation overflows, on account of all you have done and are about to do, says The Lord. And still I sent to you many in My own name, that you might be saved from yourself. Yet you rejected them all, beating some and killing others, casting them out in your pompous rage. You will not turn, and so The Father has declared your end...

WOE TO THE CHURCH CALLED MOTHER! WOE TO YOU AND YOUR APPOINTED LEADERS! WOE TO YOU AND ALL YOUR "HOLY FATHERS"! WOE TO THE CHURCH CALLED ROMAN AND CATHOLIC! WOE TO THE CHURCH FULL OF DEAD MEN'S BONES! For I have prepared a great fire, and behold, it is already kindled, and you, along with all who cleave to you, shall surely be cast into it! SAYS THE LORD.

7/2/05 **From YahuShua HaMashiach, Our Lord and Savior**
The Word of The Lord Spoken to Timothy
For Timothy, and For All Those Who Have Ears to Hear
Hearts Changed

Thus says The Lord to His servant: My son, why do you focus on that which others can not see or hear? Rather rejoice, Timothy, for I have given you eyes to see and ears to hear. Behold, all the earth proclaims the glory of The Lord, and the whole of creation testifies to the truth of who I am. Yet the truth remains hidden from the multitudes, and the testimony dwells not in the hearts of men.

Timothy, be not downhearted over your loved ones who reject Me and My Word, for they have no understanding. Their hearts remain hard and unyielding, their vision marred and narrow, their minds closed, held captive in a world which rejects God and refuses to accept Me as I truly am. Yet they shall harken in due season, wholeheartedly will they come, once their shells are cracked and they too are broken atop The Stone... *A flood of tears washing away every hurt, absolving every sin, bringing peace the kind of which only The Lord can give.*

For that which they have wrought inwardly has become a desert of arid sands, false hope and great iniquity, a wasteland of scattered stones over which they continually stumble. Yet I tell you the truth, they shall bring forth a bounty in their time, as does the desert after the much needed rains have come. For the desolate shall come to realize their need, and those who hunger and thirst for righteousness shall surely receive. I AM THE LORD.

7/3/05 **From The Lord, Our God and Savior**
The Word of The Lord Spoken to Timothy
For All Those Who Have Ears to Hear
The Lord Comes Nigh; Make the Way Straight for His Return

Thus says The Lord to the peoples of the earth: In My right hand is the power to save; and in My left, judgment, which I am about to pour out. For I am The Lord your God, The Only God, The God of Abraham, The God of Isaac, and of Jacob whose name is Israel. And behold, I sent My Only Begotten into the world, and The Word became flesh, YahuShua, Immanu El.

Again, I am sending The Holy One to you. Therefore incline your ears and listen, that you may receive true knowledge. For as it was at the first, so shall it be at the last, for I do not change. Behold, ahead of The Messiah did I send John the Baptist, the voice of one crying out in the wilderness. In John's hand I had placed the trumpet; and he made the path straight in preparation of The One coming after him, by whom all must be saved.

John indeed baptized with water and with the Word given him. And now I am sending 144,000, in the spirit of John and in the power of Elijah, to baptize with the Word of God and fire. For I have placed My words in their mouths, and the Trumpet rests securely in their hands. Therefore trust these I have sent and am sending, for they are My witnesses; they hear My voice and prepare My way before Me.

For My judgments shall fall from Heaven, upon every tribe, tongue, people and nation; My punishments shall rain down hard upon the earth and break the pride of man!

Behold, I shall remove all from their places; in My fierce anger I shall drive them out! The cities shall be laid waste and the houses shall be left desolate, for the earth shall become one vast desolation!

Yet there is sanctuary from this storm,
A way of escape has been provided;
For He is called Jesus and Christ;
YahuShua HaMashiach is His name!...

Call upon Him, do not wait!...

Call upon His name in sincerity and in truth,
And you shall surely be delivered...

Says The Lord.

7/7/05 **From YahuShua HaMashiach, Our Lord and Savior**
The Word of The Lord Spoken to Timothy
For a Brother in Christ
And For All Those Who Have Ears to Hear
The Mark

This question was asked of The Lord, for a brother in Christ:
Lord, what is the mark of the beast, in the Bible?

[The Lord answered] My son, why ask of Me such things? Rather, consider the marks you have taken. Are you clean? Where does your allegiance lie? Is it given to the things of men and to the lusts of this world? Or does it belong to God, longing always to know the deep things of Messiah, whom you call Christ? Therefore, seek first your own salvation; dwell not on outward things of evil. For evil has lost its grip on the redeemed.

Yet for the sake of all those who shall come to read these words, I shall answer you, that they may hear and know and remember: The mark, this mark of the beast, is a choice, a grave error. Yet as of this day, it remains merely an invention of man, a device, a stamp. Yet there is an evil one among men who will gain power and much prestige, who will force everyone - great and small, rich and poor, free and slave - to receive a mark in his right hand or on his forehead. The technology exists; its production has commenced. Thus that which was created for good shall be used for evil, that the few may gain control over the many, that no one may buy or sell unless they have the mark, that is the name of the beast or the number of its name, as it is written.

My son, what you seek concerning the end of the age, I have already given to My servant, John, written in the book called Revelation. And that which was given to John, I now bestow upon My servant, Timothy, that all those who have ears to hear may hear the sound of this Trumpet and escape, for the Day is at hand. For as it is written: *The Lord God does nothing without revealing His plans to His servants, the prophets.*

Therefore that which you have considered, and that which you have heard, is true. And oh how modern man glories in his own creations, taking much pride in the inventions of his mind. Look how he revels in the works of his hands. Yet they shall be his undoing, for even now he has brought destruction upon his own head. For in his pride he has opened the door to the evil one, and on account of his great arrogance has he made it possible for the man of perdition to rule over him; by his own works he has condemned himself to death!

Why, O peoples of the earth, do you forge shackles and secure them about your feet?! I tell you the truth, you are all captives, slaves to your own evil thoughts and desires! Therefore, forsake all this madness and return to Me! Call upon My name in sincerity and in truth, and you shall truly be free! For I hold all the keys; even over death and Sheol do I have complete authority. For as it is written: If The Son sets you free, you are free indeed! Says The Lord.

7/8/05 **From YahuShua HaMashiach, Our Lord and Savior**
The Word of The Lord Spoken to Timothy
For All Those Who Have Ears to Hear
**All Shall Reap That Which They Have Sown,
 Be It of Good or Evil**

Thus says The Lord concerning those who have ears yet refuse to hear, who have eyes yet refuse to see: Only those with hearts left desolate are filled with contempt. For they have not received the love of the Truth, nor do they accept Me as I truly am. Rather they hide behind corrupt doctrine and filthy tradition, covering themselves with pretense, in an attempt to shield themselves from My correction. With practiced speech and a lying tongue they twist the Scriptures, behold, they rend the Word of God, for the sake of their own pride. For they do not know Me, neither do I live in them. Thus they willingly believe the lies, and seek always to uphold the commandments of men, as they slander those sent to them.

Therefore thus says The Lord, to those who dwell in the churches of men and to all their self-appointed leaders: Why do you not receive Me?! Indeed you are unable, for you do always push out the hand! Behold, I send to you a mere man, that you might receive of My correction, yet you say he has a demon! You do always fight against Me!
Behold, this Word is Truth, the very will of The Father made known, the Word of The Lord put forth through His prophets once again. Yet you cry, *"False!"* because you find they run contrary to your preconceived notions and beliefs, as though you and your established doctrine were somehow above reproach; all the while setting up walls of falsehood, laying down traps of deceit to bar My way before Me, seeking always to fortify your position, lest I expose your masquerade.

O people of little faith, you are deceived; you have all been turned aside from the Truth! Churches of men, your doctrines are corrupt, your every tradition unclean, born of men and the harlot! She has deceived you, and yet you willingly walk in her ways!

Throughout her generations she has deceived the people; in her lust for power she has oppressed them, forcing multitudes to embrace the crooked path! She is a harlot, her ways antichrist, and yet you follow her! Behold, by her own power and authority, of which she appointed to herself, she endeavored to change My Commandments! Yet you nod your head in agreement, yes, you obey her teachings as you forsake My Sabbaths, upholding many of the same false doctrines and perverse traditions I hate!

Therefore, O churches of men, your discipline shall be severe and your abasement terrible! And you, O church of harlots, shall be stripped naked and brought to ruin! Behold, you shall be torn in pieces and left utterly desolate, to the astonishment of all people! For I do not change! Says The Lord.

So then listen closely and give ear, all you who call of yourselves Christian, all you who stone My prophets and slander those sent to you, all you who abuse My Word in Scripture and desecrate My Sabbaths; hear the Word of The Lord and give heed, be bowed down, for the mouth of The Living God has spoken: ALL YOU SOW, YOU SHALL REAP! Repent, therefore! Again I say, repent, lest you also catch fire as you watch all your works burn in the Day! For My anger is kindled against you, O churches of men! And My wrath grows in its fury, against ALL who lead My people astray!

Therefore call upon My name, in sincerity and in truth!...

Beloved ones, embrace Me as I am,
And not as you would have Me be!
Obey MY teaching and turn away
From the commandments of men!...

For I, alone, am The Way and The Truth,
The Life without end...

Says The Lord YahuShua.

7/10/05 **From The Lord, Our God and Savior**
The Word of The Lord Spoken to Timothy
For All Those Who Have Ears to Hear
The True Baptism

Thus says The Lord: Be wary of all these men in authority who dwell in the churches of men, be wary and vigilant. For they hold tightly to singleness of doctrine, teaching always that which is built upon the corrupt knowledge and understanding of men, men who refuse to let go of that which was passed down to them by their forefathers, by which they also remain blind. Therefore do not judge according to human standards, nor by that which is put forth by men as doctrine, for they are greatly misled. Rather study to show yourself approved unto God, a workman that need not be ashamed, rightly dividing the Word of Truth. For discernment with fear is righteousness.

Beloved ones, embrace the wisdom and knowledge of God, break free from all these corrupt doctrines and filthy traditions held in such high regard. For I ask you, if you dispense the food of God to the hungry, while using your own salt to salt that which has salt in itself, will not the food you offer lose its flavor and become bitter in the mouths of those who came looking to be fed?

I tell you the truth, many will there be in My Kingdom who received no baptism by water. Rather they had been fully immersed in The Word of God, enveloped in The Son's sacrifice and love, baptized in the Spirit of Truth. For most assuredly, I say to you, they have their reward. Therefore, do not cast stumbling blocks before the feet of those who love Me. Be one in Messiah, according to that which dwells inwardly in the heart. For true fellowship comes not by words spoken amongst a group of united people, nor by immersion in water.

Rather it starts with the heart, and is found in the stillness of My spirit, where My peace mends the broken and My gentle caress gladdens the heart. For all those found at the feet of The Lord are covered with grace, and those who abide in My love are indeed of one accord.

Beloved, where in The Commandments have I written all must be baptized by men to be saved? Baptism is indeed good, if it is a confession poured out from one's heart in pure belief, an outward act of faith revealing one's acceptance of their forgiveness in The Messiah. For the water of the earth can only cleanse that which is soiled on the skin. By no means can it cleanse that which is soiled in the spirit; this is reserved for the blood of The Lamb. Again I say to you, baptism by water is nothing, unless one is first washed by The Word, being baptized in the Spirit of Grace and Truth which is received in YahuShua HaMashiach, whom you call Jesus and Christ. For HE is The True Baptism, The Very Water of Life, in which all must be cleansed to receive everlasting life.

Therefore beloved, remember:
The spirit of the Word, and not the letter,
Is the way, the truth and the life...

For The Messiah is indeed coming quickly,
To baptize all in fire and glory...

Those of a wicked heart, in fire...

And those of the Spirit, in glory, forever and ever!

8/19/05 **From The Lord, Our God and Savior**
The Word of The Lord Spoken to Timothy
For Timothy, and For All Those Who Have Ears to Hear
All Have Been Purchased...
   Yet Few Have Accepted, Few Are Chosen

*This question was asked of The Lord: Lord, what does it mean in
the Book of Revelation, where it says, "The 144,000 did not defile
themselves with women; they kept themselves pure"?*

Thus says The Lord to His servant: Rather the 144,000 have
been purchased, redeemed and chosen from the earth as a special
offering, and are *spiritually* undefiled, pure *as* virgins. Timothy,
you have asked, and I have answered you plainly. Thus I tell you,
you are of the number, I have already placed you within their
ranks; My seal is upon your forehead.

Yet those who envy seek to cause doubt, by questioning your
worthiness and defilement with women. And because of this,
they reject My Word spoken to this generation. Therefore they
remain in their sins, for they want no part with Me as I truly am.
They have removed themselves far from Me, and seek to draw
others away also, that they might feel validated in their unjust
cause. Yet who The Lord has cleansed is worthy of His purpose;
call him not unworthy or defiled. For that which comes from the
heart of man does indeed defile the man, yet that which comes
from God is holy.

Therefore fear, all you who point the finger, and humble yourselves,
all you who twist My words for your own gain, lest you be found
guilty of blaspheming the Holy Spirit.

For the defilement which was written, and remains misinterpreted by men, is not defilement with the daughters of men, but defilement with the churches of men, who remain daughters of the church called mother. For she is a harlot, says The Lord. Thus spiritual purification begins with grace, and is for those whom I have chosen to become virgin in spirit, even a complete cleansing of every aspect of their lives.

All men are defiled, having fallen
Into all manner of diverse temptations;
There is none righteous in all the earth, no, not one...

Yet all who repent, in sincerity and in truth,
Are cleansed in the blood of The Lamb,
Which is pure and holy...

Therefore, those whom I have called
To be My witnesses must become pure
In heart and in spirit, set apart from the world
And the churches of men, who cease not
From polluting My name and marring
My image before the people.

Timothy, you have not sat among the prideful, nor have you kept the company of those deceived in the churches of men. You have accepted no doctrine at all. Indeed, you were like clay which had been molded by the world, yet remained unmolded in spirit.

Behold, even when you were yet in your mother's womb, I sanctified you; I ordained you a prophet, a witness for My name, an enemy to all nations. Thus you put no faith in the doctrines of the world, nor did you accept any doctrine taught in the churches of men. As for your body and mind, yes, you did become defiled by sin, of this you were guilty, as are all who have gained maturity. Yet I have taken your sins from you and remember your iniquities no more. Therefore, I ask you, what defilement remains? For what The Lord has cleansed, in the blood of The Lamb, is a new creation - *virgin*.

Behold, I am the same yesterday, today, and all tomorrows to come, says The Lord. No contradiction found. Thus all error belongs to men, exploited by the wicked one for his own evil purpose. Therefore, what I have written I have written; it stands. And that which I have written through My servant, John, stands also, though it is greatly misinterpreted, the error of which is compounded by the mistranslations of men.

Yet worse still is the interpretation of My Word by men of intellect and learning, who shroud their arrogance in pretense and hide their error under the guise of established doctrine, unprofitable servants who lead My people astray. For My Word is for all who truly seek Me and long to know My ways, even to walk in them. Thus My Word can only be accepted and understood by those who have received the love of the Truth, for they abide in Me and My spirit resides within them. For how can one who stands apart from Me know Me? And how can one who teaches his own way walk with Me in Mine?

Men do not have understanding of the Scriptures in themselves! Rather it is a gift from God, received through the Holy Spirit, given to those who have placed all their trust in The Holy One, embracing Me as I truly am.

Or have you never read this Scripture: *The fear of The Lord is the beginning of wisdom, and the knowledge of The Holy One is understanding?*
Therefore to those who have received is all revealed, and to those who have not received is all shut away. Shall the darkness understand the light? For only those of The Light, bathed in His glory, shall see; the rest left blinded.

For until one calls on the name
Of The Messiah, in sincerity and in truth,
By no means shall they receive...

For He is The One who had placed
The mud upon their eyes to heal them...

Behold, He is also The Water of Siloam
Which was sent to wash them,
That they might now see, says The Lord.

Also read: "Grafted In" - Volume Three

8/23/05 **From The Lord, Our God and Savior**
The Word of The Lord Spoken to Timothy
For All Those Who Have Ears to Hear
Abortion: Murder of the Innocent

WOE TO THOSE WHO HARM THE LITTLE ONES! WOE TO THOSE WHO SLAUGHTER MY GIFTS! AND WOE TO ALL WHO STAND IN AGREEMENT! Says The Lord. For they are and were created, sculpted delicately in fragile flesh, attached to The Vine before their very conception. For it is the fool who says in her heart, *"There is no God,"* believing she answers only to herself, as she testifies aloud, saying, *"It is my body, my choice."* YOU CHOOSE DEATH! Says The Lord. For the child within you is Mine, even as you are Mine also; your body is not your own! ALL BELONG TO THE LORD, ALL ANSWER TO ME!

Therefore, thus says The Lord: The murder of the innocent leads to the death of the guilty, who carry the innocent within them; take no part in their sin. For all who do wear equally the guilt of the mother, all seek the penalty of death; from the lawmakers to the voters, to the building owner to the workers to the suppliers, and finally to the father, if he does not take a stand to protect the unborn who are without blame.
Behold, they have brought the wrath of God upon their nation, upon their state and upon their cities, calamity upon calamity until I have laid them waste!... *Fierce is My anger, hot is My countenance, My little ones perish in all the earth! WHOLE GENERATIONS SLAUGHTERED! MULTITUDES OF CHILDREN MURDERED DAY AND NIGHT, WITHOUT CEASING! Therefore have I brought forth and appointed many days of sorrow for THIS generation! - JUDGMENT! THE GREAT AND TERRIBLE DAY OF THE LORD!*

9/3/05 **From The Lord, Our God and Savior**
The Word of The Lord Spoken to Timothy
For All Those Who Have Ears to Hear
The Judgment of God Is True and Without Question,
 Yet the Error of the People Is Great

These questions were asked of The Lord: Lord, is capital punishment OK? Are those who are cremated lost?

Thus says The Lord: The penalty of sin is death. Thus all who have sinned shall surely die, all shall lie down in death. Yet there is a people who shall not sleep, nor shall they lie down in death; a people who shall be awake at My coming, a people who have received of the divine gift, a people who know Me and in whom I am known, for I see of Myself within them. They shall be lifted up, not preceding those who have fallen asleep in Messiah. This is the first harvest and resurrection. For there is but One Way, One Truth, and One Life; from the beginning, there is but One.

Yet there is one who is cast down, who goes about to and fro in all the earth, perpetuating lies and spreading forth abomination, leading many away from the Truth. From the very beginning, satan was a deceiver and a murderer; he has never been on the side of truth. From the beginning, he has sought to ensnare My people and destroy My nation. For the heart of man is easily swayed, on account of his flesh he becomes entangled. Thus his idolatries are many, and his adulteries have no end.
Behold, hand in hand they march toward their destruction, embracing lies and rejecting Truth, as they parade their transgressions openly in the streets. For the wisdom of the wise has perished, and the knowledge of the prudent has turned to dust.

113

For the people are void, they all have itching ears. As cattle to the slaughter, or as a bird hastens to the snare, they give heed to those of clever words, failing to perceive it will cost them their life. Therefore the mouth of Sheol is open, the pit is dug deep, and the generation of My wrath shall surely be cast into it! Indeed, they shall all walk through the valley, until death comes to claim them and the grave hides them away, says The Lord.

Therefore hear the Word of My mouth and humble yourselves, O sons and daughters of men, that you may see with new eyes and restored vision: If you kill for the sake of justice, though you yourselves remain unjust, have you not transgressed twice in your spirit? Yea three times, you have sinned against The Lord your God. For man knows not the justice of God, nor can he comprehend the judgment of The Most High. YOU SLOTHFUL AND MOST WICKED GENERATION, YOU ARE ALL MURDERERS! Even to murder the murderer is murder! You do always transgress! You know nothing of the power of God, nor of My mercy revealed in The Messiah, whom you call Christ, nor are you able to search the hearts of men!

O foolish and deceived generation, if a man has committed murder and you put him to death, you have placed yourselves in the seat of judgment, making yourselves equal with God! Thus "BLASPHEMY" shall be written upon your heads, and "MURDERER" your new name! Yes punish the man who has committed murder, yet kill him not, lest he turn to Me in sincere repentance, in The Messiah's name, and be forgiven. Shall you then slaughter the sons of God, piercing the hearts of those made new?! O peoples of the earth, how long shall you tread the wide path?! How long shall you walk in the way of Cain and run greedily in the error of Balaam, holding fast in your rebellion as Korah?! For your sins are many; behold, they are increased beyond measure!

Shall sin judge sin, and institute
The punishment before the time?!...

Is not My judgment, that of capital punishment,
For all who have sinned, and annihilation
For all who refuse to repent?!...

Yet I sent My Only Begotten Son
To suffer your sentences for you;
Therefore, you do greatly err...

Peoples of the earth, where are your hearts?!
Err on the side of hope and salvation
In Messiah, where one can not err!

Therefore concerning those who kill the body, yet can not harm the soul, I say this: He who murders his brother has committed great evil. Even he who has conceived of murder in his heart is guilty. And those who carry out capital punishment are of the same. For they have put themselves in the judgment seat; behold, they have placed themselves upon My throne! Yet you know not what tomorrow will bring, nor can you look upon the heart of man; even all his thoughts are hidden from you.

Thus only I shall make an end of evil. Only I shall destroy the wicked of heart and cast the sons of satan into eternal darkness, into the void of lifeless nothingness. For only The One who grants life can take it away. I AM THE LORD! Or have you forgotten whom you shall fear, The One alone who can destroy both body and soul?

Behold, the sins of this generation reach unto heaven, a murderous and most wicked people, a great multitude who stand in agreement, a whole generation seeking the penalty of death as they shake their fists at Heaven! Yes, by your own admission you are guilty! Behold, according to your own laws, YOU should be put to death, YOU are the ones who should be sitting in the chair! HYPOCRITES! You have destroyed yourselves!

FOOLISH GENERATION, YOUR LIFE IS NOT YOUR OWN! Apart from Me, there is no wisdom! Apart from The Holy One, there is no life! Apart from The Vine, there are no branches! Behold, the leaves wither and the fruit has been cast down, for the people have no favor with God. Thus every dry branch must be broken off and cast into the fire, all corrupt fruit must be left and tread down. For the temple of God has lost its form; its comeliness has departed, every chamber is empty. For the heart of man is void, his countenance unyielding. Thus the pride of man has become a chasm, both deep and wide, says The Lord.

Therefore, thus says The Lord your Redeemer, The Holy One of Israel: Tear down the temple of God, and I shall raise it up again! For all who have died but sleep, yet I shall raise them up again. And of those who are Mine, I shall not lose one, for I am The Lord and I shall raise them up again. Even those cremated and those long since turned to dust shall rise. For from the dust you came forth, by My knowledge were you made, and by My breath you became living souls.

Can not God raise up children to Abraham, from the very stones, if He so chooses? This I have already told you. Why then, O peoples of the earth, do you rant and rave and wail like the heathen, as one with no hope? Where is your trust?

Indeed, you have forgotten your God, and are greatly deceived; you do not know Me, nor will you believe. For if you knew Me, then you would know The Father also, and understand that all things are possible with God.

Therefore, let those who ask in faith receive, and let those who believe have understanding. For the fear of The Lord is indeed the beginning of wisdom. For I have already told you, that neither man nor angel can truly kill another, nor is satan able to raise the dead. Only The One who formed it can raise it up again, and only by the hand of Him who created it shall it be utterly destroyed. Thus if one refuses to be restored in the image of God, which I am, he shall surely perish. He shall be blotted out, his life forfeit. Indeed, it shall be as though he had never been.

> Therefore repent, and receive of Me as I am,
> And not as you would have Me be,
> That you may be truly born again...
>
> For I am the perfect reflection of The Father,
> The image of The Invisible God...
>
> I died, behold, I am risen,
> And by My life are you saved...
>
> That you might become the perfect reflection of Me,
> The One alone in whom is everlasting life...
>
> Says The Lord.

9/3/05 **From YahuShua HaMashiach, Our Lord and Savior**
The Word of The Lord Spoken to Timothy
For All Those Who Have Ears to Hear
(Regarding suicide)
Twice Murdered

Thus says The Lord: I have looked upon those who strike themselves down, upon all who have been ensnared by the devil. For the sin of suicide is very grievous, a sin which only multiplies suffering and increases pain; of which the dead have no knowledge, for there is only silence in the grave.

Therefore, hear and understand: If one heavy-laden with sorrow, with hopelessness and pain, ends their own life, they have indeed sinned. For to kill is to kill, even of one's self. Yet I tell you the truth, they are twice murdered; slain first in their heart by the devil, then in their body at their own hand. Are they lost? No. For even one dead at their own hand, coerced by the devil, will live again. For I am He who shall call forth both the first and the second.

For all who have sinned are dead in their sins, yet in Me they are made alive again, as many as drink My blood and eat My flesh. For I am The Life Without End, The Only Fountain of Living Waters, The Bread of God which came down from Heaven and gave life to the world... *Behold, from the beginning I had overcome all things; from the very foundation of the world, I AM HE, The Resurrection and The Life!*

9/6/05 **From YahuShua HaMashiach, Our Lord and Savior**
The Word of The Lord Spoken to Timothy
For All Those Who Have Ears to Hear
One Truth, One Church, One Body - No Walls

This question was asked of The Lord: Lord, what of the Seventh Day Adventist Church, and their claim to be the true church and remnant?

Thus says The Lord: Again I say to you, My church has no walls, and is called by no other name except the name The Father has given Me. Its members are of one mind and one spirit, of one love, one flock with one Shepherd, a people set apart who keep The Commandments of The Father and remain faithful to The Son, striving always to walk in My ways. For those who truly know Me dwell in Me, and I in them. For they are Mine, even as I am theirs also - My body, My bride.

Therefore woe to any church of men, who claims to be the true church and remnant. Woe, I say to them. For they have placed themselves in the seat of The Father, and therefore remain under God's judgment. For none walk according to the Truth, not one accepts Me as I truly am; all have gone astray, teaching as doctrine the commandments of men.

Beloved, no one can come to Me, unless The Father who sent Me draws them to Me. And only those who accept Me as I truly am are of My body, for The Truth resides within them and is revealed by their works. Yes, even these stumble in their walk, for they are but flesh.

Yet I am He who searches the
Hearts and minds, I know My own;
I know whose love is steadfast,
Whose faith is unmoving...

And this is the True Church
My people long for, the remnant
Which now is and is yet to come...

For it is not found outwardly in the world,
But inwardly, in the temple of God...

I am The Lord.

10/7/05 **From The Lord, Our God and Savior**
The Word of The Lord Spoken to Timothy
For All Those Who Have Ears to Hear
As God Is Three Aspects, All as One,
So Too Is the Coming of The Son of Man

Thus says The Lord: If The Son of Man is coming on the clouds of heaven with power and great glory, and every eye shall see Him, how then does He also come as a thief?

Here is wisdom: The Son of Man comes at a day and hour unknown, to spoil the house of the strong man. And that which belongs to The Lord shall be taken, and that which is of the strong man shall be left. For The Son of Man comes first as spirit poured out on the nations, to call upon His elect. Behold, He shall pass through the multitudes and peer deep into the heart of every vessel, and bundle them together. And on a day which no one knows, at an hour no one can predict, The Son of Man shall come as a thief and steal them away. Then shall the lawless one be revealed, whom The Lord will consume with the breath of His mouth and destroy with the brightness of His coming, as it is written. I AM THE LORD.

10/7/05 **From The Lord, Our God and Savior**
The Word of The Lord Spoken to Timothy
For the Churches of Men
And For All Those Who Have Ears to Hear
I Will Take My People OUT OF

Thus says The Lord: Churches of men, you do always twist the Scriptures! You cease not from adding to and taking away from the Word of God, as you continue to stand firm upon your own cracked foundations which your forefathers laid! - Foundation upon foundation throughout your generations, built ever higher according to the pride and vanity of men, an arrogance which has no equal!

How long shall you contend with Me? How long shall you pervert the Truth? Churches of men, shall I lie to My prophets and give them false testimony?! Or did you think I have ceased from making My plans known, that I have altogether turned back from sending them? Certainly not! For I am The Lord, and I do not change! Therefore, let every cracked foundation crumble and every house fall with a great crash! Let the glory of man be turned backward, until the pride of man is bowed down and the arrogance of man is utterly humiliated! For The Lord alone shall be exalted in that day, as it is written.

Thus says The Lord: Humble yourselves, O churches of arrogance, and pray that you are not left standing upon the earth in bewilderment and tears, in the day I gather up My treasured ones and steal away My elect, those counted worthy to escape all these things which shall soon come to pass, the first to stand in the presence of The Son of Man, the first to be sheltered from My fury. Behold, the angels of Heaven shall ascend and descend upon The Son of Man, until the harvest is made complete.

Therefore, again I say to you, humble yourselves! For pride has blinded your eyes and arrogance has stopped your ears! REPENT! And pray double for those YOU have led from the Truth! For you preach and teach in the name of another messiah, a false christ who looks nothing like Me, a molded image which you have shaped to fit your own corrupt doctrines and perverse traditions, polluting My name and My glory as you continue to twist and segregate the Scriptures to your own hurt! Says The Lord.

Therefore, blessed are those who
Come out from among them...

Blessed are those who obey God rather than men...

Blessed are those who place their trust
In The Son of God, striving always to walk
In His ways and keep His commandments;
They shall surely be taken out of this place...

Yet woe to all those who disobey The Son,
Woe to all who turn aside from The Way
And forsake The Commandments,
For the wrath of God remains upon them.

11/25/05 **From The Lord, Our God and Savior**
The Word of The Lord Spoken to Timothy
For All Those Who Have Ears to Hear
Do Not Be Tempted by the World,
  For Its Ways Lead Only to Blasphemy and Sin

*This question was asked of The Lord, for several family members:
Lord, may we still give gifts to our loved ones, as long as it doesn't
take place on the 25th of December, and if we do not call it
Christmas?*

Thus says The Lord of Heaven and Earth: In these things of sin,
which are altogether an abomination before The Lord, TAKE NO
PART! Make no compromise, nor attempt to go roundabout; be
completely separate. Turn your back on all these commandments
of men which pollute My name and My glory, stop drinking from
these polluted fountains! For I hate all these filthy traditions,
I loathe the sight of them! They are corrupt, evil works and
adulteries, harlotries passed down from generation to generation,
idolatries of every kind! Says The Lord.

*Thus says The Lord to all those who say they love Me, yet do not
remain in My love:* Do you really know Me? And if you long to
know Me as I truly am, then let go of this world and forsake its
evil ways. Come out from among them and be separate; take no
part in that which is unclean, and I will receive you.
Yet I hear you saying, *"But I do these things with a pure heart.
The Lord will understand, for I do these things out of love."* Yes,
all things born of love are good and well-pleasing to The Lord.
For I know your hearts, beloved, even to your innermost desires
and intentions.

Yet those who love Me obey My commands and give heed to the leading of My spirit, for the two are in agreement. It is written: *God is love*. And if I am love, then obey Me as I have loved you; remember My decrees and obey My Commandments. Reveal to every onlooker that I am indeed your First Love, and I alone deserve your worship.

Thus says The Risen One: Therefore no more give your love or attention to the things of this world, for they are passing away. Neither shall you love anyone more than Me. Or have you never read these Scriptures: *He who loves father or mother more than Me is not worthy of Me; and he who loves son or daughter more than Me is not worthy of Me; and friendship with the world is enmity with God?* Therefore honor Me in spirit and in truth, in accordance with the Scriptures. Stand apart from the ways of this world, and cast away those things which pollute My name and My glory; crucify your lives of old and follow Me!

Beloved ones, the Scriptures are not malleable,
The Commandments do not change!...

For The Truth is absolute, forever standing on a hill,
Bright and shining, immovable, unbreakable!...

The Everlasting Stone which has become
The Head of the Corner, The Great Mountain
Which fills the whole earth! Says The Lord.

Also read: "Obey God" - Volume Four

12/1/05 **From The Lord, Our God and Savior**
The Word of The Lord Spoken to Timothy
For All Those Who Have Ears to Hear
Judgment, Transgression and The Word

Thus says The Lord: I am The Lord your God, He who stretched out the heavens and laid the foundations of the earth, The Maker of all things. Yes I AM HE, The Creator of Heaven and Earth, The One alone who sits on high, molding and shaping that which I have created by Him who is forever seated at My right hand. The Father and The Son are One.

Behold, even to man did I grant this power, the power to create or to destroy. Yet within man dwells a corrupted spirit. And so he goes out and comes in, corrupting his way before him, leaving mourning in his wake; creating that which brings harm to himself, destroying that which was to sustain him, even to the murdering of the innocent; desecrating that which is pure, polluting the things of God, as he turns his back on his Creator.

Thus I must judge the peoples of the earth; behold, I shall surely testify against them and utter My strong rebuke. For as it is written, so shall it be: *I shall come, and I shall not keep silent! A fire shall devour before Me, and a great storm shall rage all around Me! I shall call to the heavens above and to the earth beneath, and judge all people! Indeed, all shall give an account on that day, even of every idle word.*

Yet let My faithful ones, all who have made a covenant with Me by sacrifice, be gathered to Me, and let them be judged according to the New Covenant; let The Holy Sacrifice stand in their place and speak on their behalf.

For only the rejection of The Holy Covenant leads to judgment and death; or the acceptance thereof, from judgment into life. For I am a just God and a Savior; My mercy endures forever, My judgment is righteous, and My justice lasts throughout the generations. Behold, Heaven is My throne, and the earth My footstool, says The Lord.

For I had sent to you My Son, in whom the fullness of God dwells, God in the flesh, Immanu El; a man without sin, blameless, who willingly gave up His life for all who have fallen under judgment, that those who are willing might pass from death to life, from darkness into The Light of Life.

For He carried the weight of the world's sin
To the cross, and crucified sin through His suffering;
The penalty of sin abolished as He fell asleep,
The Victory established for all time upon His rising...

Thus He will be your judge
At the Last Day, O peoples of the earth,
Because He is both God and man...

Therefore, blessed are all those
In whom He sees of Himself,
For these have already passed from
Judgment into life, seated forever at His right hand.

Therefore hear the Word of The Lord, for thus says The Lord: Do not be deceived; let satan gain no foothold. For there is but One God and One Savior, One Deliverer in the Day of Wrath.

Again, I say to you, do not be deceived. Satan can not change his visage and become man. He is what he is, and remains who he became to this day. He is heylel, son of the morning, with a heart like the abyss. And those fallen are like him, corrupted by those same things which consume him.

Yet satan has indeed appeared to men, sending them strong delusions, preying upon that which already dwells within them; even imitating Mary, the mother of The Messiah, deceiving those who remain ignorant of the Truth, leading a multitude away into false worship and idolatry.

So then satan only imitates the truth, for there is no truth in him. When he tells a lie, he is only doing what comes natural to him, because he is a liar and the father of all lies. Thus he does indeed wear many disguises, and delights in leading My people astray. For by clever words and dark speeches he bears false witness, leading multitudes away into faiths which are dead - FALSE RELIGIONS! DETESTABLE PRACTICES! ABOMINATIONS!

YahuShua HaMashiach is The Gift, He is The Only Way; there is salvation in no other, nor any other name under Heaven by which you must be saved. Thus ALL religions of this world are an abomination in the eyes of The Most High God! Every one of them pollutes the land and spreads forth like a plague! Behold, even those who bear My name have become like them! Not one worships Me in spirit or in truth, all have gone astray! Corrupt workers, arrogant assemblies, you worship yourselves!

Yes even you, O churches of men, have corrupted the Word of Truth, and do not cease from polluting My name! You misuse My name and abuse My Word, subverting the people through false doctrine and filthy tradition! You encourage them to forsake My Commandments and ignore My every decree!

In the name of The Holy One, you cause My people to sin! By permission, UNDER GRACE, you encourage them to transgress The Commandments of God, teaching and preaching to them another messiah, adding to and taking away from My Word to uphold your own way, and all for the sake of unjust gain! Shall I not discipline you for these things?! Shall I not bring down My hand hard upon you?! Shall I not come forth swiftly and wipe ALL religions from the face of the earth?!

Yet true faith has a name, and true religion yields fruit of the same: A Bride who obeys the voice of her Husband and walks in His ways, a people worthy to be called by His name. Yet the light has departed from the churches of men, The Word of Truth is hidden from their eyes. All is corrupt and dying, darkness fills the earth.

And so The Word was sent, and came into
The world to seek and to save the lost...

And behold, He is coming again, to deliver His own,
All those who believe and live by The Word;
And to destroy those who fight against The Word,
For they too are bound by The Word...

For The Word stands forever.,
Immovable and everlasting, unchangeable,
Having complete authority over all things,
The light and the dark, the righteous and the wicked...

Indeed, the whole universe is set within
The confines of His will, giving heed to Him
Who created it, forever and ever... Amen.

12/15/05 From YahuShua HaMashiach, Our Lord and Savior
The Word of The Lord Spoken to Timothy
For All Those Who Have Ears to Hear
Heed the Call

Thus says The Lord: The time approaches quickly, and is already here, when My servant shall speak as never before. And those who have ears to hear will listen and come out. Yet those who hate the sound of this Trumpet will turn and fight against Me. For Timothy shall wield My words like a sword, and many shall be pierced and struck through - some to hope and salvation, and many more to refinement and tears; and still others to condemnation, all those who refuse to repent, those who hold fast in their rebellion to the end. For My words are fire, singeing the forehead of the arrogant, setting the countenance of the prideful ablaze, twin daggers piercing the heart of every hearer.

Therefore hear the Word of The Lord,
And heed the call...

For it is a call to repentance, a shout
And a witness, a proclamation of Truth...

A trumpet of alarm and war, a declaration
Of judgment, a strong rebuke...

Says The Lord.

12/16/05 **From The Lord, Our God and Savior**
The Word of The Lord Spoken to Timothy
For All Those Who Have Ears to Hear
(Regarding the modern holidays of men)
Transgression

Thus says The Lord God: This world has altogether become a house
of harlots, a whole generation who ceases not from committing
fornication with the pagan and the heathen, reveling always in
those things I hate! - A most perverse generation who desecrates
the name of The Messiah, a foolish people who do always take the
name of The Lord in vain!

Behold, all remain shackled to this world, captivated by sin,
caught up in the ways of the world and men! Even those within
the churches of men will not heed My voice, nor will they receive
My correction; choosing rather to mingle honor with dishonor,
praise with blasphemy, and purity with sin!

Therefore stop breaking My Commandments
In The Messiah's name, O churches of men!...

You shall not associate His name with sin,
Nor shall you honor Him with pagan rituals
And idolatrous traditions, lest I reject you
As I rejected the pagans before you!

Repent, therefore, and give Me glory; worship Me in spirit and in truth, and call upon The Name! For He alone shall deliver you in the Day of Wrath, if you so choose to embrace Him as He truly is; He being the very same who shall also destroy the wicked and bring terrible judgment upon the rebellious, upon great and small, rich and poor, bond and free, upon all who forsake My Law and push out the hand against the Word of My Commandment!

For by Him were you made a vessel unto honor, yet you have all become vessels of dishonor, heaping to yourselves vanities and sin! Therefore, because you are not ashamed of all these abominations which you have committed, but walk proudly, you shall be the first to fall among those who fall, at the time I punish this world for its iniquity and cast down the multitudes for their wickedness! For I am The Lord, and I do not change!

Therefore hear My words, all you proud blasphemers, all you modern pharisees who pervert the Truth, for thus says The Lord: How long shall you desecrate the name of The Messiah, and set yourselves up as an authority?! Behold, as vines of wickedness you bring forth only bitter fruit, propagating corrupt doctrine and perverse tradition among the people like a plague, doctrines and traditions I hate! YAHUSHUA, whom you call Jesus and Christ, is The True Vine! And only those who bear fruit in accordance with His likeness are His branches. And I shall surely prune every branch which grows from Him, that it may bear even more fruit. Yet you say, *"Here I am, I also grow from The Vine!"* You are all liars, a malignancy growing where you should not, dry branches meet to be broken off and cast into the fire!

Peoples of the earth, the Wrath of The Lamb is coming! Did you think I would stay silent during the time appointed?! Did you think I would not set the time and declare the season?! For I am a jealous God and great in power, AND I DO NOT CHANGE!

Thus I shall speak plainly, for you are a most rebellious and hard-hearted people, a most foolish and deceived generation: These modern holidays called Christmas, Easter, Halloween and the like, are an abomination in the eyes of The Most High God.

Therefore in My jealousy and in the fire of My wrath, I shall destroy all your pagan traditions, and tear apart every perverse holiday of man! Behold, I shall wipe them from the face of the earth on that day, and no more shall you break My Commandments and revel in sin in The Messiah's name!

> *Behold, My countenance is turned*
> *Against you, O churches of men!...*
>
> *For you have blasphemed My name*
> *Without ceasing, polluting the name*
> *Of The Messiah days without end!*

You have placed the commandments of men above The Commandments of God, saying within yourselves, *"We are the only authority among men."* How long shall you walk in the ways of the harlot and commit adultery with the pagan?! How long shall you turn your ear away from hearing The Holy Law?! Thus your worship is not accepted, and your prayers are an abomination!

Churches of men, stop your vain babbling, for you do always twist the Scriptures of Truth! BE SILENT BEFORE YOUR GOD! For your traditions are heresy, and your holidays are proof! Purge all this blasphemy from your lips, therefore, step back from your corrupt teachings, and take an account! HUMBLE YOURSELVES! For I am indeed calling you out!

Know you not, that you have all become as the pagan and the heathen, by which all your holidays have their origins?! ABOMINATION! This world has seduced you, and the harlot has led you into temptation! She shall be stripped naked and left desolate in the day of her calamity, broken because of her iniquities, put to death because of her denial of the Truth, crushed beneath the feet of The Holy One of Israel!

Therefore hear the Word of The Lord and give heed, for thus declares The Lord: One Commandment broken are all Commandments broken. One sin committed in The Messiah's name are all sins accounted to you. One sin repented in His name, all are forgiven you. For I know your thoughts, My children, even your innermost intentions, and I know whether or not you are fully converted in your hearts. And though you may lie to yourselves, and bear false witness in the sight of many witnesses, nothing is hidden from the eyes of God - every lie exposed, every heart laid bare, in the Day I rise up and judge the earth.

Come to Me, therefore, in sincerity and in truth;
Humble yourselves in The Messiah's name...

For He is The True Light, utterly void of darkness,
The Only Way to follow, The Truth Absolute;
By Him alone shall you walk into everlasting life...

For only those who walk in Him shall find Me,
And only those in union with Him shall know Me...

Says The Lord.

1/8/06 **From YahuShua HaMashiach, Our Lord and Savior**
The Word of The Lord Spoken to Timothy
For All Those Who Have Ears to Hear
Living Sacrifices

Thus says The Lord: My children, do you love Me? Then do as I command you. Grow wise in Me, and live according to My Word, even according to all these Letters I have given you, by which I have set all these crooked paths straight. For My every word is Scripture, My every Letter truth. Be cognizant of My comings and goings. For I have indeed come to live in those who have received of Me, those who obey My voice and embrace Me as I truly am.

Again, I say to you, honor Me first with your ways, then with your mouth. For honor only spoken of is but wind, the veil of the hypocrite who knows not where he is going, having no remorse over where he has been. For how can one who professes to love Me live contrary to Me? Beloved ones, I love you as I love The Father. In the same way, whoever loves Me loves The Father also. I obey The Father in all things, because I love The Father and The Father is in Me. Likewise those who are truly My disciples obey My voice, because they love Me and I live in them.

So then, walk in My ways and be for Me examples, letting your light so shine before men, that they may see your good works and glorify your Father in Heaven, as it is written. Beloved ones, show them the Way by your faith and obedience, that they too may come to walk beside Me, even upon the Highway of Holiness, each at their appointed time, each in due season.

For I tell you the truth, to walk where The Son of God walks, you must become like Me; crucifying your lives of old, separating yourselves from the bitter enmity which is of this world and the churches of men, living sacrifices who seek to please The Father in all their ways.

For it is written: *If anyone desires to come after Me, let him deny himself and take up his cross, and follow Me. For whoever desires to save his life will lose it, but whoever loses his life for My sake will find it. For what profit is it to a man if he gains the whole world, and loses his own soul? Or what will a man give in exchange for his soul?* Therefore, those who strive to hold onto their life in this world will lose it, having already become dead men's bones in a wasteland of many sorrows, leading and following others on the wide path to destruction.

Beloved, what are all these things of this world compared with your life? What is their worth? And what of all these works of man? Are they not passing away? Again I ask you, what is their value? I tell you the truth, whoever loves anything in this world, more than Me, is not worthy of Me. For I am The Only Way, The Only Truth and The Only Life. There is nothing apart from Me.

Therefore, come and follow Me...

For I am called Jesus The Christ...

My name: YahuShua HaMashiach,
The only name under Heaven
By which you must be saved.

1/14/06 **From The Lord, Our God and Savior**
The Word of The Lord Spoken to Timothy
For All Those Who Have Ears to Hear
Proclaim NOT the Hell of the Churches of Men

Thus says The Lord: Listen, all you churches of men! Shall I, even I, torment My beloved?! SATAN IS THE TORMENTOR! Thus by your own mouths, you have unwittingly called your God, satan! Repent therefore, mend your ways and your doings! Stop profaning My name and desecrating the Glory of My majesty, for you have surely blasphemed the Spirit of Truth!

Again I say, repent, and have greater understanding of My Mercy, which endures forever. For The Son of Man did indeed sleep in the heart of the earth, His tomb, for three days and three nights, yet by no means did He descend into the evils of man's imaginings! Therefore forsake these corrupt doctrines, for they are most perverse! Become again a child of God, and seek to know Me as I truly am.

Beloved ones, the eternal state of My punishment is the second death, the grave from which one shall never be raised. For they have been cast out, forever separated from God and their part in life. So then those under condemnation are dead. In no way are they part of the living, nor are they living in torment; they know nothing at all. Their inheritance is lost, they have been blotted out, broken vessels of dishonor received by the earth once again.

*Thus all those who believe in The Son
And obey His voice shall rise and live...*

*Yet those who hate The Son will not see Life,
For the wrath of God remains upon them, says The Lord.*

1/31/06 **From The Lord, Our God and Savior**
The Word of The Lord Spoken to Timothy
For All Those Who Have Ears to Hear
**To the Church Who Dwells in the Midst Of
And Sits Upon Seven Hills**

*Thus says The Lord God of Israel, The God of Abraham, The
God of Isaac, The God of Jacob, The God of all:* I AM THE
I AM, The Only God. I am The All in All, Maker of all that is
heaven and earth. I AM. And nothing in all creation exists apart
from Me, for even all things have come into being by My voice.
For I am YAHUWAH, He who causes to be; even I am He,
YAHUSHUA, by whom all things consist.
Yet you, O unholy church of men, have polluted My name! You
have departed from The Way, and you have desecrated The Holy
Covenant! Behold, you have altogether despised My Word and
My Law! For you do always pick the scab and refuse the ointment,
a people covered with sores! Thus you shall receive of the curse in
full! Says The Lord God. Yes, according to your works, so shall
you receive recompense in full, until you are utterly consumed!

*Therefore hear the Word of The Lord, for thus says The Lord, yes
I, The Only Lord of Hosts:* The Word of My mouth speaks, and
so it comes to pass. I think, and so it is and shall be. And behold,
I curse, and it is cursed. For I cast down the wicked and cause the
lofty to fall. I throw down the strongholds of the rebellious and
break apart every false foundation.
For I AM HE who has punished great kings and brought plagues
upon their people. I AM HE who has cast down the mighty and
destroyed whole nations. Behold, I abase the pride of the pagan
and punish the wickedness of the heathen with death!

I break the idols in pieces and cause the graven image to fall on its face! For I am a great king, says The Lord, and My name is to be feared among the nations!

Yet I am not without mercy, for My promises stand and My Holy Covenant endures forever. Therefore, when one comes to Me in the name of The Son, in sincerity and in truth, they are forgiven, even forever and ever. Amen. For I said, *"Let there be a Lamb without spot or blemish, sacrificed for the atonement of sin,"* and so it was, *"And let The Lamb be The Son of God, The Holy One of Israel, in whom all the nations of the earth shall be blessed,"* and so it is, forever and ever! Sing halleluYah! Let My people cry out, *"God is with us!"*

Yet you have not sung, nor have I heard you cry out in the name of The Holy One of Israel, nor have you given thanks in His holy name! YOU REFUSE TO DRINK FROM MY CUP! Instead you pollute it, you defile it, as you pour it upon the ground; coming before Me in the name of those who went before you, of whom you have not known, offering up supplications in the name of the dead; having altogether become as the pagan and the heathen, as those who worshiped the queen of heaven, teaching as doctrine abomination, laying one transgression upon another throughout your generations! Shall I not then require it at your hand?!

And yet your pomp reaches higher than the mountains, and your false piety extends to the ends of the earth! - *WOE TO YOU! Woe to your sons and daughters! Woe to every disciple who follows you and drinks from the cups of your fornications, taking part in your abominations! WOE TO ALL PEOPLE, WHO HIDE IN THE BOSOM OF THE PRINCE OF DARKNESS!*

Thus says The Lord God, who is and was and is to come, The Almighty: As I have spoken, so shall I speak; as I am, so shall I be. Therefore, hear the Word of My mouth and give heed to My speech, and turn from this evil way you uphold, lest I come upon you suddenly and tear you in pieces! Says The Lord.
For among you are wicked men, who like fowlers lie in wait and set traps, that they might catch men. Behold, with practiced speech and a lying tongue they ensnare them, that they might go into captivity together! As a cage full of detestable birds, so are all your houses of worship, O unholy church of men!

> *Behold, your leaders have grown fat*
> *With deceit, truth has perished among them;*
> *It has altogether been cut off from their mouth!...*

> *For your seers swear falsely,*
> *And your leaders do not cease from speaking*
> *Blasphemies with a practiced and lying tongue,*
> *And your appointed kings and bishops*
> *Rule by their own authority!...*

> *And oh how your people love to have it so...*

> *Yet what will you do in the end?*

Thus says The Lord God, whose throne is set high above the heavens, The Creator of Heaven and Earth: As I have spoken, so shall I speak; as I am, so shall I be. Therefore hear the Word of My mouth, and give heed to My speech, and turn from this wicked way you have chosen, lest I come upon you suddenly and tear you in pieces! Says The Lord.

For The Lord God hates abomination, yet vines of wickedness have sprung up, reaching to the ends of the earth. For the fruit of the people is corrupt, their bounty wickedness, producing only rebellion against The Lord! Yet you, O church of harlots, are worse still! For with what can I compare you, and who are you like? You are a whole congregation of sly and deceitful snakes, a vicious den of vipers from which a great hissing has come forth against The Lord and His anointed, a den of thieves who cease not from robbing Me, captive children whose fathers persecuted and murdered those sent to them!

Throughout your generations, you have been murderers! From the beginning, you were scoundrels! Even to this day you persecute My messengers, and stone those sent to you in word and by deed, that you might continue to poison your own people; behold, your heresies have no end! SHALL I NOT PUNISH YOU FOR THESE THINGS?! SHALL I NOT AVENGE MYSELF UPON A CHURCH SUCH AS THIS?!

Yet you say, *"We are sovereign. We are set apart from the nations and sit as queen. We set the times and declare the seasons. See, we have given birth to many kings, and have grown rich beyond measure. Thus our princes shall reign supreme."*

Therefore, thus declares The Sovereign Lord who reigns from Heaven: Because you have not shut your mouth from speaking blasphemies, and have not drawn back your hand from all your abominations, to both practice them and to teach them, and because you have endeavored to change The Commandments of The Lord, even to set yourselves up as the standard, declaring your own glory before men, AND BECAUSE YOU HAVE POLLUTED THE HOLY COVENANT BY YOUR EVERY WORD AND DEED, so also shall I open My mouth against you, so also shall I stretch out My hand against you, until you are utterly consumed! Declares The Lord.

Therefore take up a lamentation on the desolate heights, bring forth a bitter weeping in all the earth! FOR THE LORD HAS REJECTED AND FORSAKEN THE GENERATION OF HIS WRATH!

O unholy church of men, I take no pleasure in you. You are an abhorrence to Me, your faith is dead, and the fruit of your doings brings forth death, says The Lord. For you do not give heed to My words, nor do you obey My Commandments; My every statute you have torn asunder. You do always reject My Word; from My ways you are far removed.

Behold, you have taken it upon yourselves to change MY Word and MY Commandments, teaching as law the doctrines and traditions of men, which I hate, to the continual blaspheming of My spirit! How long shall I suffer you?! I can not endure all this iniquity! You are perverse, a church overflowing with iniquity, harlotries beyond measure! Your offerings are not accepted, all your supplications are rejected; behold, they are a foul stench in My nostrils, a rancid taste in My mouth! Therefore you must be purged, I must vomit you out!

O unholy church of men, mother of all fornications, how long shall you tempt The Lord your God?! How long shall you bring before Me defiled offerings, making supplications in the name of the dead?! How long shall you deceive yourselves, as you continue to place your hope in those who have fallen asleep?! For I tell you the truth, even by all you say and do, do you cause your people to sin, even to crucify their Savior again and again in their hearts.

For the people come to you, to you and your appointed "fathers", seeking forgiveness, which I said you shall not do. Your appointed fathers are guilty; they remain in their sins! Nor can praying in the name of Mary, using vain repetition, save you, which I said you shall not do.

THE SONS OF MEN CAN NOT FORGIVE SINS! MARY IS NOT THE WAY! Mary was My beloved servant and vessel, who also was in need of redemption by Him who created her and through whom she was made. Mary sleeps, she is dead, and her sepulcher remains with you to this day.

Is she assured of life in The Kingdom? She is. Because though she bore The Victory, she humbled herself before Him, knowing in herself that The Son she bore first bore her; being both her Son and her Father, her Lord and her God from Heaven; also being her brother, both being children of David and of God in the earthly places.

I tell you the truth, all have sinned, all have fallen short of glory. There is none righteous, no, not one. Shall you then pray to the vessel, or to The Maker who formed it? And shall you hold the handmaiden of The Lord in high regard, and make for yourselves graven images, though I said this you shall not do?

Therefore I tell you plainly, by your own hands
You have transgressed The Commandment,
And by your own fingers you have sinned
Against The Lord your God!...

YEA, BY ALL YOUR DOINGS, YOU HAVE
SURELY FORSAKEN AND BETRAYED
THE SON OF THE LIVING GOD!

Behold, even your consciences are defiled, and upon your knees you commit idolatry without ceasing! Did Mary suffer for your iniquities? Did Mary bear your sins on the tree? Was Mary crucified for you?

Was Mary raised from the dead, and by her life do you now live? Can anyone in need of redemption redeem another?! Only He, who is completely blameless, may redeem those who have fallen. Therefore if one commits themselves to a faith which is dead, then with the dead they must sleep, having denied The Truth and The Life sent to them, crucified and raised, The Lord your Righteousness, The Only Way.

Therefore thus says The Lord God, The Holy One of Israel: Stop worshiping the dead! Worship Me by Him who alone is holy, being altogether as The Father, the very same as God. For before the foundation of the world, I AM, with The Christ forever seated at My right hand; The Father and The Son are One. By Him do all things consist, and through Him all was made, even all these worlds.
HYPOCRITES! WOE TO YOU! Woe to you who testify falsely on My behalf! Woe to you who teach as doctrine the commandments of men! Woe to you who pervert the Way of The Lord among the people, and profane My holy things! I DO NOT KNOW YOU, NOR DO YOU HAVE ANY PART WITH ME AT ALL! For the Way of The Lord is set apart and holy, My Law is holy, and My Commandments, holy, just and good, says The Lord.

Thus says The Lord, whose way is in the whirlwind and in the storm, and the clouds are the dust of His feet: O unholy church of adulteries, you speak as though you know Me, yet you do not know Me. You have forsaken Me! For you are an estranged woman, who knows not that she is accursed. For the musings of your heart have been evil from your beginnings; from your very foundation your wickedness has not ceased!

Therefore I will indeed draw near
To you for JUDGMENT!
I will indeed stretch out My hand
Against you for RECOMPENSE!
And you shall be torn in pieces! ...

For you have robbed Me, says The Lord,
And have not ceased from perverting
My way amongst the people!...

Behold, you continue to pollute My name
In all the earth, even to this day!

Therefore, turn! Says The Lord. Turn aside from this wicked way you uphold, from this evil path you have chosen, and return to Me! Turn aside, and now follow The Shepherd in spirit and in truth, and I also shall return to you. Hear His voice and obey the Word of His mouth, heed His every commandment; turn not to the right hand, nor to the left, but walk in His ways.

Beloved children, I say this once again, so you may be saved: Come out! Come out from among them and be separate! Says The Lord. And no more touch what is unclean, and I will receive you! Cast away the commandments of men, and obey not the word of your forefathers. Turn away from the counsel of your appointed bishops and kings, and shut your ears to the words of your priests and false fathers; fully shun the ways of your founders.

For their every doctrine rests upon the sands of abomination, all their ways are corrupt. And no more give reverence to your "holy see", for this is most contemptible in My sight. Break free from all this insolence before The Lord, and I may yet have mercy upon you.

Beloved children, there is but One Way...

YahuShua HaMashiach,
Yes, He who is called Jesus The Christ,
He is The Only Way...

Therefore follow close behind Him,
In His very footsteps, and you shall
Surely live and not die...

Says The Lord whose dominion is everlasting
And whose authority is absolute,
The Only Lord God of Hosts, The I AM.

VOLUME THREE

2/8/06 **From The Lord, Our God and Savior**
The Word of The Lord Spoken to Timothy
For All Those Who Have Ears to Hear
Deceptions

This question was asked of The Lord: Lord, what do you say about new age spirituality, psychics, mediums, buddhism and the like?

Thus says The Lord: All is wickedness, deceptions clothed in falsehoods, presented to the masses under the guise of so-called truth and enlightenment, the wide path leading to destruction. For those who embrace such things cast stumbling stones at their own feet, and those who teach such things teach doctrines of demons, and shall surely fall into the pit.

Beware. For these teachings are of the spirit called antichrist; propagated by those sent out by the evil one to disguise and pervert the Truth amongst the people, to deceive the whole world (and if it were possible, even the elect); cunning ones who seek only to steal, kill and destroy, to the devouring of whole nations. For the thoughts and desires of the people are perverse. They practice abomination, and do not retain God in their thoughts. They are consumed by lust, easily devoured by their own evil thoughts and desires.

Therefore, again I say to you, beware. For evil comes in many forms and shall only increase by measure, reaching unto new heights in wickedness. Behold, right has become wrong; and wrong has become right, and the right of the individual who has become a god unto themselves. For My children have removed themselves far from Me, searching in vain for they know not what.

For I tell you the truth, what they call god is nothing! - Dead works, useless faith, all in all a leading away from The Truth; lies upon lies, deception hidden within deception, both great and subtle, vanity and vexation of spirit; falsehoods passed down from one generation to the next, deceptions built upon the ever-shifting sands of religion, philosophy and science, masquerading as truth!

For the evil one does indeed wear many disguises by which he ensnares the people, clever contrivances both subtle and obvious; stones of stumbling, rocks of offense, abominations hidden under the guise of peace and enlightenment, full of self and self-indulgence - DELUSION! Yet the fulfillment they seek through meditation and enlightenment leads only to spiritual starvation and bitter thirst, as they wander aimlessly through a vast desert of lies wherein all dead men's bones are found, hidden within the mirage of inner peace.

Peoples of the earth, YahuShua HaMashiach
Is The Fulfillment of all things,
The Truth and Understanding you seek,
The Meaning of Life!...

HE is The Bread which came down
From Heaven to feed those who hunger,
The Fountain of Living Waters for those
Who thirst, The Prince of Peace...

The ONLY Way, The ONLY Truth, The ONLY Life...

Says The Lord God.

150

2/10/06 **From The Lord, Our God and Savior**
The Word of The Lord Spoken to Timothy
For All Those Who Have Ears to Hear
The Last Trump

I AM COME! Says The Lord. Therefore arise and give answer, O peoples of the earth! Who is the face and image of The Invisible God?! Who?! It is He I have sent, The One who is and was and is to come! Behold, He shall wait no longer, for the Day of The Lord is at hand and the time appointed draws near! For The Son of Man shall enter in and gather them together, He shall surely pass through and prepare the harvest - HE SHALL REAP!

Therefore hear the Word of The Lord, for thus says The Lord: My spirit is poured out. My watchmen are called, My prophets sent; they prepare My way before Me. And if you are willing to receive it, they are John and Elijah, My witnesses, even 144,000; and behold, they shall surely baptize with My Word and fire. Who else shall I send?! Who will go for Me?! Who will noise in the four corners and shout from the rooftops?

WATCHMEN, stand up and blow the Trumpet, for the Great and Terrible Day of The Lord draws near! PEOPLES OF THE EARTH, repent and be spared, for The Thief is about to enter the house and take His spoil! Behold, He has entered the hearts of the penitent already, and has but to call out, and they shall be snatched away. CHURCHES OF MEN, let My people go! For The Master is coming quickly, and He shall surely purge every temple and tear down every house, which pollutes My name and desecrates the glory of My majesty. Therefore do not wait, beloved ones, COME OUT FROM AMONG THEM! For the Day of Judgment is at hand.

Behold, judgment shall rain down from Heaven upon every tribe, tongue and people - RECOMPENSE FOR ALL NATIONS! Calamity upon calamity shall overtake the land, disaster shall reach into every corner, even to the ends of the earth! For who can hide from the face of God revealed in His hot displeasure, burning in the fierceness of His wrath?! Who is able to drink from the cup of My indignation, and live?! For it is written: *Unless those days were shortened no flesh would be saved. For the heavens shall be set on fire above, and the earth shall become a desolation beneath. Yet whoever calls upon the name of The Lord, in sincerity and in truth, shall be delivered, says The Lord.*

For thus says The Lord, to the generation of His wrath: I have trumpeted to you, yet you cover your ears. I shall show great signs and wonders, the likes of which have never been seen (indeed many signs are made plain already), yet you shall cover your eyes. Indeed you refuse to repent, neither will you humble yourselves and consider. For your hearts are hard, your countenances unyielding, a vile people who despise The Truth!

Therefore judgment is coming quickly, and shall fall hard upon the desolate, the high-minded and the hypocrite - ALL shall be broken; some broken and uplifted, and many broken and condemned. Behold, before the sixth seal is broken, I shall deal to the hard-hearted a glancing blow: One shall be taken, and the other left. For the innocent shall be taken, and the upright in heart shall be hidden, as many as receive My words and also do them. Behold, even those asleep in Messiah shall come forth, and they too shall be gone from this place, for I know My own... *The earth shall starve, all light gathered and taken, darkness, thick clouds and darkness, the Great and Terrible Day of The Lord.*

Therefore hear the Word of The Lord, for thus declares The Lord: Travesty, great travesty is coming and is already here; even the abomination which causes desolation shall be revealed. Atrocities and war shall increase, perversions of every kind shall reach unto new heights in wickedness, as injustice upon injustice is perpetrated in every land, to the rending of the hearts of all people.

Thus I have declared the Day and set the hour: JUDGMENT for all who fight against Me! RECOMPENSE for all who harm My little ones or persecute My messengers! REFINEMENT for those who refuse to embrace Me as I truly am!... *Yet glory for those who glory in Him who gave His life as a ransom, deliverance for those who obey The Son, sanctuary for the innocent.*

Therefore love The Lord your God
With your whole heart, and find sanctuary
In The One through whom you were made...

Kiss The Son!...

For He alone is The Loving Mercy of God,
Your only Salvation...

The Way, The Truth, The Life.

2/17/06 **From The Lord, Our God and Savior**
The Word of The Lord Spoken to Timothy
For All Those Who Have Ears to Hear
The Mountains Shall Crumble and Fall Upon the Desolate

I am The God of Jacob, The God of Isaac, The God of Abraham; I am The I AM. I am God alone; there is no other.

Therefore hear the Word of The Lord and give heed, for thus says The Lord to this most wicked generation, to the last of these kingdoms of men: You are maimed! You have altogether become as one whose ears have been cut off! For you will in no wise hear Me, nor are you able! This world has seduced you, and eagerly do you embrace the seduction! Thus your portion shall be sorrow, and your lot the grave! For the wicked shall lie down in death, and the evil of heart shall be struck down - Broken off! Blotted out!

Behold, even you, O churches of men, have been seduced! For you do not cease from committing fornication with the harlot! Indeed you have embraced many lovers, lying down in beds of false doctrine, covering yourselves with the filth of the pagan and the heathen, committing many acts of adultery by your traditions, as you continue to indulge in those things which I hate!
YOU HAVE CAUSED MY PEOPLE TO SIN! YOU HAVE ALTOGETHER TURNED THEM ASIDE FROM THE TRUTH! For you have preached to them another messiah, a false christ, passed down to you by your forefathers, an idol arrayed in purple and scarlet, which even now you mold to your own likeness, according to your own perverse desires and arrogant assumptions! - Blind guides! Foolish children!

YOU ALL SLEEP! Yea, you fold your hands to rest, that you may remain at ease in your slumber! Awake! Free yourselves from the deluge of lies, from this great flood of sin! AWAKE! And go and wash yourselves in the pool of Siloam, yea, immerse yourselves in The Healing Pool of God, which was sent. Beloved, wash yourselves, make yourselves clean, and come out from among them! Be separate from all these commandments of men, from all these false doctrines and filthy traditions, and I will receive you!

Yet you refuse Me, nor will you come out. For you want no part with Me as I truly am. Thus you remain under judgment, and the shadow of death covers you. Behold, My own people sin against Me, for they are *not* My people. For they do always testify falsely, as they continue to pervert My name in all the earth. Therefore every lampstand shall be removed from its place, all light gathered and taken; darkness, thick clouds and darkness, cover the face of the earth.

Beloved children, you have rejected Life!
You have turned your backs on Forgiveness!
WHY HAVE YOU FORSAKEN ME?! ...

My heart bleeds with sorrow,
As I look upon the works of your hands!
Anguish grabs hold of Me,
As I search your hearts and minds!
Deep mourning fills Me, as I stretch out
My hand to bring destruction upon you!...

Great and bitter sorrows, unending grief,
My children have departed from Me.

Thus says The Holy One of Israel, to this lost and dying generation; thus says He who died and is alive forevermore: I am The Only Way by which you shall enter, having ripped the curtain in two; I am The Open Door by which all My beloved shall pass through. Yet you refuse to come to Me, nor will you accept Me as I truly am. How then shall you enter? How then shall you pass through?

Behold, I had sent to you My apostles, that you might learn of My ways. I had sent to you My prophets, that you might hear the Word of My mouth and receive of My correction. Indeed throughout your generations, I sent to you many servants, as lambs amongst wolves, yet you persecuted and slandered them all. And still I send more, behold, even a multitude as The Father wills, yet as in all times past you will stone them in word and by deed.

Therefore, woe! Woe to the arrogant scoffer and the high-minded hypocrite! Woe to all who take the name of The Lord in vain! All your works shall come to an abrupt end, and that which you spew at My chosen shall return atop your own head! For My prophets are sent and prepare My way before Me, sounding the alarm, trumpeting My strong rebuke.

Behold, they shall call all people to repent and warn every nation; yes, they shall give a shout and blow the Trumpet. And whether you will hear or whether you will forbear, they shall surely sing. For it has been appointed to My witnesses to sing a new song, of which only they know and shall be revealed. And behold, they shall sing with a loud voice in concert, to every tribe, tongue, people and nation. And whether the multitudes will hear or forbear, My servants shall surely sing. For the song must be sung and is sung already.

Therefore thus says The Lord God, The Only Holy Father, Creator of Heaven and Earth: Call upon the name of The Messiah, and listen to those I send. For the time of judgment is at hand, the Day of The Lord draws near.

Peoples of the earth, do you not feel My quaking footsteps? Do you not feel the earth tremble? Behold, the mountains shall crumble and fall upon the desolate, every high place shall be broken down. Therefore as it is written: *Kiss The Son, lest He be angry and you perish in the way, when His wrath is kindled but a little.* For most assuredly, I say to you, the fire is already kindled, and on a day you did not look for and at an hour you did not expect, the cup of My fury shall be poured out; behold, it shall be imparted in full!

Therefore, blessed are those who call upon the name
Of The Messiah, in sincerity and in truth,
For the Spirit of God dwells within them...

Blessed are those who seek refuge in Him,
For they shall find it...

Blessed are all those who love and
Obey The Son, for they shall be delivered...

Says The Lord.

2/24/06 **From The Lord, Our God and Savior**
The Word of The Lord Spoken to Timothy
For All Those Who Have Ears to Hear
Woe to the Captives of This World

Harken to My Word, O house of Jacob, listen to My voice, all you captives of Israel, and let all in the isles receive understanding, for the mouth of The Living God has spoken. Indeed let every tribe, tongue, people and nation hear the Word of The Lord. From those who dwell in the desolate lands, to all those who abide in the fenced cities, to all those who spread forth across the land, even unto the ends of the earth, hear the voice of The Living God...
For thus says The Lord: Come out and humble yourselves, O peoples of the earth! Repent of your evil deeds, turn aside from all this iniquity and return to Me! For you have forsaken Me! Days without end you deny My name and shake your fists at Heaven, as you reject The Salvation of God; behold, you spit upon The Name and desecrate My Word, without ceasing! Therefore harken to My voice, says The Lord, for I am come! And behold, judgment shall blaze before Me and great desolation after!...

Woe to all who forget God and parade
Their whoredoms openly in the streets!
You shall by no means escape the
Day of Wrath when it comes!
For I shall deal with you swiftly, even
Recompense in full according to the example[1]!

158

Woe to every high mountain! Woe to every uplifted hill!
Woe to all high places, to everything high and lofty!
WOE TO ALL WHO SEEK TO EXALT
THEMSELVES ABOVE THE MOST HIGH!...

Woe to the giants of this world
And to the mighty oppressor!
Woe to all who step on the fingers
Of the poor and steal from the needy!
Woe to all who conspire together
In secret, to do My people harm!...

And woe, even three times woe,
To all who harm the little ones
And those not yet born from the womb!...

WOE TO ALL WHO MURDER THE INNOCENT,
AND TO ALL WHO STAND IN AGREEMENT!
A double portion of wrath is reserved for you!

For I tell you the truth, not one spring of water flows in purity, not one piece of bread is offered freely or without leaven. All is corrupt, dead men's bones in a wasteland of iniquity and sin. Every table is covered with flies, a feast of abominations is always before their eyes, leaving them void and desolate.

For none harken, nor does one truly give heed, for all cry aloud, saying, "Cast these shackles from us! Let us alone, for we go our own way! Our knowledge transcends Heaven, our egos reign!" Thus they have made their covenant with death, and with the grave they are in agreement.

Therefore take up a lamentation on the desolate heights, for The Lord has rejected and forsaken the generation of His wrath! Yea, cry out to The Lord in sincerity and in truth, with deep remorse over all you have done, and I may yet have mercy upon you. Cry out to The Lord your God, for there is no other, fall down at the feet of your Savior, for there is but One, and confess, saying, "We have done an evil thing, we have committed great iniquity throughout the land! We are desolate, starving and in bitter thirst! Heal us, O Lord! For we have eaten up all the bread, broken every staff, and defecated in the pools of living water from which we were to drink! Surely we are wretched, miserable, poor, blind, deaf and naked!... Save us, O Lord!"

Therefore thus says The Lord God, to those near and to those who remain afar off: Beloved ones, I have saved you already, having sent The Lamb of God slain from the foundation of the world. He was come into the world, and you would not receive Him... *Blessed are those who have received Him; Grace covers them.*

Behold, He is coming again, and He have I poured out on every nation, yet you are offended in Him... *Blessed are the thirsty who have drunk deeply from His cup; they are filled with His glory.*

Behold, He shall call out, He shall surely gather, yet you will neither see nor hear Him... *Blessed are those who have eyes to see and ears to hear, for they shall surely be gone from this place.*

Yet now the time has come for this generation to drink from another cup; behold, they shall taste of it to the fullest! For it is the chalice of My reckoning, and it shall consume them! Thus as I punished My enemies in all times past, so also shall I stretch out My hand against this most wicked generation. For I am The Lord, and I do not change.

> Even so, blessed are all those who call on the name
> Of The Lord in that day, for as it is written:
>
> It shall come to pass that whoever calls
> On the name of The Lord shall be saved...
>
> For in Mount Zion and in Jerusalem,
> There shall be deliverance among the
> Remnant whom The Lord shall call.

1. 2 Peter 2:6; Jude 1:7

3/19/06 **From The Lord, Our God and Savior**
The Word of The Lord Spoken to Timothy
For Timothy, and For All Those Who Have Ears to Hear
The Watchman

Thus says The Lord: Abominations swell in the holy lands; great wickedness fills the entire earth! Sins of every kind are committed without ceasing, and perversion is celebrated openly in the streets. Vines of wickedness grow unimpeded, spreading forth iniquity, growing and spreading and putting down roots. Behold, they climb the walls and enter in through the cracks, as they seek new ways to invade every stronghold and break down every barrier.

Therefore hear the Word of My mouth, Timothy, and give heed, for the time has come: I have ordained you a prophet to the nations, and you shall be for Me a mouthpiece and a witness, a watchman crying out in the midst of this desolate land, saying, *"Prepare the way of The Lord! Set all these crooked paths straight!"*
Behold, as an adamant stone I have set you against them, a rock of offense which can not be broken, a stone of stumbling which can not be moved. Therefore, My son, take what I have given you and convict this generation of its evil ways - reprove, rebuke, and exhort. For I shall kindle a fire within you, and into your ears I shall speak, and through you I shall make My plans known. For I am The Lord, and I do not change.
For there are many who claim to know Me, yet do not really know Me. There are many who are wise in their own eyes, yet of My ways they have no knowledge. Yes, there are many who will come out and fight against you, doing so in the name by which I am called among them.

They shall slander you, and spit upon you, and seek to do you harm. Indeed, they shall persecute you in word and by deed, saying, "*Look at this man! He is unlearned, and yet he speaks to us with authority. Shall he teach us?! How dare he correct us! For we know The Lord and His will and have served Him our whole lives. Is this not one of the prophets, the kind of which The Lord spoke about, who would come speaking and doing miracles, that he might fool even the elect?*"

Yet do not listen to them, Timothy. Do not be turned aside, nor go after them; do not be moved. Give heed to none of their arrogant and dark speeches, listen to not one word that proceeds from their mouths.

Be not turned to the right hand,
Nor to the left, but go straight forward,
Proclaiming My Word by all manner
Of speaking and devices...

For those who glorify Me in The Messiah's name,
And obey My Commandments, are true;
They are by no means false...

For My spirit dwells within them,
And I Myself have sent them...

I AM THE LORD.

3/19/06 **From The Lord, Our God and Savior**
The Word of The Lord Spoken to Timothy
For All Those Who Have Ears to Hear
Desolations Are Determined

Thus says The Lord God of Israel: Woe to the kingdoms of this world! Woe to the false religions of this world! The atheist shall have it far better than you, when the wrath of the great and dreadful God has come! Woe to the king of the north! Woe to the kings from the rising of the sun! Woe to the king of Persia and the people of violence! Woe to every nation and people, who say, *"Come, let us put an end to Israel as a nation. Let us utterly destroy them, that the name of Israel may be remembered no more!"...* BEHOLD, I AM AGAINST YOU! Says The Lord God.

Thus says The Lord, to the king of the north: Come and mount up your troops, and take flight. Call upon your agreement with those of the rising sun. Honor your covenant with the people of violence. Cast your devices and launch all your weapons of war. Come against My chosen people and the land promised to their forefathers, forever! COME! Says The Lord. Fulfill the evil desires of your wicked hearts. For you shall fall, and you shall not be found! Says The Lord of Hosts. You shall be a valley of dead and dry bones, buried in the land you came to destroy, for it shall consume you! - Food for the birds, dwelling place of the worm.
Therefore come, I say! Come, and leave your spoil and your rotting flesh! For you shall surely stumble, you shall fall, and you shall not be found! And by your falling shall the name of The Lord be glorified in every land, even unto the ends of the earth! For this is but an awakening, and many shall behold it, the mighty and awesome power of The Lord!

Behold, the earth shall be shaken, the clouds shall burst! I shall command pestilences to come upon you; they shall cleave to you and drink your blood, and you shall be driven mad. For you shall stumble, you shall fall, and you shall not be found! (Save a sixth part whose hearts I know; they shall return home and be spared.) For in your eagerness to spoil shall you become the spoil, and sustain My people seven days.

Swiftly shall I destroy this great multitude who come out to fight against Me, who seek to destroy My people, Israel! For they shall be driven to the ground by fire, by hail, and by thick darkness! FOR STRONG IS THE LORD WHO DEFENDS ISRAEL!

Behold, My countenance has changed! My face is set hard against you, O enemies of Israel! My arm is outstretched and ready for battle! Thus that which is written shall be fulfilled, and that which is determined shall be done, and you shall be left utterly desolate! Then all shall know, I AM THE LORD!

Yet understand this, O house of Israel: I do not do this for your sake, but for My holy name's sake. For My name is profaned among the nations. And you, O Israel, have not obeyed My Word, neither have you walked in The Way I have shown you. For you yet reject The One who I had sent to you, The Holy One who was glorified upon the tree. Thus His blood remains upon you. For you are the children of your fathers, the descendants of those who killed The Author of Life!

Thus I have spoken it,
And it shall surely come to pass...

Says The Lord of Power and Glory.

3/29/06 **From The Lord, Our God and Savior**
The Word of The Lord Spoken to Timothy
For All Those Who Have Ears to Hear
You Shall Not Desecrate the Sabbath

Thus says The Lord God: You shall not desecrate the Sabbath, the seventh day of the week, which I have commanded you to remember and keep holy. For as I had spoken it to My servant Moses, so it is and shall be, even to this day. And as I had spoken it before the congregation, so shall it be done. Yea, with the blowing of the great trumpet, with lightnings and thunderings, did I declare My Law; before the tribes of Israel, and in the presence of angels, did I put My power on open display. Behold, by My own finger was it engravened upon tablets of stone, and by the power of My spirit is it established within the hearts of the penitent.

Yet the churches of men forsake The Law, and the peoples of this world seek to tear down My Commandments! Thus they shall surely die! For transgression of The Law is sin, and the penalty of sin is death. Yet a New Covenant I have sent to you in YahuShua The Messiah, to save you from the penalty of that which you have forsaken. Therefore, you shall live because of Him and set your steps aright, according to that which He upholds and has magnified in Himself, He being the only One who is without sin, having kept every tittle of The Law - blameless.

For it is written: *It is easier for the heavens and the earth to pass away, than for one tittle of The Law to fail.* For the spirit of The Law is shown in The Messiah's vesture, He being the same One who taught you The Law anew, by His example and by His every word and deed. For The Law is fulfilled in The Messiah; indeed, He is the goal at which the Torah aims. Thus He is The Lord of The Law and of the Sabbath.

So then give answer, O churches of men: If He is The Lord of the Sabbath, having obeyed My every command, why do you not follow Him? You say you follow Him and honor Me, yet most assuredly, I say to you, you shall all be found liars in the Day of Reckoning! Says The Lord.

And you, O church called Roman and Catholic, how We mourn for you! For you have been judged, and shall be left utterly desolate in the Day of The Lord's Anger! You say you speak for Me and have The Messiah's authority, yet I tell you, you have trampled upon the grave of The Resurrected One, making His sacrifice of no effect! WOE TO ALL WHO BLASPHEME THE SPIRIT!

Throughout your generations you have not ceased from transgressing The Law by your traditions! Even to this day you embrace every foul and contemptible doctrine, reveling in those things I hate! Behold, you pollute the name of The Messiah by all you say and do, as you lead the people astray!

> *O unholy church of adulteries, mother of all*
> *Fornications and lies, your destruction draws near!*
> *You have become Egypt; LET MY PEOPLE GO!...*

> *Stop desecrating My Sabbaths!*
> *The seventh day is the Sabbath,*
> *Which I had ordained from the beginning!...*

> *Cease from your heresies, hold your tongue*
> *From your blasphemies, turn back from this*
> *Wicked way you have chosen, AND REPENT,*
> *And I may yet have mercy upon you!...*

> *For I am The Lord, and I DO NOT CHANGE!*

Therefore heed My words and bow down, O unholy church of men! Hear the Word of The Lord, and be broken in pieces! For The Holy One is coming quickly and will take from you His own; He shall snatch them from your very breast! And no more shall My children receive nourishment from you! No more shall they be held captive under the veil of your deceptions! The light shall be taken from you, and you shall be left all alone, utterly estranged, on account of your unending adulteries and for the multitude of your whoredoms, which you performed in MY NAME!

Thus your fate lies with him who is coming, the wicked one who shall lead many into perdition and death. You shall bear him a son, a man who bears the number of his name, his prophet. Yet you will not be alone when desolations come; you and your enemy, Ishmael, shall receive recompense in full. For you both remain children of your father, the devil.

Behold, The Mighty and Strong One
Shall return and take from the earth
His own, and great recompense
Shall be poured out on all nations...

He shall come in power and great glory,
And Judgment shall sit...

Yet all who come out from among them,
And call upon the name of The Holy One of Israel,
In spirit and in truth, shall be delivered...

Says The Lord.

3/30/06 **From The Lord, Our God and Savior**
The Word of The Lord Spoken to Timothy
For All Those Who Have Ears to Hear
Culmination

Thus says The Lord, The God of Israel, The Only Lord of Hosts:
My anger is aroused and shall not be quenched, until every tall
tower is torn down and shaken to dust, and not one fenced city is
left standing! In My hot displeasure, I shall turn My hand against
the earth, and smite every bird, beast and crawling thing! Every
fish shall die, every creature of the sea shall perish, when I strike
the waters! I shall not relent nor turn back, until every blade of
grass is burned up, and every tree has been stricken and bears
neither leaf nor fruit! The earth shall be forsaken for a time and
made utterly desolate, with the kingdoms of men left in ruins!

Therefore gather together, O children of the man of perdition,
all you who bear the number of his name; come and gather
against My Holy Mountain! Yes, look up and behold the Glory
of God wrought in His Mighty and Strong One, The Holy One
of Israel, and prepare to meet your end! - Consumed in His glory,
cut asunder by the sword of His mouth! For you are accursed in
My sight, and there shall be none to deliver! Your bodies shall
consume away; your eyes in their sockets, your tongues in your
mouths, your flesh from your bones! For thus is the reward of all
who come out to fight against Me in that day!... It is finished.

Behold a new day, the seventh, even one thousand years! The
kingdoms of this world have become The Kingdom of God and
His Messiah, and He shall reign forever and ever! Says The Lord.

4/7/06 **From The Lord, Our God and Savior**
The Word of The Lord Spoken to Timothy
For All Those Who Have Ears to Hear
The Truth Absolute

Thus says The God of Israel, Lord of Heaven and Earth, of all that is seen and unseen, known and unknown, The God of all: There is One Truth, One Absolute, One Constant in all creation, in whom the fullness of God dwells - YahuShua HaMashiach.

All else is fantasy, great vexation of spirit. For the people are corrupt; by the deceits of their own hearts are they led away. My beloved are misled, they have all gone astray, a whole generation scattered upon the wind. For the ways of men are an abhorrence to Me, their every religion is an abomination. The sins of men are great, and their iniquity increases beyond measure.

Behold, they make for themselves molded images, useless things, and by the mouths of wicked men every false way is upheld in vain. For the people have no knowledge, nor do they understand. They are perverse, a most wicked generation, a people who hold out their cup with both hands, that they might fill themselves with abomination. Behold, the broth of abominable things is in their vessels, yet they are eager to drink. They are foolish and can not discern.

The works of men are evil, even from their youth. Thus the little children shall be My inheritance, and the babes My jewels. For the innocent come forth as lights shining out of darkness, gifts born from the womb. They are precious; to be cherished is every child in their youth. For the innocent are of more value than gold and silver, prized above precious stones.

Therefore, woe to this world and all who dwell in it! WOE TO ALL WHO AFFLICT MY LITTLE ONES! SAYS THE LORD. For I shall strike the earth in My wrath and punish the wicked! I shall strike the earth, and bring swift discipline upon all who lead My people from The Truth! In My great anger, I shall strike them down and bring everlasting punishment upon the evil of heart, for death is reserved for the wicked! - A valley of dead and dry bones, darkness and blackness, a void of lifeless nothingness!

Behold, I shall pour out in My anger and destroy in My fury! With eternal fire, I shall take vengeance upon all My enemies, until they are utterly consumed! For thus is the second death prepared for the wicked; thus is the second death, in which the evil of heart shall be consumed: Destruction and annihilation, blotted out! - *The death of which the redeemed in Messiah need not fear; for they have passed from death to Life, from despair to Joy, and from judgment to Salvation; bought for a price, purchased in blood, the blood of The Lamb.*

Therefore come to Me, My beloved little ones, for you know My face! Come forth, O sons and daughters of God, for The Lord has redeemed you! Come out, My people, for The Holy One of Israel has called you by name! Do not look back, nor hesitate; turn not the head, nor twist the shoulder. Beloved ones, do not look back! For abomination dwells there, Sodom and Gomorrah!

Thus the time of My watchmen has come, the Day of Punishment is made clear. Behold, it waits at the doors and is about to come in, terrible judgment poured out without mixture! - Destruction of the cities! The distress of all nations! WOE TO THE SONS OF MEN! WOE TO THE INHABITANTS OF THE EARTH, FOR NOW SHALL BE YOUR PERPLEXITY! SAYS THE LORD.

Therefore, thus says The Lord God: Great patience and steadfast faith is required. For great and terrible things are coming, days which have no equal. For upon the earth, evil of every kind proliferates unfettered. Iniquity is upheld and righteousness is trampled underfoot. Damnable heresies are taught in the churches, and blasphemy is heard within the synagogues. Temples of false gods litter the face of the earth, and mosques pollute the land like a plague - abomination, blasphemies without end, lies upon lies fed to the masses as truth! Shall I not come forth and destroy?! Shall I not come out swiftly and take vengeance upon My enemies?! Shall I not bring swift destruction upon them, until not one stone is left upon another?!

THE DAYS ARE EVIL! The light of the eye has darkened, iniquity fills the heart, and sins of every kind come forth from the people without respite! They do not relent, nor has one truly turned aside! For out of the abundance of the heart the mouth speaks, and those void of the Spirit can not discern. Therefore those with unclean lips prosper, and the desolate kiss them upon the mouth.

For this is a most vile generation, a wholly ignorant and deceived people who can not discern, nor will they consider. For they hate the one who rebukes at the gate, and despise the one who speaks a message from God. Shall I not cause the earth to tremble for this?! Shall it not break apart under their feet?! For I shall open the mouth of sheol, and a great multitude shall fall into it. The nations shall mourn, and all those who remain shall be overcome with grief. For from the least, even to the greatest, they have all forsaken The Word of The Lord!

Therefore, I call My beloved to choose starvation, to forsake all this worldly food. For only that which comes down from Heaven has life in it, and only those who eat of the manna which I shall give them shall be satisfied; yea, they shall be lifted up, high upon healing wings! For this world is awash in sin, every cup overflows with abomination, every way leads to death. Thus those who take pleasure in unrighteousness shall be cut off, and those who choose evil shall be condemned. And so it begins, the short season of him cast down, when evil reigns in all the earth.

Thus says The Lord, The Risen One: Therefore, I call My beloved ones to be sober and vigilant, because their enemy, the adversary, stalks about like a roaring lion, seeking whom he might devour. Behold, he stalks his prey and grabs hold by that which dwells within their hearts. Therefore, beloved, take every thought captive and resist the devil. Believe not the lies, nor give into fear, nor doubt; be steadfast, immovable, abounding in faith. For I am with you. For as it is written: *I am the image of The Invisible God, The Firstborn over all creation. By Me were all things created, both visible and invisible, in the heavens and on earth. Whether thrones or dominions, or principalities or powers, all things that are and were created were created through Me and for Me. I am before all things, and in Me all things consist.*
Therefore, give heed to My words and understand. For as I had spoken to My friends in times past, so now do I also speak to you. For the time has come and is coming and is already here, when all signs and wonders shall be made manifest, when all prophecy shall be fulfilled.

Rejoice, for your redemption draws near! And though the time of great sorrows has come in, hold fast, for these days shall be shortened... *No more pain, no more tears, no more death, all sorrows passing away, rebirth, a time of refreshing which shall never end.*

Therefore, remember My words and have peace:

One God...

One Son, The Only Way to The Father...

One Truth, One Word, One Messiah, One Spirit; One Food, One Bread and One Drink...

One Body...

Of which I am all, The All in All.

Amen.

4/14/06 **From The Lord, Our God and Savior**
The Word of The Lord Spoken to Timothy
For All Those Who Have Ears to Hear
The Vineyard

Thus says The Lord: Peoples of the earth, I had sent to you The Messiah, The Sower of the seeds of salvation. Yet to you, He has become an object of scorn and His words cause for disdain. For you do always contend with Me, a most arrogant and deceived people who revile My Word and reject My Commandments, saying, *"I answer to no one, nor to any god. I am who I am, and I go my own way."* For truth has perished among you; it has altogether been cut off from your mouth.

Therefore are the pleasant fields left desolate, and the peaceful pastures laid waste, for there is no latter rain. For the heart of this generation has turned against Me. Their consciences are defiled as they embrace every evil thought and intention, a base people lost in their own bitterness, who turn justice into wormwood and cast righteousness to the ground.

My vineyard has produced wild grapes!
Behold, roots of rottenness plunge deep,
As great vines of wickedness reach
Unto the ends of the earth!...

Therefore I must break down the walls,
And tear out the hedges, and destroy
All these briers and thorns...

I must tread them down,
Until nothing remains! Says The Lord.

Therefore thus says The Lord to the oppressor, to the haughty, the high-minded and the hypocrite: Mankind shall be cast down! I shall throw down the kingdoms of men and bring terrible judgment upon the wicked! The oppressor shall be cut in pieces and the haughty broken, the high-minded abased and the hypocrite put to shame!

Thus the prideful shall in no wise escape the Day of The Lord, and the insolent shall be left to wallow in the darkness of their own understanding. For all the children of disobedience must walk through the valley, to the shedding of many tears. For as it is written: *There shall be wailing in the public squares, and in every street they shall cry, "Woe is me! Woe is me!" They shall summon the farmer to mourning and call for the skillful lamenters to wail on their behalf. And in all vineyards, there shall be wailing. For I shall surely pass through, says The Lord.*

4/17/06 **From The Lord, Our God and Savior**
The Word of The Lord Spoken to Timothy
For All Those Who Have Ears to Hear
Stricken

Thus says The Lord God: This world is stricken, a corrupt tree which bears only bitter fruit! You have done this, O peoples of the earth! You have done this, O men of power and wealth, all you people of excess! YOU HAVE DONE THIS! For the sake of greed, to fulfill your insatiable appetites and ever-increasing lusts, YOU HAVE DESTROYED THE GARDEN!
Therefore cut down the tree and burn the branches! Break apart the stump and pull up the roots!... **For thus declares The Lord:** As you have sown, SO SHALL YOU REAP! And that which you have withheld from the poor and the needy shall be taken from you, and you shall suffer! Behold, even all you have wrought in the earth shall return atop your own heads, for I shall strike you down and lay you waste! - Desolation upon desolation, calamity upon calamity, plagues and famine until you are utterly consumed!

Behold, My people are afflicted, and My faithful
Ones are persecuted, imprisoned and put to death;
My little ones are brought to harm, and the innocent
Are murdered in droves, CAST OFF AS REFUSE!...

Therefore the afflicted shall be given wealth beyond
Imagining, and the meek shall inherit the earth;
The little ones shall be taken, and the innocent
Shall return home; and they shall be My sons
And daughters, forever, life without end.

Yet you, O most wicked generation, shall be cut off! I shall cast you out, and you shall remain outside the gates! For I do not know you! Says The Lord. There shall be wailing and gnashing of teeth.

For thus says The Lord to the generation of His wrath: As a lion springs forth suddenly from its hiding place and lays hold of the prey, so shall I break the neck of this generation and drag it away, until every last remnant of your wickedness is devoured! Behold, you shall be broken without hand, and the wickedness which dwells in the midst of you shall be torn in pieces! And who among the nations shall deliver you from the mouth of The Lion?!

For I am risen up in My anger, I am come forth in My fury! Therefore let every way crack and every foundation crumble; let the earth give way! Let the high places fall with a great crash, and let every false image perish before the great and awesome power of The Lord!

See, your wealth has come to nothing, O peoples of the earth. For as it is written: *Your wealth shall rot away, your fine clothes shall be eaten by moths, your gold and silver shall become worthless, and shall be for a witness against you in the Day of Wrath, and shall eat your flesh like fire.* Thus all the treasure, which you have heaped up against the Day, shall bury you.

Therefore kneel, kneel before The Lord of Hosts, humble yourselves before The King! Kiss The Son! For in YahuShua alone is your salvation, in Messiah alone is there deliverance in the Day of Wrath, your only escape. For He is The Lamb; behold, He is also The Lion!... Yet you will forsake Him in the name of another.

Did you think, O most wicked generation, the man of perdition could save you from the Day of Wrath?! Did you think you could escape the Day of Judgment, which I pronounced from the beginning?! You are deceived, even as he is deceived!

For the reign of evil shall be abolished,
The wicked stricken and the evil of heart blotted out,
Extinguished in the lake of My burning heart...

For My heart is set ablaze in My anger,
And My countenance burns like a raging fire;
My sadness is infinite, the weight of
Unending sorrow covers Me...

For as I live, says The Lord,
I take no pleasure in the destruction
Of the wicked, but call all in the earth
To repent, to turn from their evil ways...

And return to Me.

4/19/06 **From The Lord, Our God and Savior**
The Word of The Lord Spoken to Timothy
For All Those Who Have Ears to Hear
(Regarding the Feast of Unleavened Bread)
Unleavened

Thus says The Lord, The Risen One, your Redeemer: I had come
to you as a man, clothed in the flesh, humble; My glory set aside,
God become man, Immanu El... Living as all have lived in the
body, yet not as man lives in the spirit; for I am clean, having no
sin in My body, nor in My spirit, having obeyed every command
of The Father - blameless.

Thus says The Lord God: Behold The Lamb of God without spot
or blemish, sent to die for the sins of the world, bearing the full
weight of transgression in His own body; the perfect sacrifice,
acceptable to God, whereby all men are reconciled to The Father
if they so choose to receive of The Free Gift, becoming once again
My sons and daughters, free to enter the Garden and My love,
from which they shall never again depart.

Thus says The Risen Lamb: Therefore, as I have unleavened all
men by My sacrifice, in the same way must those who live in Me
crucify their lives daily, bearing their cross after Me. For the first
six days of the feast shall be for a physical representation of My
command to you: *You are forgiven, now go out and sin no more.*
Be then separate from the ways of this world and the churches of
men, and be for Me a strange and peculiar people who remain
in My love, even as I kept The Father's commands and remain in
His love.

And the seventh day, it is the consummation of the six gone before, a holy convocation, the cleansing completed, a rest from all works against temptation and the many snares of the evil one. For I am coming quickly, and I shall make a complete end of all iniquity, of all things which lead My people into sin. For I had come at the first to unleaven all men, to heal the hearts of all who receive of Me, to bring peace to the minds of all who believe in Me, to set the captives free - I am The Passover! And now I am returning to make a complete end of all leaven which fills this world; behold, in a week and in the Day shall I accomplish it. Then rest, peace, one thousand years.

So then, My children, even all who gather together in My name, have understanding of the Plan of the Ages. In the sixth day, the leaven of sin entered the Garden; and on the seventh, God rested, and blessed the seventh day and sanctified it. Thus here is wisdom: *Six days, creation; the seventh, rest, holy. Six days since Adam; the seventh, rest, holy. Six days shall you labor; the seventh, rest, holy. Six days shall you feast; the seventh, rest, holy.*

Therefore, eat and drink in remembrance of Me;
Be filled with the glory of The Lord!
For I died; behold, I am risen!...

Says The Amen, The Firstborn from the dead,
YahuShua HaMashiach, Lord and Savior of men.

4/21/06 **From YahuShua HaMashiach, Our Lord and Savior**
The Word of The Lord Spoken to Timothy
For All Those Who Have Ears to Hear
I AM RISEN!

*Thus says The Everlasting who would be man, Immanu El: I was
born into the world of the virgin, the chosen vessel by which the
salvation of man would come... Growing... Living as all men, yet
remaining unspotted from the world, blameless...*

*Born to die, suffering as no man could endure, the healing of many
in the blood of sprinkling... Death... My spirit committed to The
Father, all things accomplished, the cup of The Father consumed...*

*The grain of wheat, The Holy Seed, has fallen and died, planted in
the heart of the earth for three days and three nights... For I gave
My life as a ransom for many, even unto death; I have the power to
lay down My life, and behold, I have the power to take it up again.*

I AM THE RESURRECTION AND THE LIFE!...

*And all who believe in Me shall not die, but live,
For I shall raise them up at the Last Day!...*

*No more tears, no more death, no more pain,
For the old order of things has passed away;
All things restored in glory, the glory of everlasting life!...*

*I AM RISEN! YOUR REDEEMER LIVES!
Says The Holy One of Israel.*

5/23/06 **From YahuShua HaMashiach, Our Lord and Savior**
The Word of The Lord Spoken to Timothy
For All Those Who Have Ears to Hear
Awake, All You Churches of Men

Thus says The Lord, your Redeemer: I AM COME - I have come already and shall also return; I shall gather My elect and come on the clouds of heaven, with power and great glory. Yet you of this world do not believe. Beloved ones, how is it you do not understand My speech? Behold, I proclaim it through your own kindred and countrymen, in a familiar tongue, yet you can not bear to listen; indeed, you refuse to hear! For your hearts remain far from Me, married to a world of unbridled sin, caught up in a deluge of lies, false truths called science and religion which deny My name and steal from My glory!

Beloved, I AM THE TRUTH, which was born into the world to testify! Yet you of this world will in no wise hear Me! Yes, even you who dwell in the churches of men reject Me, refusing to accept Me as I truly am! Woe to you, therefore! Woe, I say to you! Woe to all who reject My words and hold fast to the doctrines and traditions of men!

Thus says The Lord, to all those who call of themselves Christian: Beloved, do I live in you? Do you even know My name? For I tell you the truth, you all slumber, you have all fallen asleep. In beds filled with man's conceit, overlain with purple and scarlet, you have lain down and remain at ease.

Behold, upon false foundations of corrupt doctrine and filthy tradition, you build up high walls with untempered mortar - church after church, denomination after denomination, walking always in the commandments of men!

YOU HAVE WROUGHT IN VAIN! For I tell you the truth, your every church shall come to nothing - every house devastated, all denominations brought to ruin! For I have not dwelt there!

> *Repent therefore, and tear down all you*
> *Have built up in My name, for yourselves,*
> *Of yourselves, to your own glory...*

> *Tear it all down, and begin again in Me...*

> *Obey My Word as it is written,*
> *Cast off all you have written,*
> *And walk no more in the way*
> *Set forth by the founders...*

> *Break up this fallow ground, and sow*
> *No more among all these briers and thorns,*
> *And I may yet receive you, says The Lord.*

Churches of men, hold your lamps up, so I may see your faces. Shine your lamps on your houses, that I may behold your good works, all these grand works you boast of in My name, saying, *"Lord, Lord, have we not prophesied in Your name, cast out demons in Your name, and done many wonderful works in Your name?"* Yet most assuredly, I say to you, I do not know you!

Your lamps have gone out, and you have nothing at all with which to relight them. Neither are you willing to go out and receive from those I send, for you do always offend. Thus you shall remain in your darkened houses, folding your hands to sleep, until destitution overtakes you and scarcity drives you out.

For I have purposed disaster upon every house of worship, until every church is torn down and every denomination is left in ruins. Therefore come out from among them, and embrace The True Light and receive of the pure oil, says The Lord.

Beloved, how long shall I wait for you? How long will you put Me last, as one who is made to wait in an outer room? How long shall you forget My Sabbaths and forsake My Holy Days? How long shall you pollute My name and forsake The Commandments of God, in the name of Grace?!

Beloved, follow Me as I am, and not as you would have Me be! Walk in MY ways, and forsake all these commandments of men! For I dwell not in any church made by human hands... *I dwell in the hearts of men! I live in those who love Me and obey My commands; I abide with those who continually seek My face and long to know Me as I truly am; I dwell in the temple of God made by HIS hands!*

Therefore again, I call you to repent, to repent in sincerity and in truth; to return to your First Love, to walk in the first works; to embrace The Word of God anew and bring forth works worthy of repentance, that you may truly be born again. For there is only One Way, Only One Truth Absolute, Only One Life without end... *I am He, beloved! I AM HE!*

Therefore awake, all you churches of men,
And listen to the sound of this Trumpet...

Be wide awake and very sober, pay close attention,
For the mouth of The Living God has spoken...

Says The Holy One of Israel.

6/5/06 **From The Lord, Our God and Savior**
The Word of The Lord Spoken to Timothy
For All Those Who Have Ears to Hear
To the Church Which Bears the Name, Jehovah

Thus says The Lord: You have all gone astray, you are lost and void of understanding. Your knowledge is corrupt and shall come to nothing; indeed, all your works shall burn in the Day. For you have not known Me, nor will you accept Me as I truly am, having segregated the Scriptures, both adding to and taking away to uphold your own way, polluting My name and My Glory, to the continual blaspheming of the Spirit.

Thus you remain desolate, void of the Spirit, listening only to the sound of your own voices - LIES! A multitude of subtle deceptions, knowledge and commandments brought forth by MEN! Men of vanity who seek after human praise, saying, *"We alone are righteous, we alone understand God, and we will fulfill His Word. Are we not His chosen elect, the sent?"*

Hypocrites, shall you speak for The Most High and declare My Word before the people, though I have not sent you?! Modern pharisees, stop speaking, for you do always bear false witness! You proclaim another Messiah, of which your forefathers formed in their own image! DESECRATION!

O arrogant church of men, you know nothing yet as you ought to know, nor have you any wisdom at all! For you remain trapped, grievously entangled, caught in your own snare! Put away your pride therefore, that you may see! Cast off all this bitter arrogance, that you may hear! For it is the humble, penitent man who shall know God. And to know The Son is to know The Father, for The Father and The Son are One...

For in the beginning was The Word, and The Word was with God and The Word was God; and behold, The Word became flesh and dwelt among you, Immanu El.

*Thus YahuShua is both Messiah and Lord,
The ONLY Way, The ONLY Truth, The ONLY Life...*

*Therefore embrace Him as He truly is,
And not as you would have Him be;
Only then will you begin to know Me,
Only then will you begin to see...*

*Yet continue to bear false witness,
And only by great tribulation
Shall you come into glory...*

Says The Lord.

6/28/06 **From The Lord, Our God and Savior**
The Word of The Lord Spoken to Timothy
For The Lord's Little Flock
And For All Those Who Have Ears to Hear
Abide in the Doctrine of The Messiah

Thus says The Lord: I have spoken, yet those of hardened hearts refuse to harken to My voice. I have written it with parchment and ink through My prophets, behold, I have etched My words in stone with My own finger, yet who has received My message? Who has obeyed My Word, as it is written? I tell you the truth, only those fully converted in their innermost parts have accepted My message, and only those who truly love Me obey My Word. For they remain in My love and delight in My Commandments, knowing I AM WHO I AM.

So then what of all these smoking firebrands who surround you, who do always rebel against Me in word and by deed? Hypocrites! Shall My children profess to know Me with their lips, and then go and sin before My face in that selfsame hour?! They do continually transgress; neither do they abide in the doctrine of The Messiah.

Beloved ones, to abide in the doctrine of The Messiah is not mere proclamation or belief. To abide in His doctrine is to LIVE by His words, a shining example of righteousness, striving always to make your love perfect through obedience, that those close to you, even to the passerby, may see your good works and glorify your Father in Heaven. For it is written: *One does not live on bread and water alone, but by every word that comes from the mouth of God.* So then do not just give voice and preach, but ABIDE in the doctrine of The Messiah... *By example shall you lead them, says The Lord.*

7/16/06 **From The Lord, Our God and Savior**
The Word of The Lord Spoken to Timothy
For All Those Who Have Ears to Hear
**The Dust Has Been Shaken Off the Feet of God's Messengers
   As a Testament Against You, O Churches of Men**

Hear the Word of The Lord, all you insolent children, and give ear, all you desolate houses, for thus says The Lord to those who dwell within the churches of men: Shall you come and stand before Me in your temples made by human hands, and say you are delivered, then go in that selfsame hour and pollute My name by all you say and do?! Desecration! Blasphemy!

How dare you kneel before Me in repentance, as a show before your brethren, adorning yourselves with pretense! You are not delivered! Your offerings are not accepted, neither will I hear your pleas. For you have surely taken the name of The Lord in vain! For not one of you strives to make your repentance full, nor are you willing to forgive all who have sinned against you. Thus your repentance has become unrepentance, and your words wind.

Behold, you quote My Word instant in and out of season, yet not one of you obeys My Word! As a wife who ceases not from committing adultery, you continue to defile My name by your corrupt doctrines and filthy traditions, even to the embracing of all these holidays of men, which I hate! STOP BREAKING MY COMMANDMENTS! For they do remain atop your marred heads, says The Lord.

Churches of men, know you not, to worship anything or anyone other than The Father through The Son is false worship?! Know you not, to love any image or material possession more than Me is idol worship?! And to uphold any tradition which stems from idolatry is idolatry?! YOU WORSHIP YOURSELVES!

189

Churches of men, know you not, to speak of Me falsely or to call on My name in unbelief or for a pretense, or to associate My name or The Messiah's with any doctrine or tradition which I have not decreed, is to take the name of The Lord in vain?! DESECRATION! ANTICHRIST!

Churches of men, know you not, the seventh day of the week is the day you shall remember and keep holy, and do no works therein except that which is good and upholds the cause of the fatherless, the widow and the needy?! SUNDAY IS NOT THE SABBATH! SATURDAY YOU SHALL KEEP! For I do NOT change! Nor have I commanded any other day, neither has the thought entered My mind! How long shall you cleave to the harlot?! How long shall you walk in her ways?!

Churches of men, shall you continue to dishonor your father and mother, by all you say and do?! UNGRATEFUL HYPOCRITES! Shall you continue to commit murder?! For you hate the one who rebukes at the gate, and despise the one who speaks a message from God. Thus in the hating of your brother, you are all guilty of murder in your hearts!

Behold, even some of you, who call of yourselves Christian, are in favor of capital punishment. Yet again I say to you, even to murder the murderer is murder! Worse still there are some among you, who are in favor of this so-called "right to choose"! THEY HAVE CHOSEN DEATH! THEY HAVE SURELY CONDEMNED THEMSELVES! And all who cast their lot with those who murder the innocent shall be left outside The City! I AM THE LORD.

Churches of men, shall you continue to commit adultery in your hearts without pause?! Know you not, to even look upon another with lust in your heart is adultery?! Behold, even every doctrine and tradition born of men is adultery against God! How long shall you rob Me and steal from your neighbor, for you do always bear false witness of Me, lying to your neighbor and to yourself!

For I tell you the truth, you know neither Me nor My will, nor have you heard My voice at any time! And shall you continue, without ceasing, to covet that which you do not possess?! Be set apart from this world, and come out of the churches of men. Only then will you begin to see, only then shall you receive ears to hear.

> O arrogant generation, how shall
> I humble you that you may be saved?!...

> For I tell you the truth, only those who are
> Truly converted in their hearts shall be delivered;
> Only those who have the Testimony of The Messiah
> AND keep The Commandments shall escape...

> Thus I have shaken the dust off the feet of
> My messengers as a testament against you,
> I have set apart My elect...

> And of your houses,
> See, I have left them to you desolate...

> Says The Lord.

7/27/06 **From The Lord, Our God and Savior**
The Word of The Lord Spoken to Timothy
For The Lord's Little Flock
And For All Those Who Have Ears to Hear
Death and Deliverance

Thus says The Lord: The wicked shall surely fall by the word of their own mouth, and by their works shall they stumble into the pit; behold, by their every word and deed have they condemned themselves to death. Yet if these same ones turn from their iniquity, and call upon Me in the name of The Messiah, they shall live and not die; they shall surely be delivered! For they have called upon The Name, the only name under Heaven by which you must be saved. For He is called Jesus and Christ - His name: YAHUSHUA HAMASHIACH, both Lord and Savior of men.

I tell you the truth, the very moment one has
A change of heart do they pass from judgment into life...

For I know the hearts of men,
And their thoughts are not at all hidden from Me;
Behold, I look upon their innermost desires,
I know every hidden intention...

Therefore when one calls upon Me,
I know, I see, I hear, regardless of the name
By which they have come to know Me, says The Lord...

For there is but One God and One Savior, and I AM HE.

Yet understand this: In times past I overlooked the ignorance of the people. Yet now I command all people everywhere to repent in sincerity and in truth. In like manner, I have overlooked the ignorance of those who call The Messiah by another name. Yet now I command all who have ears to hear, to call upon His name as it is, was, and has always been, and not as they presume it to be. Indeed I am calling all tribes, tongues, peoples and nations to embrace Him as He truly is, and not as the churches of men would have Him be, says The Lord.

8/4/06 **From The Lord, Our God and Savior**
The Word of The Lord Spoken to Timothy
For All Those Who Have Ears to Hear
Hallowed Ground

Thus says The Lord God of Israel: As I have commanded it, so shall it be done. As I have spoken it, so shall it come to pass. As I have purposed it, so shall it be accomplished. For My glory, all shall be fulfilled.

Thus that which I have spoken by My prophets shall surely be. And though they stumble, they shall by no means fall, for they do continually humble themselves before Me. Therefore, blessed is the man who comes to Me ashamed of his trespasses, whose heart is full of grief on account of his sins, for I am faithful to forgive his sins. Indeed I shall lift him up, and set his feet upon hallowed ground.

Thus says The Holy One of Israel: My servants, remove your sandals from your feet. For wheresoever you come to Me, I am there, and wheresoever you hear the sound of My voice is hallowed ground. For I have come to abide in My temples, to sanctify them, a continual washing.

For all men stumble, none having obeyed My voice unto pure righteousness, no, not one. Yet those I am sending have been anointed in My own blood; behold, I have placed My seal upon them. And yes they stumble, for they are but men, yet they do not fall; behold, they shall endure for My name's sake and bring glory to My name, even to the end of this age.

For My mercy endures forever. And those who receive of My Mercy shall likewise endure, forever, says The Lord.

9/4/06 **From The Lord, Our God and Savior**
The Word of The Lord Spoken to Timothy
For All Those Who Have Ears to Hear
Chosen Vessels

Thus says The Lord: There are many who count themselves worthy, as vessels of honor. Yet they are corrupt, having been filled with all manner of falsehood, bitter doctrine and perverse tradition; men in authority who know not The Truth nor do I reside within them, modern pharisees who in My name feed the masses spoiled food, scraps from which even the dogs turn away, doctrines and traditions I hate, works which shall be burned up in the Day.

Therefore I have gathered to Myself a special offering, of the number, empty vessels void of all doctrine taught within the churches of men. And though these have sinned in the body, as all men, they are fully immersed in the Spirit of Truth, enveloped in The Son's sacrifice, cleansed in the blood of The Lamb... *Behold the chosen vessels of The Lord. They are washed and made clean, both in body and spirit, remade, vessels of honor, meet for The Master's use. Behold, they are filled with the pure water, of which they shall continually pour into the cups of the thirsty. I AM THE LORD.*

Yet what of all these other vessels filled with all manner of bitter and foul doctrine? Shall I pour the pure water into these, mixing the pure with the polluted and the clean with the corrupt? Surely not. For they have sat long and unmoving, their contents stagnant and rank, fermenting. Thus when vessels such as these fill the cups of the thirsty, My people become ill, even drunk by the contents.

For none are able to perceive the Truth as it really is, nor will they accept it when it comes. They have all become intoxicated, they are all drunk! They are intoxicated with the doctrines of men, they are drunk with the ways of this world! They are corrupt, their works abominable! There is none righteous, no, not one! Therefore every vessel of dishonor shall be broken, all contents purged in the heat of the Great and Terrible Day of The Lord!

How easily men give heed
To the cleansing of the sin of the body,
Yet oh how they resist the cleansing of the spirit...

For they do always resist the Truth, believing within
Themselves they are already clean, deceiving themselves...

For this reason I have set apart a special offering,
Even 144,000, My witnesses, who are cleansed and
Made ready, men of promise who shall go for Me...

I am The Lord.

11/9/06 **From YahuShua HaMashiach, Our Lord and Savior**
The Word of The Lord Spoken to Timothy
For Someone Who Asked if They Can Still Serve
The Lord as a Pastor Even Though They Are Homosexual,
And For All Those Who Have Ears to Hear
Blessed Are Those Who Overcome For My Name's Sake

Thus says The Lord to His servant, whom He loves: You seek Me, and this is very good. Yet if you wish to please Me, then you must first become My disciple, a devoted servant who walks in My ways.

My son, I have not forsaken you. If you ask of Me forgiveness, I shall surely forgive you, even for all you have done. Yet to continue in those same sins, for which you had sought forgiveness, is most unpleasant in My sight. For by doing so, you have made My forgiveness of no effect. For that which requires forgiveness is the very same from which you must depart, lest your repentance become unrepentance, crucifying Me again and again in your heart.

For repentance is more than the asking;
It must come from a deep desire to be set free
In My love, followed by a sincere unyielding commitment
To make your love perfect through obedience...

The shedding of the skin of this world,
The crucifying of your old man with his sinful ways...

The putting on of the new man who is renewed
In the knowledge of The Holy One, conforming to
The image of Him who created him, says The Lord.

My son, there is none righteous in all the world, no, not one. All have sinned and fall short of the Glory of God. Behold, even Timothy, a man who I have given to hear My voice, does continually stumble. Yet when he is weak, he becomes strong. For My grace is sufficient for him, and My strength is made perfect in his weakness.

For he does not cease from coming to Me, laying himself at My feet in repentance, taking full responsibility for his actions, remorseful over those things which yet cause him to stumble, being fully tempted as all men. For I have not yet delivered My people out of temptation, nor has the evil one been bound in the abyss (this time is not yet). Yet from the power of sin, which is death, I have surely delivered you - if you so choose to receive of Me fully, if you so choose to embrace Me as I truly am, if you so choose to remain in My love[1].

Therefore you know the answer to your question already, for all is written in the Scriptures of Truth. Shall one, who does that which is an abomination in the eyes of God, serve Me? He may not. For as it is written: *No one who actively engages in or passively practices homosexuality shall inherit The Kingdom of God.* Behold, even all who voice their agreement shall be left outside the gate, says The Lord.

Yet if one comes to Me and asks of Me forgiveness, even a continual washing in My own blood, he shall surely have it; even if he comes to Me seven times, or seventy times seven times, he shall be forgiven. For I forgive all those who come to Me in sincerity and in truth, and draw near to those of a contrite heart, delivering those of a humble spirit.

Beloved, by this then shall our love be made perfect...

You shall abstain from that which is not lawful,
And make every effort to depart from that
Which is an abomination in the eyes of God...

You must strive to be completely separate
From that life, presenting your body
As a living sacrifice to The Lord...

Blameless.

For that which is unnatural is universally known, though the men and women of this world deny it. And that which is against God shall be purged by fire. Even all that offends shall be destroyed and come to a swift end.

Therefore, My son, take up your cross and follow Me as I am, and not as you or the churches of men would have Me be. For as it is written: *Whoever loves their mother, father, sister, brother, child or close friend, more than Me, is not worthy of Me. And he who does not take up his cross and follow after Me is not worthy of Me. For he who holds onto his life in this world will lose it, yet he who gives up his life for My sake will find it.*

So then, do I call you to serve Me? I do, if you are willing to serve Me in all righteousness, without compromise. Do I then require that you be perfect? No. For there is none perfect, save The Holy One of Israel. Rather I require that you strive to be unto Me a servant of pure heart, of pure intention, a disciple who loves Me with all his heart, understanding and strength, and also loves his neighbor as himself. For it is written and remains standing, that one can not be crowned unless they strive lawfully.

My son, I am the fulfillment of The Law, the very goal at which the Torah aims. Thus all those who embrace Me are freed from the curse of The Law, but by no means are they now free to forsake The Law. Rather let The Law be written in your heart, for now you are under grace, and by the power of My own spirit are you now able to keep The Law... *Beloved, come to Me and receive! Let Me wash you and make you clean, that you may now arise and walk in My ways.*

Therefore, again I say to you, serve Me as I am and not as you would have Me be. Yet turn away unto strange flesh, and I shall also turn away from you, leaving you in the midst of the earth, until you are truly ready to give up your life for My sake. My son, come out from among them and be separate, and I shall give you a cool drink of water, for you are yet thirsty.

.

Hear My words and understand;
For My words are life for those who walk in them;
And if you walk in them, then you are really My disciple...

Says The Lord.

1. John 15:1-14

200

11/12/06 **From The Lord, Our God and Savior**
The Word of The Lord Spoken to Timothy
For Timothy, and For All Those Who Have Ears to Hear
A Rock of Offense

Thus says The Lord to His servant: Timothy, I have sent you out amongst My sheep, as a young shepherd who lacks experience, as one who has little knowledge of My flock. Yet from your birth, I set you apart for My purpose. Yea, before your formation in the womb, I appointed you a prophet to the nations. Thus you shall go for Me and be to My people a light, a beacon shining amidst the darkness of the end of this age, a voice shouting in desolate places calling them out.

You shall be for Me a witness, a rock of offense
Which I have placed at the feet of the rebellious
And set against the churches of men,
Causing them to stumble...

For I have put My words in your mouth,
And by the power of My spirit have I
Caused you to write all these words...

Each Letter a spear with which I shall pierce
The heart of this people, every Volume a sword
By which I shall divide them asunder...

A rod and a staff for those who believe...

I AM THE LORD.

Timothy, I have made you a watchman for the people. Therefore you shall hear the Word of My mouth, and warn them from Me. Yet their ears are dull, their countenances set and their hearts unyielding. For they are haughty and do always reject the Word of God. Indeed My words have become an object of scorn among them, and in My ways they find no delight. Therefore I shall increase in you seven-fold, and cause this Word to become as a blaring trumpet in the ears of this people, a thorn in the side of this nation which can not be removed, and you shall be perceived as an enemy to all men.

Behold, I have set you apart for My glory; an empty vessel of dishonor, of which I have cleansed and filled unto great honor; a man who shall be hated and persecuted by those of this world, yet rejoiced over by angels.

For even those who claim to be of My sheepfold shall come to hate you with a profound and bitter hatred, to the casting of many stones in word and by deed. For they have not known Me. Thus I have called you out of the world, and shall also send you back into the world, even to the churches of men.

For as it was written of My prophets of old,
So in like manner have I appointed you:

I have made your face strong against their faces,
And your forehead strong against their foreheads;
Like adamant stone, harder than flint,
I have made your forehead...

For I have set you over nations and over kingdoms,
To root out and to pull down, to destroy
And to throw down, to build and to plant;
For I am The Lord, and I do not change.

11/12/06 **From YahuShua HaMashiach, Our Lord and Savior**
The Word of The Lord Spoken to Timothy
For All Those Who Have Ears to Hear
Follow Me

Thus says The Lord, your Teacher: God is just in everything. And if The Father's justice is not partial, then it shall surely come to pass in these latter days, that those who have placed themselves first shall be last, and those who were seen as last shall be first partakers of The Glory.

For what shall I do and what shall I say, to all these who call of themselves Christian, to a people who invoke My Word in Scripture, yet in that selfsame hour disobey it? Shall I reward the arrogant for their disobedience and the prideful for their pomp? Shall any who teach as doctrine the commandments of men escape the Day of The Lord? For of My servants I require meekness and fear, rightly dividing the Word of Truth unto the edification of the people - not in justification of themselves, by themselves, to their own glory.

Therefore thus says The Lord, to all those who call of themselves Christian: Do you really know Me? Have you truly received of Me? And if you have received of Me, how is it you do not abide in Me? Where is the fruit of My spirit, which you say lives in you? I tell you the truth, I have not seen it! And of My gifts, what have you done with them? My lost sheep, where have you laid them? They lie next to your faith, which has also been misplaced.

Indeed many of you have asked of Me forgiveness,
And I have washed you in My own blood;
Are you not then married to Me?...

How is it then that you still play the harlot,
Returning to those things which are not lawful,
Taking pleasure in those things I hate?...

Thus as it is written, I will surely
Correct and discipline all those I love...

For I do not change.

Therefore I have called forth the watchmen, My prophets, of whom you shall know by their fruits and by their sword (the fruits of which the devil can not duplicate - imitate, yes; duplicate, no). Therefore, woe to those who do not embrace their words and ignore their correction. For it would have been better for you if you had never met them, nor heard them, and remained in ignorance. Yet you have heard them. Thus you are bound by their words, a cord which can not be cut.

Therefore woe to all those who come against them, for you have lifted up your heel against ME! Says The Lord. Indeed all who stone them in word or by deed shall not be gathered, nor shall they escape. For I shall leave them in the midst of the fire, left unto refinement in the Great and Terrible Day of The Lord. There shall be wailing and gnashing of teeth.

Therefore listen closely and take My words to heart,
All you who call of yourselves Christian:
I ask you, do you really love Me?...

Then follow Me...

Beloved ones, listen closely and take My words to heart,
All you who call of yourselves Christian:
Do you really love Me?...

Then obey My Word! Follow Me!...

Beloved, listen closely and take My words to heart,
All you who call of yourselves Christian:
Do you really love Me?!...

Then heed My voice and come out! FOLLOW ME!

1/5/07 **From The Lord, Our God and Savior**
The Word of The Lord Spoken to Timothy
For All Those Who Have Ears to Hear
(Regarding the Holy Spirit)
I Am With You Always

*Question asked by Timothy: Lord, can You help me better
understand John 16:13-15?*

Thus says The Lord to His servant: Timothy, think not in
earthly terms, nor consider by human means. Rather know and
understand, that which I have poured out is spirit and truth.
For the Spirit is not a person, as one separate. Rather it is a gift,
a blessing received through The Messiah. For as it is written:
Streams of life-giving water will pour out from His side. Therefore
that which you receive is of God and of Messiah, for The Father
and The Son are one. Thus the Comforter is of The Son and The
Father also.

Thus says The Lord, your Teacher: This is why I said, the Spirit
shall not speak of itself as one separate, but shall take of Mine and
reveal it to you. For the fullness of The Father dwells in The Son,
and that which is The Father's is The Son's also. My son, the Spirit
and The Messiah are completely one, even as I and The Father
are One. For I tell you the truth, all The Father wills is made
manifest through Me. Thus the Spirit is given so you may really
know Me, and receive strength to walk in My ways. For I am with
you always, even to the end of this age.

And behold, there is a day coming
Quickly when you shall be changed,
And no longer shall I dwell only in you,
But you shall dwell also in Me...

Then shall you understand the fullness of who I am...

For as it is written:
Now you see in a mirror dimly, but then face to face;
Now you know in part, but then you shall
Know just as you are also known.

1/22/07 **From The Lord, Our God and Savior**
The Word of The Lord Spoken to Timothy
For All Those Who Have Ears to Hear
Rebellion, Recompense, Reformation

Thus says The Lord of Hosts: I have stretched out My hand to this dying people, I have opened My mouth to speak to this lost and most wicked generation, a people who do always cover their ears and hide their faces, lest they be made to give an account. Indeed, they are wise in their own eyes, and from the Way they have departed. For as it is written: *They are wise to do evil, but to do good they have no knowledge.*
Thus all I have purposed to do shall be done, it shall surely come to pass, and you, yes you, O most wicked generation, shall be astonished, horribly afraid! For I shall confound the multitudes, and the people shall be dismayed! Therefore run and hide; conceal yourselves in the clefts of the rocks and hide your faces! For the power of The Lord shall surely be put on open display!
For what is this generation to Me? Are you not a people exceedingly great in number, a people whose cities cover the face of the earth like the stars fill the heavens? And though you build and make for yourselves a name, I shall surely throw down! For before Me is a whole generation whose every inclination is evil continually, a most rebellious people who do not cease from fighting against Me! Says The Lord.
Not since the days of Noah, when the wickedness of man was great in the earth, have I beheld a generation such as this! - A people who are wise in their own eyes, who parade their whoredoms openly, without restraint, a most vile people whose transgressions increase beyond measure, whose sin reaches unto heaven!

Behold, they seek out evil to embrace it, and the grave that they might lie down in it, a so-called modern people who make for themselves laws, that they might practice abomination freely, even to the murdering of the innocent without fear of reprisal!

Behold, they run from evil to evil, that they might provoke Me to anger! Yes, they run to and fro in all the earth, committing evil and practicing abomination, for their wickedness has no end! They oppress the poor, and the right of the needy they do not defend! The widows and the fatherless are cast aside, and the meek are trampled underfoot!

Day and night you exalt yourselves, O sons of men!
Every day you walk proudly in your rebellion,
And every night you practice abomination!...

Shall you steal, kill and destroy,
For the sake of your own glory?!
How long shall you bring forth
Only works of unrighteousness?!
How long shall you run greedily for gain,
Fueled by your never-ending lusts?!...

YOUR WICKEDNESS OVERFLOWS, A PEOPLE
WHOSE COVETOUSNESS HAS NO EQUAL!

And what is this I see among all these so-called people of faith, among all these multitudes who claim to be a people for My name? Behold, in MY NAME they commit abomination, provoking Me to anger!

In MY NAME, they make great spectacles of themselves, as they twist the Scriptures for evil gain! In MY NAME, they teach as doctrine the commandments of men; lawlessness is widely accepted! THEY HAVE SURELY TAKEN THE NAME OF THE LORD IN VAIN!

Therefore, I shall turn their glory into shame, I shall make of them a desolation and their people an object of scorn, and they shall bear the reproach of all nations! Behold, I shall break all these unruly branches, for they can in no wise be grafted in! For I am The Lord, and I do not change!

Yet in My mercy, I set watchmen over them, saying, *"Listen to the sound of the trumpet, heed the voice of The Living God, and embrace My correction. For I do not change."* But they said, *"We will not listen, nor will we give heed, nor will we embrace The Lord's correction. For we love our whitewashed palaces, and will never depart from these houses which are called by our name. Yes, we love the sound of our own voices, and we have brought glory to our name."* Thus I shall continue to speak. I shall open My mouth in the former manner and speak to this most ungodly generation. Yes, I shall surely make My plans known and warn the people; I shall rebuke them sharply and declare all their wrongdoings, as in the days of old. For I do not change, says The Lord.

Did I not speak in times past by the mouths of My servants, the prophets? And was I not also speaking to you, O foolish and deceived generation? Yet they would not give heed to My words, nor would they listen, and so all I had purposed to do to them was fulfilled. Thus upon you also will I bring all I have spoken by My servants the prophets, both the former and the latter, even to this day. For you also refuse to give heed to My words, nor will you listen, nor will you turn aside from your evil ways, provoking Me to anger! Says The Lord.

And as for you, Timothy, you must proclaim My words, both the former and the latter. You must blow the Trumpet and warn the people. For as I had spoken by My prophet of old, so now do I also speak by you. Therefore prophesy against them, saying...

> The Lord shall roar from Heaven and thunder from His Holy Mountain; He shall roar mightily against His people! He shall give a shout like the one who treads grapes, and rebuke the inhabitants of the earth! All the people shall hear Him; behold, the sound of His voice shall echo in all the earth!
> For The Lord has a controversy with the nations; He shall pass judgment on all mankind, and the wicked shall be handed over to the sword. Disaster shall go forth from nation to nation, and a great storm shall be raised up from the uttermost parts of the earth. On that day, the slain of The Lord shall be from one end of the earth to the other. Yet they shall not be lamented, nor gathered, nor buried, but lie as refuse upon the ground.
> Therefore wail, all you shepherds! Says The Lord. Wallow in the dust and cry aloud, all you leaders among men! For the Days of Brokenness have come upon you, and the Day of Slaughter is about to come in! For I will surely break you; like a clay pot you shall fall and shatter upon the ground!
> The shepherds shall be unable to flee, and the leaders shall have no escape! Behold, the wailing of the shepherds shall be great, and the cry of the leaders shall resound in every nation! For I shall plunder their pastures and all the peaceable dwellings shall be cut down! Says The Lord in His fierce anger.

Therefore, prepare in the desert the way of The Lord!
Make a straight path in these dry and parched lands,
For The Holy One of Israel!...

Let every valley be exalted,
And every mountain and hill brought low!
Let the crooked places be made straight,
And the rough places smooth!...

For The Glory of The Lord shall be
Revealed from Heaven, and all
People shall behold it together!...

For I am The Lord, and I do not change.

2/2/07 **From The Lord, Our God and Savior**
The Word of The Lord Spoken to Timothy
For Timothy, and For All Those Who Have Ears to Hear
Grafted In

Thus says The Lord to His servant: Timothy, why do you beseech
The Lord your God in such a manner? Have I not given you your
heart's desire? Stop stifling the Spirit, and break free from doubt.
For doubt is your enemy, a clever adversary, a false witness, the
work of the evil one in an attempt to bar your way before Me.
Therefore cast off the unfruitful works of the devil, and embrace
that which I have given you, and you shall surely be established.
Let not doubt nor fear rule over you any longer. You need only
turn to Me and believe, for all I have spoken shall surely come
to pass.

And yet you ask of these things written in the book called
Revelation, and of the 144,000. Why do you doubt? Have I not
said, *"You are chosen, and you shall go for Me"?* Therefore listen,
and also understand: I am no respecter of persons, for all in The
Messiah are of one body. So then your appointment is not by
lineage nor heritage, but of Messiah. And what of those of the line
of Israel who reject The Messiah, shall they go for Me? Surely not.
For they are broken off, until such time I choose to graft them in
again. And if I choose one such as you, Timothy, whom I have
plucked from among the Gentiles and grafted in, are you not then
the same as those who remain in the olive tree?

Again, only those in union with The Messiah shall go for Me. For
if you are adopted into the family of Abraham, then of Abraham
you are. If I have grafted you into the branch of Levi, then of the
Levites you are and as a Levite you shall serve. And if you grow
from The True Vine, and I Myself have pruned you, then you shall
indeed bear much fruit in My name.

Therefore let no man, nor any doctrine conceived within the churches of men, lead you astray. Do not be swayed, nor doubt, on account of all their lofty assertions, which they falsely call truth. For upon their heads is a veil held fast by the pride and arrogance of men, men in authority who teach and preach in My name, though I have not sent them. For they do always bear false witness, saying, *"I see, I see!"* though they themselves remain blinded. Their knowledge is corrupt, not one has heard the voice of The Living God, nor will they embrace Me as I truly am.

For as it is written:
When I swear an oath, I swear by Myself,
For there is none greater...

Therefore who I choose, I choose!...

I AM THE LORD.

2/6/07 **From YahuShua HaMashiach, Our Lord and Savior**
The Word of The Lord Spoken to Timothy
For a Brother in Christ
And For All Those Who Have Ears to Hear
Born Again

Thus says The Lord: It is written, that none shall enter The Kingdom of Heaven, unless they are born again. For all are born physically, of human parents, by great travail into a world of sin. So then to enter The Kingdom of Heaven, one must also be born again, of the Spirit, set apart from this world and from all that is sin.

My son, you are being born again even now, from the first moment you came to Me in repentance, even to this day. For I am faithful. And yet you ask, *"How can this be?"* questioning My words spoken to My servant, where I said, *"You must be born again and again."* My son, I have spoken, and all I have written through My servant Timothy stands; no contradiction found. Rather it is the understanding of men, which remains lacking. Therefore if one comes to Me in repentance, with sincere remorse over their sins, they shall surely be born again - even again and again, as they strive to make their repentance full.

Yet I tell you a mystery: It has been appointed to those who are born twice to die once, but by no means shall they die a second time. Yet those who do not come to Me in repentance shall be born once and die twice. Yet there are some among this generation who shall never taste death, having already passed from judgment into life. Thus to My chosen elect, there is a death of the body unto resurrection.

Yet for those still living at My return, there is a death of another kind - the crucifying of your old man with his sinful ways, the putting on of the new man who is renewed in the knowledge of the Truth, restored in the image of Him who created him.

Thus when one is born into this world,
The child and the mother suffer the pangs
Of childbirth, until the birth is complete...

In the same way, those born of the Spirit shall suffer travail;
For they are not yet separated from their flesh
Or this world, in which they continually stumble...

So then being born again is the process by which
You are restored in the image of God,
A continual washing, until you come into glory.

My son, I died for the forgiveness of your sins - those of today, yesterday, and those sins of tomorrow. Yet man does continually stumble over his flesh, being tempted in a world filled with sin. And so he must continually come to Me, and even seventy times seven times shall I cleanse him and lift him up. And so to Timothy, I have spoken and said that he must be born again and again, until I present him to The Father clean.

This is not rebirth in the Spirit again and again, but rather the process by which Timothy sheds the skin of this world, as he crucifies his old man with his sinful ways and puts on this new man I have given him, in Me and of Me.

And so there is one rebirth in the Spirit (the moment one's heart is irrevocably changed), but many rebirths of man's spirit, because of his continual sin, fear, doubt and temptation. Therefore as it was with My servant, Sha'ul (also known as Paul), so likewise shall it be with My servants of this day: *You must die daily.*

And still in another place you ask, concerning those who teach in My name, *"Why must these become, again, children of God?"* This is not rebirth in the Spirit, but rather a correction and a washing. For these have strayed off the path, though they claim to follow Me. And when one strays off the path and follows after the world, teaching in the churches of men doctrines of demons, I ask you, what father have they chosen and whose child have they become?

And so with a firm hand, I will surely correct and discipline all those I love, so they may return to Me and become again children of God. For indeed, small is the gate and narrow is the way into Heaven. And no man who thinks himself righteous may enter, called Christian or otherwise.

So then, My son, you are reborn in the Spirit and have embraced the new heart I have given you, but by no means is this birth complete. For you are indeed that fruit which is still ripening, as you have said. In this you have spoken well, by the wisdom I have given you. For as it is written: *I am The True Vine, and My Father is The Vinedresser. Every branch in Me that does not bear fruit He takes away; and every branch that bears fruit He prunes, that it may bear even more fruit.*

My son, you have bore much fruit in My name,
And shall continue to do so until the day I finish you,
The day you become completely new...

For as a babe is born naked and wrapped in soft linens,
So also shall My people be reborn -
Naked, void of the things of this world,
Clothed in fine linens of white...

Behold, the corruptible has put on incorruption,
And the mortal immortality, as it is written...

Says The Lord.

2/15/07 **From The Lord, Our God and Savior**
The Word of The Lord Spoken to Timothy
For the United Church of God
And For All Those Who Have Ears to Hear
Under God

To the church at The Lord's right hand, hear the Word of The Lord, for thus says The Lord: Many of you remain seated at My right hand, because of your faith and those good works which you have done in accordance with My will. So then call yourself no more "The United Church of God." Rather call yourself "The United Church in YahuShua The Messiah, Under God."

My children, do you sit next to Me on My throne? Or is it My body in which you dwell? The Messiah is The Church, His name is YahuShua, and He is the body in which My children dwell. By Him and through Him are all things, and to Him shall My children flock. He is your Shepherd, and by His shed blood are you made sons and daughters of God.

Yes, many of you are of His body
And remain seated at His right hand...

Therefore continue in the Way I have
Shown you, resting firmly in The Messiah,
Being an immovable stone for His name...

Turn not to the right hand, nor to the left,
But continue straight forward, according to
The Scriptures and that which I speak to you this day.

For in your doings I am well pleased. For you have kept My Commandments and remembered My Holy Days, and have not departed from My Sabbaths, even the seventh day of each week, which I had commanded My people to remember and keep holy, yes, even to all who are grafted in.

Indeed, you have sought to be separate from those things I hate, forsaking that which is detestable in My sight, even all these filthy holidays of men which man celebrates in ignorance and sin, to the desecrating of The Messiah's name. Thus you have not made your members to be members of a harlot. Therefore great shall be your reward in Heaven. For all sin is not equal; only My forgiveness is equal.

Yet remember this, that you may be humbled in your service toward Me: No church named of men is the true church, not one. Rather each member individually, who believes in The Messiah and obeys His voice, in whom His spirit dwells, make up the True Church of His body - no walls, only spirit and truth. Therefore, O church of men, if you seek to strive on toward perfection, hear My words and forbear not. Take to heart all I have given you, and make it not a point of contention; nor pollute your good works with pride, nor use them as a measuring stick by which you count others unworthy. For I alone sit as judge, I alone correct and discipline all those I love.

Rather take all I have given you, both in knowledge and understanding, and remain students. Do not cease from studying to show yourself approved unto God, a workman that need not be ashamed, rightly dividing the Word of Truth, as it is written.

Beloved, heed My words and listen closely to My speech; for thus says The Lord to the church at His right hand, if you do indeed seek to remain at My right hand: Forbear not, nor reject My Word spoken to this generation, lest I leave you unto refinement also.

For your robes have been made white, washed in the blood of The Lamb. Yet many of your daughters have gone their own way, returning to the ways of this world and the harlot, doing those things which are most unseemly in My sight - forsaking My Sabbaths and embracing those doctrines and traditions I hate, even all these holidays of men which I loathe in My zeal! Therefore be strong, yea, be very strong, and make every effort to turn them back again, lest they be torn in pieces when I stretch out My hand against the harlot and bring calamity upon the churches of men.

Again, I say to you, strive toward perfection, yet do not think yourselves above reproach. Embrace My words, obey that which I have spoken to this generation, and you shall surely escape all these things which I am about to do. For as it was in the days of Lot, when I brought him out of the city, so likewise shall I deliver My people in the Day of Wrath. For those in whom The Messiah dwells must be taken out of the way. Then shall I judge the earth and strike the nations. For I do not change.

Therefore give heed to My words and embrace My correction, that you may see with greater eyes. Or have you forgotten this truth: *No prophecy or scripture is to be interpreted by an individual on their own? For prophecy has never come as a result of human power or by the will of man. Rather those chosen received ears to hear, and by the power of My spirit and according to My will, they became mouthpieces of The Most High God.* For all I speak is Scripture and Truth, a plumb line by which all these crooked paths shall be set straight, says The Lord.

Therefore, hear and understand
The love and severity of God...

For those who forsake Me and trample
Upon the name of The Holy One of Israel,
Rejecting Me and My Word, great adversity,
Refinement in the Day of The Lord...

Yet for those who embrace Me
And My Word, cleaving to Him
In whom the fullness of God dwells,
Escape, sanctuary in the house of The Lord.

Again I say to you, heed My words and embrace My correction; remain in My love. For you have indeed done many things well, according to My Word in the Scriptures. And only by these things for which you yet lack understanding have you erred.

Therefore hear and understand the truth of baptism, of which you hold in such high regard, and be careful that you do not make it a rod or measuring stick by which you judge others; nor make baptism by water more than it was ordained to be, lest you make the cross of The Messiah of no effect. For like circumcision, so is baptism; neither is necessary for salvation. For you need only look to the thief on the cross, and have understanding. For one who had not known baptism by water was assured of salvation, though his sin was great, having confessed before The Messiah with a sincere and penitent heart.

And in that same moment he was forgiven, and will enter into paradise at the Last Day, as Messiah had spoken it, saying, "*In truth I speak to you this day, you shall be with Me in paradise.*"

For as it is written: *Many will there be in My Kingdom who received no baptism by water. Rather they had been fully immersed in The Word of God, enveloped in The Son's sacrifice and love, baptized in the Spirit of Truth. For most assuredly, I say to you, they have their reward. Therefore, do not cast stumbling blocks before the feet of those who love Me. Be one in Messiah, according to that which dwells inwardly in the heart. For true fellowship comes not by words spoken amongst a group of united people, nor by immersion in water. Rather it starts with the heart, and is found in the stillness of My spirit, where My peace mends the broken and My gentle caress gladdens the heart. For all those found at the feet of The Lord are covered with grace, and those who abide in My love are indeed of one accord.*
Beloved, where in The Commandments have I written all must be baptized by men to be saved? Baptism is indeed good, if it is a confession poured out from one's heart in pure belief, an outward act of faith revealing one's acceptance of their forgiveness in The Messiah. For the water of the earth can only cleanse that which is soiled on the skin. By no means can it cleanse that which is soiled in the spirit; this is reserved for the blood of The Lamb. Again I say to you, baptism by water is nothing, unless one is first washed by The Word, being baptized in the Spirit of Grace and Truth which is received in YahuShua HaMashiach, whom you call Jesus and Christ. For HE is The True Baptism, The Very Water of Life, in which all must be cleansed to receive everlasting life.

Therefore beloved, remember:
The spirit of the Word, and not the letter,
Is the way, the truth and the life...

For The Messiah is indeed coming quickly,
To baptize all in fire and glory...

Those of a wicked heart, in fire...

And those of the Spirit, in glory, forever and ever!...

Says The Lord.

3/20/07 **From YahuShua HaMashiach, Our Lord and Savior**
The Word of The Lord Spoken to Timothy
For All Those Who Have Ears to Hear
Keep The Passover

Thus says The Lord: My children, keep The Passover. Keep it according to the New Covenant, in faith and love, and remember.

Yet you who call of yourselves Christian do always dishonor Me. Behold, you pollute the glory of My sacrifice with filthy traditions and desecrate My resurrection with pagan practices, forsaking those things which you were to keep holy and remember, nor will you incline the ear. Churches of men, know you not that in these Seven (the Holy Days) is wisdom and understanding, the very mind of God?! Yet you choose vanities on top of vanities, embracing corrupt doctrine and pagan-laced tradition, placing your stamp of approval on them. For you are a most perverse and adulterous generation.

Churches of men, I am not of this world, yet you are of this world. Thus only those who obey My voice trust in Me, and only those who embrace Me as I truly am are set apart. For I live in them and they follow Me. You claim you trust in Me and that I live in you, yet not one of you obeys My voice; indeed, you ignore My example and refuse to walk in My ways. For if I truly lived in you, then you would do as I did.

Beloved, follow Me! Keep the Passover, honor the Holy Days, and remember the Sabbath. Only then will you begin to see, only then will you understand. For the Holy Days are revelation, every Sabbath a blessing, a sign between Me and you that you may know I am The Lord who sanctifies you.

And behold, four are fulfilled:
Salvation assured, sin and death overcome,
The Spirit given...

Three are coming quickly:
Sin destroyed, evil bound,
My seat taken, Judgment...

A new day, even one thousand years...

Then a short season, consummation...

An everlasting day in The Lord!...

Amen, and amen.

VOLUME FOUR

6/26/07 **From YahuShua HaMashiach, Our Lord and Savior**
The Word of The Lord Spoken to Timothy
For a Brother in Christ
And For All Those Who Have Ears to Hear
Without Spot or Blemish

This question was asked: Was YahuShua ever ill? It is written: "I was sick and you visited Me." It is hard to imagine that He could be scourged and crucified, but never suffered a migraine.

Thus says The Lord to His servant: My son, I came to minister, not to be ministered to. I came to heal the sick, even all who came asking; I bore their infirmities. By no means did I, Myself, become sick, for The Father allowed nothing to keep Me from My purpose.

I came down to you in the flesh, to live as a man, to be fully tempted as man, yet I did not suffer illness of the body, nor did I sin. For The Father made the body and mind to be one; not to suffer illness, but to abide in health. So as I came from The Father, and The Father is in Me and I am in The Father, so in like manner was My body, incorruptible; the kind of which even Adam was given, and would have kept to this day if he had not transgressed. For he who is without sin has everlasting life; death has no power over him.

My son, I carried the infirmities of all those who came to Me in faith. In the same way, I carried their sin though I had no part in sin Myself. I am completely clean, and because of this, all who come to Me in sincerity and in truth are clean also.

My son, I carried the weight of the world's sin
To the cross, and crucified sin through My suffering;
The penalty of sin abolished as I fell asleep,
The Victory established for all time upon My rising...

For I am and will always be The Perfect Lamb,
Without spot or blemish, given up for many...

The Restoration of All Things...

Says The Lord.

7/25/07 **From The Lord, Our God and Savior**
The Word of The Lord Spoken to Timothy
For a Sister in Christ
And For All Those Who Have Ears to Hear
**Mistranslation and Misinterpretation Leading to
   Great Obscurity Among Many Faces**

*Regarding Genesis 9, where Noah drank too much wine, and
Ham, his son, saw him naked and uncovered: Some churches
and Christians believe and teach that Noah cursed Ham and his
son because Ham committed a homosexual act with Noah, while
Noah was drunk from the wine. Others believe that Ham had
sexual relations with his mother, while Noah was drunk from the
wine, and this is why Canaan and Ham were cursed. And still
others believe that Ham impregnated his mother, while Noah was
drunk from the wine, who later gave birth to Canaan. These same
churches use Leviticus as "evidence" for their beliefs.*

*Question asked by Timothy, for a sister in Christ: Lord, are these
teachings correct?*

Thus says The Lord: Beloved daughter, hear and understand that
which I have spoken through Timothy already. And be very careful
that you do not deny My Word, nor add to, nor take away from it.
For I am The Lord, and I do not change. And if I do not change,
then I shall surely correct and discipline My own; even to the
rebuking of all these churches of men, who do always speak in My
name without permission, willfully forgetting that no prophecy of
Scripture is to be interpreted by an individual on his own.

231

For no prophecy or Scripture has ever come about by the power of man's will. Rather those chosen were given ears to hear My voice, and by the power of My spirit, according to My will, they shared My message.

Therefore here is truth and wisdom concerning these blasphemies, of which you have accepted: In the days of Noah there was much violence and great perversion upon the face of the earth, and so the wrath of God came upon all the inhabitants of the earth in those days. And none were saved except those counted worthy to escape, those who had walked uprightly before Me, obeying My every word. These, having hearts which were right and good, were spared.

Yet I tell you, if even one of these eight souls were not of a right heart, they would have by no means entered the ark. For all appointed to wrath received of wrath and were consumed. Yet these eight lived not as the multitude, but stood apart, choosing rather to trust in My voice and obey My commands, and it was accounted to them as righteousness. So then by no means did these of Noah's household commit that which is a disgrace to their parents and to themselves, committing that which is altogether worthy of death.

Beloved, you see with tainted eyes,
Through a veil of purple and scarlet;
Remove this veil, and see with new eyes and restored vision;
Discern rightly and look upon My words as they are,
And not as you or the churches would have them be...

For My Word is pure, and I am indeed
A shield to those who put their trust in Me.

Therefore do not add to My words, lest I rebuke you and you be found a liar, as it is written. For only I may add to My Word, yea, an unveiling of the Word's majesty, both subtle and brilliant, that you may have greater understanding. I alone shall take what man has made crooked, and set it straight once again. For I tell you the truth, the translations of men are greatly erred, which leads to an even greater misinterpretation of My Word by the churches of men, who seek not the Truth as it is but long for that which is malleable, embracing only that which yields to their own perverse desires and expectations.

Beloved, hear and understand, and grow wise according to this wisdom I have given you, and no more listen to the churches of men. Be wary of their scholars, and stop your ears from hearing the arrogant speeches of all these men in authority; be wary and vigilant. For they hold tightly to singleness of doctrine, teaching always that which is built upon the corrupt knowledge and vain understanding of men, men who refuse to let go of that which was passed down to them by their forefathers, by which they also remain blind, doctrines and traditions I hate! For they hold onto judgment, seeking always to expose the darkness in men, though they themselves continue to embrace every contemptuous word and deed, perverting My Word and polluting My name before many witnesses. Thus the day is coming and is already here, when all they have wrought in My name shall be tried, it shall surely be tested, and found wanting, declares The Lord.

Beloved, you lack knowledge and have no understanding; you know not the will of The Most High God. Therefore I will speak plainly, that you may discern your error and repent: There is no mention of a forbidden sexual act, nor the "uncovering of one's nakedness" as it is ambiguously referred to in certain translations of men.

Rather Ham saw his father naked, and then told his brothers, as it is written. Thus Noah's anger was not aroused because of an act worthy of death, but on account of shame. And it was I, by Noah, who cursed Canaan, the father of the Canaanites, according to that which was yet to be. For that which was spoken through Noah was according to prophecy, which later came to be written and was also fulfilled. I AM THE LORD.

Therefore again I say to you,
Even to all who call of themselves Christian,
Stop adding to and taking away from My Word,
To uphold your own perverse way!...

Says The Lord.

11/19/07 **From The Lord, Our God and Savior**
The Word of The Lord Spoken to Timothy
For All Those Who Have Ears to Hear
The Day of Astonishment

Thus says The Lord: The time has come and is already here, when all shall be fulfilled; behold, the consummation of all things is at hand! The time has come for the stone to grow very heavy, a yoke upon the necks of all nations. And though many shall gather together seeking to cast it off, they shall be broken in pieces. For they shall stumble, they shall fall, and the weight of their rebellion shall crush them in the day of their calamity, when the foolhardy come out to fight against Me.

> *For I shall stretch out My hand against the nations,*
> *And My strength shall be made fully known;*
> *Behold, My name shall resound in all the earth,*
> *From the uttermost isles even unto the beloved city...*

> *Therefore let the nations be awestruck*
> *In astonishment at the power of The Lord!*
> *Let all people be utterly amazed at the*
> *Mighty works of The Holy One of Israel!...*

> *Declares The Lord.*

4/17/08 **From YahuShua HaMashiach, Our Lord and Savior**
The Word of The Lord Spoken to Timothy
For a Brother in Christ
And For All Those Who Have Ears to Hear
Integrity With All Trust

Thus says The Lord to His servant: My son, I have come to live in you, and you have begun to walk in Me; therefore embrace Me fully. For one who loves Me is not ashamed of My ways, neither do they hide what they are doing. How is it then that you hide that which is good and bears fruit in righteousness, and submit to that which is corrupt and bears only bitter fruit, leading to vexation of spirit? Rather as it is written: *Let your light so shine before men, that they may see your good works and glorify your Father in Heaven.*

My son, fear not, your beloved will soon awake. Yet for now she remains a stone of stumbling at your feet. Yet you compound the error, by making that which you do seem veiled and sinister in the eyes of the ignorant and arrogant alike. For that done in a corner, or in secret, is not of Me; for that held in secret is akin to a lie. And that which you hide from others, concerning Me and My will, is to deny Me. Know you not, that to love anyone more than Me is to be unworthy of Me? Yet I remain faithful.

My son, put dishonesty far from you. For by this you have made your sincere testimony void in the eyes of others, and your good works suspect. Rather be willing to endure persecution for doing what is right, in obedience to God, for this is acceptable with God. Let them speak against you for doing what is right, yet no more give them occasion to speak against you for your wrongdoings; give the adversary no platform at all.

My son, hear My words, yet do not act rashly in an attempt to rectify your error; rather in quiet boldness shine forth. Have peace, for I have seen your heart. And that which I see is a sincere hunger and thirst for righteousness - I AM HE. Therefore strive to walk as I walked, and they will see, for every veil is lifted in Me. Be steadfast and forthcoming; make honesty your companion and integrity your close friend.

Love your enemies, bless those who curse you,
Do good to those who hate you, and pray for those
Who spitefully use you and persecute you,
That you may truly be a son of your
Father in Heaven, as it is written...

My son, lead by example, with quiet boldness
And steadfast trust, and they will begin to see...

Says The Lord.

5/24/08 **From YahuShua HaMashiach, Our Lord and Savior**
The Word of The Lord Spoken to Timothy
For His Brothers in Christ
And For All Those Who Have Ears to Hear
Who Is First?

My beloved sons, whom I have also called friends, trust in Me. Stop denying My name, and cease from covering over My doings. For I have indeed called you, yet you have kept secret that which I said to show before all, and quieted that which I commanded be trumpeted loudly. Therefore give heed to My voice, embrace the leading of My spirit, and do those things which are right and good in My eyes; proclaim the Truth, speak it aloud, and no more hide what you are doing. For though you say, *"I shall keep the peace,"* there is no peace. And though within your heart, you have said, *"I shall serve in secret,"* I tell you the truth, you have surely denied Me. Therefore let your 'Yes,' be 'Yes,' and your 'No,' 'No,' as it is written.

Therefore gird up your loins like men, and serve Me in sincerity and in truth, or serve Me not. For it is far better to do nothing, than to deny Me by concealed works and dark speeches. Nor shall you attempt to justify yourselves by false and erred parables, which you did not receive from Me. For you deal not with children, nor with those who feign ignorance, but with those of your own household, of which you were to be the head.

Thus you are to blame. For by your actions you have added to their quandary, when instead you should have quickly set all these crooked paths straight.

For it is written: *Whoever confesses Me before men, him I will also confess before My Father who is in Heaven. But whoever denies Me before men, him I will also deny before My Father who is in Heaven. Do not think that I came to bring peace on earth; I did not come to bring peace but a sword. For I have come to set a man against his father, a daughter against her mother, and a daughter-in-law against her mother-in-law; and a man's enemies will be those of his own household. For he who loves father or mother, more than Me, is not worthy of Me. And he who loves son or daughter, more than Me, is not worthy of Me. And he who does not take his cross and follow after Me is not worthy of Me. He who finds his life will lose it, and he who loses his life for My sake will find it.*

Thus that which I had spoken
To My servant, Kefa, I say also to you:
Do you love Me more than these?...

Then feed My sheep, and take care of My lambs...

Says The Lord.

9/29/08 **From YahuShua HaMashiach, Our Lord and Savior**
The Word of The Lord Spoken to Timothy
For The Lord's Little Flock
And For All Those Who Have Ears to Hear
The Cups of the Thirsty

Thus says The Lord: I am come, I dwell with My people. And behold, I shall also return and gather My own - some before, and many more after.

Therefore thus says The Lord to His servants: Those of you who have received My Word must walk in it. And those of you who have not received must depart for a time. Yet you also shall receive when your time comes. For The Father will make it possible for you to do so.

Therefore to those of you who remain, I say this: Come and drink fully of that which is sweet. Come and drink also of that which you perceive to be bitter and very hard to swallow. Ingest it fully, for it too shall become sweet when understanding comes.

Beloved ones, receive of Me and
Partake of My words; take your fill!...

Then go out and share it with all
Those held captive in this world;
Fill the cups of the thirsty...

And oh how blessed are those who receive,
For they shall surely be delivered.

Yet concerning those who refuse to drink, those who hold up the hand and shoot out the lip, pour it out upon the ground in front of them. For again I say to you: *Whoever receives My message receives Me, and I sanctify them. Yet whoever does not receive My message is against Me; and he who does not gather with Me scatters abroad...* They shall not escape!

Yet take hope, beloved ones, for even among this most arrogant and high-minded generation, there is a remnant of whom I know. For in this also is the glory of God revealed. For that poured out as a testament against them does indeed contain wrath, yet from wrath shall also come forth repentance and deliverance among the remnant whom The Lord shall call.

4/6/09 **From YahuShua HaMashiach, Our Lord and Savior**
The Word of The Lord Spoken to Timothy
For The Lord's Little Flock
And For All Those Who Have Ears to Hear
Awaken... Partake of The Living Bread

Thus says The Lord YahuShua: There are none here who have come into perfection, a finishing of that which I Myself have planted within you and watered...

Therefore, understand the Word of My mouth and that which is set before you, even upon each of your plates: I have bore you, even twice have you come forth; first by water and blood in the flesh, and a second time in the Spirit, yea even a third time when you shall come into glory. And behold, that which is first sown in your hearts is The Living Word. And that which grows from Me bears fruit, according to the food and drink I provide, the written Word. Therefore both are necessary, yet one must be first.

Yet understand this:
One who is awakened can not remain so,
Unless they receive of Me and also
Eat of that which I provide...

Therefore abide in Me,
And partake daily of My supper...

Says The Lord.

242

6/2/09 **From YahuShua HaMashiach, Our Lord and Savior**
The Word of The Lord Spoken to Timothy
For All Those Who Have Ears to Hear
From Betrayal to Victory

Timothy, this question of Judas has come up before Me once again. Therefore because you have humbled yourself before Me, sincerely seeking to know the truth of the matter, even if it meant your own correction, not at all doubting the Scriptures of Truth or My Word in the Volumes, I will answer you, and for the sake of those who seek to know Me as I truly am. So then let all those who have ears to hear, hear and gain wisdom.

For thus says The Lord: Before you in the Scriptures of Truth you see the man called Judas, who by receiving the bribe betrayed The Son of Man. Yet afterward, out of extreme remorse, he took the money (the price for which I had been weighed) and cast it down at the feet of the guilty. Therefore Judas could not buy a field with the money he did not have, nor did it enter his mind. Rather those of evil and hardened hearts bought the field to bury those who they saw as unworthy, whereby a sign was also given and fulfilled by Judas, written in his own blood; and so it remains to this day, the desolate Field of Blood.

Therefore, again I say to you, stumble not over the letter, nor be confused by gossip; nor let perverse interpretations and biased translations lead you astray, by which the churches of men have marred My Word and My Glory before the people. Stop judging by human standards! Discern by right standards, according to My love and the knowledge you have received in Me; see with greater eyes! For I tell you the truth, Judas shall be with Me in paradise.

Beloved ones, I forgive all who return to Me;
Even the one in ninety-nine who goes astray,
Even the one among twelve who betrays Me...

For I am The Lord...

And of all those The Father
Has given Me, I shall not lose one.

And though Judas was indeed lost according to the flesh, he was not lost according to the spirit. For he repented in sincerity and in truth, confessing his sin with extreme remorse. And though he died before Me, his sins I bore also, crucifying them upon the tree.

Therefore awake and give answer, all you who call of yourselves Christian: Who among you has not gone astray? Who among you has not betrayed Me? Who among you has not sinned? Who among you has not denied The Son of The Living God?! Therefore, again I say to you, all those who repent in My name, with sincere remorse in their hearts, are saved. For I am The One who makes it possible for them to do so.

And though some have fallen asleep in death, and others are slain, even by their own hand, I ask you, shall death have the last word? BY NO MEANS! For I shall raise them up at the Last Day! For I have granted them the victory, even as I am The Victory, being the Firstfruits from death... *Even as those given Me shall likewise be first when the shout is made, says The Lord.*

6/25/09 **From YahuShua HaMashiach, Our Lord and Savior**
The Word of The Lord Spoken to Timothy
For All Those Who Have Ears to Hear
Hold Fast and Do Not Waver

Thus says The Lord to His servants: Beloved, prepare your hearts and do not abandon hope. Though much death draws near and the pain of death increases in every corner, though heavy sorrows overtake the land and tears fill your eyes, hold fast; embrace Me fully and do not waver.

Beloved, receive My words and also do them, obey all My commands, for I am with you. For those who love Me obey My voice and walk in My ways. They recognize those I send and the Word given them. Yes, these are they who keep The Commandments of God and testify of My glory without ceasing, and their testimony is true.

Thus at the appointed time I will surely gather them to Myself, some before and many more after, for I know My own. Beloved, I know when each will come to Me, I know every trial and tribulation. Therefore, again I say to you, call on My name in this time of darkness, in this time of great calamity and fear. Hold fast through all these tears, endure in these times of trouble.

Fear not, for I have overcome the world; I hold the keys of death and Sheol, and The Book of Life is held securely in My right hand. No one can steal you from My love; no one can pluck you from My hand; no one can break off what I have grafted in. For that which I revealed to My servant is true: *I know you as you are and as you will be, with Me where I am, says The Lord YahuShua.*

7/20/09 **From The Lord, Our God and Savior**
The Word of The Lord Spoken to Timothy
For All Those Who Have Ears to Hear
(Regarding the false doctrine of hell and eternal torment)
Evil Blotted Out, Righteousness Reigns

Thus says The Lord: When My will is fulfilled to the last, and the wicked become ashes under the soles of your feet, indeed when all things are completed, satan shall be no more. Or do you also see with tainted eyes and blurred vision, as those within the churches of men? For the veil remains and is held fast atop their heads; behold, their lies do not cease! For the churches of men do always bear false witness of Me; they think I have altogether become like them! Thus I will rebuke them, and list all My charges against them. Therefore consider and pray. Seek My face with a fervent desire to know Me as I truly am, that you may worship Me in spirit and in truth.

Therefore hear My words and gain wisdom, for thus says The Lord: If in My Word, as it was written in the beginning by My chosen people, there was no trace of this doctrine of hell and eternal torment, as it is commonly spoken of amongst the churches of men, how has it now come to be in the New Covenant Scriptures? Again, I say to you, consider and pray, and seek My face by Him who alone is the image of The Invisible God. For only through The Son shall the true nature of The Father be revealed.

Beloved ones, be wise and vigilant; do not be deceived. For as it is written: *From the very beginning satan was a murderer and has never been on the side of truth, because there is no truth in him. When he tells a lie, he is only doing what is natural to him, because he is a liar and the father of all lies.*

Thus from the beginning he sought to ensnare My people, saying, *"You will not surely die."* [1] And still to this day, the lie is widely spoken of and accepted, even fiercely defended by the churches of men for the sake of pride. For they uphold the lie, teaching that whether one believes and accepts The Son, or whether one forbears and rejects The Life, all have eternal life in Heaven or in hell - BELIEVE THEM NOT! See with greater eyes, for I do not change! I do not grant eternal life to the wicked, in any form, nor shall the evil of heart see everlasting life. Their existence shall be taken from them, they shall surely be blotted out.

Again, I say to you, those under condemnation are dead. In no way are they part of the living, nor are they living in torment; they know nothing at all. For the churches of men are foolish, and their leaders teach doctrines of devils.

Therefore come out from among them,
And be separate from all these corrupt
Doctrines and perverse traditions...

For as it is written:
Do not be conformed to this world, but be transformed
By the renewing of your mind in The Beloved,
That you may prove what is good and acceptable
Before God, according to His will, which is perfect...

I AM THE LORD.

---

1. *Genesis 3:4*

7/27/09 **From YahuShua HaMashiach, Our Lord and Savior**
The Word of The Lord Spoken to Timothy
For a Sister in Christ
And For All Those Who Have Ears to Hear
I Search the Hearts and Minds

This question was asked of The Lord, for a sister in Christ: Lord, are You coming only for those who are looking for You?

Thus says The Lord YahuShua: Your question is answered in this: I know My own. Thus I am coming for those who are Mine, all those in whom I see of Myself and for the little ones who remain in their innocence, for all who remain blameless. For those who have received of Me look always to The Blessed Hope, their hearts filled with joyful expectation. For they have been awakened to the Truth, and long to know Me as I truly am.

Yet there are many who say they love Me, yet do not walk in My ways. For they do always resist the Truth, persecuting and slandering all those I send. Thus these shall suffer great loss, yet they too shall be delivered - yet so as through fire, as it is written. For those who hold fast to the veil refuse to discern, nor will they receive correction. They have altogether gone astray and remain at ease in their slumber. Indeed their own arrogance has deceived them, and on account of their pride they are held captive, bound with cords of man-made doctrine, ensnared by filthy tradition, walking always in the commandments of men. Thus they must be left to refinement, a great humbling in the Day of The Lord.

Yet even amongst the churches of men there is a hidden treasure, a select few who shall escape, a humble penitent people whose hearts speak true, in spite of their error.

For I am The Lord...

I alone search the hearts and minds...

And whether they be of the first
Or of the second, I know My own.

7/30/09 **From The Lord, Our God and Savior**
The Word of The Lord Spoken to Timothy
For a Brother in Christ
And For All Those Who Have Ears to Hear
Feed My Sheep

*This question was asked of The Lord, for a brother in Christ:
Lord, how is he to satisfy the scrutiny of a scoffer, who says that
the Letters contradict Scripture, saying, "My children" in the
Letter "Transgression" to those that altogether forsake The Lord
YahuShua, before they have repented to become "children of God"?*

Thus says The Lord: My son, answer not the obstinate, nor strive
with those who reject My Word out of hand, nor give answer to
those who seek to tear down My words. For by doing so you have
agreed that their point is valid, though you argue.
Is My Word in need of human power or wisdom to uphold it?
That which proceeds from My mouth at present is foremost, and
shall not be put second to My Word spoken aforetime. Neither is
one a foundation for the other, as though the Word proceeding
from My own mouth is in need of anything to uphold it; nor is
any other witness required to prove My Word as My own, when I
Myself have spoken it.
What I speak, I speak by Myself; and that which I have sworn in
My wrath, I swear by Myself - IT STANDS! And you, O most
arrogant and deceitful generation, shall live by it! Says The Lord.
And if you forbear and reject My words, and refuse to heed My
correction, you shall come to know the power of The Lord in the
Day of Wrath, for you shall surely be left in the midst of it.

Behold, I shall stretch out My hand in My anger, and the whole world shall fall under the shadow of My judgment. Then you will know, I AM THE LORD, and it was indeed I who had spoken it!

Therefore, My son, I shall answer you simply, to keep your foot from stumbling. (Yet of the scoffers, let them stumble until the time be changed.) Who among all these created ones, whether on the earth or under the earth or those in Heaven, who of these are not My children? And who among these, at present, is blotted out? And who among men has done right? Answer if you know. There is none righteous in all the earth, no, not one.

For I tell you a mystery: If all being alive in the flesh are dead, then how is it you remain alive? (I speak not of salvation in The Messiah, but of those with breath.) For all remain in The Father, all are attached to The Vine, unless they are broken off and cast into the fire.

So then ALL people are My children...

Yet among My children, only those
Who fully embrace The Son of Salvation
And obey His voice are given the right
To be called children of God...

Receiving their inheritance according
To the seed of which they have become
And now are, grafted into My olive tree.

Therefore, again I tell you, the time has come and the day is near, when the harvest shall be gathered together, the bundles tied and set in their places. And all who reject The Life will no more be My children, they shall cease. They shall be broken off and thrown into the fire, and like dry branches they will be burned up, utterly consumed. And of those who remain in The Vine and bear fruit, these shall receive life anew, even life everlasting.

So then, My son, you have searched the Scriptures and have seen, yet only dimly. And of the scoffers, they remain blind, not at all willing to go and wash their faces, that their eyes might be opened. Nor do they seek Me in truth according to the Spirit, which can only be received in Messiah; He is not in them. Thus the mud remains, the scales have yet to fall from their eyes.

Therefore stay separate from those
Who shoot out the lip, from all who reject
This Word and slander My messengers...

Rather feed those who come
Seeking bread in sincerity and in truth,
Those who seek to know Me as I truly am,
Those who carry Messiah within them...

Feed My sheep, says The Lord.

10/28/09 **From YahuShua HaMashiach, Our Lord and Savior**
The Word of The Lord Spoken to Timothy During Men's
Fellowship, For All Those Who Have Ears to Hear
Wholly of The Lord

Thus says The Lord to His servants: My sons, who you are at home reveals the person you remain. Therefore, do not be as the hypocrite who has two faces. For I see all your doings, I know your hearts.

Thus the servant I call must be wholly of The Lord, at all times and in every season - one who serves Me in open and in secret, one who keeps The Lord close to his heart and present in all his thoughts, seeking always to please Me. Whether he is seen by men or hidden from their eyes, whether he is at home or in a public place, whether he is trumpeting My Word openly in the streets or has entered into his closet in quiet supplication, I tell you the truth, I have seen it. For I know all his comings and goings, and his thoughts are not at all hidden from Me.

Again, I tell you, who you are at home is who you are...

For by a man's actions is his heart revealed,
And by his mouth is he defined before others...

Therefore honor Me first at home, among your beloved,
As I have taught you; then go out and testify...

For My every word is Scripture, My every Letter truth.

My sons, speak My name aloud and reveal My glory to the world. Share My words with your kindred, and trumpet My strong rebuke against your nation, sounding the alarm among your countrymen; be bold in word and by deed.

Yet again I tell you, do not be as the hypocrite, who honors Me with his lips though his heart remains far from Me. For his actions testify against him, and that which he does in secret reveals the corrupt fruit of the same.

Therefore let My servants be given fully to their task, let them serve Me without distraction. Let each man first order his steps before Me in righteousness, setting his own house in order, then shall he be meet for The Master's use, prepared for every good work.

And if My servant does indeed strive to keep his way straight, endeavoring also to set his household in order, taking a stand, he shall surely receive his reward. Yet if his spouse refuses to give heed and attempts to bar his way, let her depart, and let My servant proceed with his task; let him go forth in the name of The Lord. For all who seek to bar My way before Me shall be left desolate, and all who fight against Me and slander My messengers shall suffer many tears, even to the rebellious children. (Yet not the young ones, for they are Mine.) I AM THE LORD.

11/19/09 **From The Lord, Our God and Savior**
The Word of The Lord Spoken to Timothy
For The Lord's Little Flock
And For All Those Who Have Ears to Hear
(Regarding a video which showed children being
"Slain in the spirit" at a church assembly)
The Innocent Are Mine

Thus says The Lord: How long must I speak to that which is obvious, little flock? Must My servant be drawn away continually to feed you, as though you were yet babes? How is it you still question, though within your heart the truth of the matter is made known by the Spirit, which cries, *"False!"*? When will you open your eyes and see? When will you lay yourselves down and hear? When will you empty yourselves, that you may truly discern?

Therefore because your eyes are slow in seeing and your ears dull of hearing, your mind congested with the many deceits of this world, this is what The Lord your God says: WOE TO THOSE WHO LEAD MY LAMBS ASTRAY! WOE, I SAY TO THEM! Woe to all who feed lies to the little ones and cause them to sin! For as it is written: *It would be better for them if a millstone were hung around their neck, and they were drowned in the depths of the sea, than to suffer My wrath over these little ones!*
Therefore woe to those who uphold perverse and bitter doctrine; your discipline shall be most severe! Woe to those who pollute My name, in word and by deed; for you have brought shame upon your own heads, and disgrace to all your houses which you call by My name! Woe to all who take advantage of the ignorant and pollute the minds of the innocent!

WOE TO ALL WHO HARM MY LITTLE ONES! For I shall stretch out My hand against you; indeed, a double portion of wrath is reserved for you!

Behold, I shall stretch out My hand and bring harm upon the wicked, and strike those who slaughter the innocent, until I have destroyed them in all the earth! For My wrath remains upon all who have taken part, upon all who voice their agreement! And yes double, even double again, upon all who murder My precious gifts! Declares The Lord.

Therefore, beloved, turn away from the
Churches of men and take a stand
Against the wickedness of this world,
And no more give any credence to that
Which you behold on the screen...

Rather fall down and pray, wail and bring forth
Many tears, on behalf of those perishing...

Yet of the little ones you need not pray,
Nor make intercession, for they are Mine,
And I shall surely hide them away...

Says The Lord.

12/17/09 **From YahuShua HaMashiach, Our Lord and Savior**
The Word of The Lord Spoken to Timothy
During an Online Fellowship, For The Lord's Little Flock
And For All Those Who Have Ears to Hear
Come to Me; No More Time to Tarry

Thus says The Lord: Beloved, how long shall you tarry? How long shall you remain unmoved? How long shall you fail to raise your voices? What is it you wait for? Have I not drawn you to the sound of this Trumpet? Have not I, even I, pierced your hardened hearts with these words? Have I not blessed you with a multitude of words in your hearing?

Behold, I have placed My Word in front of you; indeed every Letter is within your reach. Beloved, take your fill! Stop listening to the adversary! Stop judging My Word! For one who is a judge has ceased from being a hearer, and has also cut themselves off from being a doer, leaving them desolate.

Beloved, each minute you withhold does your faith weaken, each second you hesitate does your trust break. Therefore come to Me quickly, and sup with Me at My table. And when you have taken your fill, stand up and blow the Trumpet; go and tell your neighbors. And when they refuse to hear, go into the streets and tell the stranger. And when they turn away, go and seek out the homeless, the fatherless and the widow.

Beloved, share My Word! Tell them of My sacrifice, and of The Glory which is and was and shall soon return, and is also coming quickly in power and great glory. Place My Letters in the hands of all who are willing to receive them, doing so in My name. And to the rest, let it be to them as a trumpet of alarm and war, a declaration of judgment, a stern warning, a strong rebuke.

Beloved, I have spoken, and behold I am speaking again. For I am The Lord, and I do not change. Therefore no longer be confused on account of your flesh, nor let your minds deceive you. For you have One Master; I AM HE. Come to Me in sincerity and in truth, humble yourselves and cast off all this worldly knowledge, that you may see Me as I truly am. For I tell you plainly, Timothy is My prophet, yet you must look past him. Look past him, beloved, and tell Me what you see? Tell Me, who is there?

[Fellowship Participants] YahuShua! You, Lord.

[YahuShua] You have answered well. And if I am there, and you have recognized both Me and My Word, then where must I be also? For the one who I have given to hear My voice shall indeed prophesy. And those who have eyes to see will recognize My words, and those who have ears to hear shall surely receive them. Yet only those who truly love Me will obey My voice and walk in that which is given. Yet for one to know Me as I truly am, they must receive of My spirit and embrace Me fully, whereby they shall see with new eyes and restored vision. Therefore I ask you once again, do you really love Me?

[Fellowship Participants] Yes, Lord.

[YahuShua] Then make Me your treasure! For you are Mine already, even as I had set you apart for My glory from the beginning.

[YahuShua] Therefore, again I ask you, do you really know Me? For I have always known you; even from the beginning you were Mine. And if you have always been Mine, then come to Me as you are, and withhold not; embrace Me fully, that I may reign in your hearts. Ask no more in doubt, nor seek Me in passing; ask as one dying of thirst, as one who is starving in this world, as one with few breaths left, suffocating in this world of sin. Ask, and be broken atop this Stone - It is time!

12/17/09 **From YahuShua HaMashiach, Our Lord and Savior**
The Word of The Lord Spoken to Timothy
For The Lord's Little Flock
And For All Those Who Have Ears to Hear
Addendum to "Come to Me; No More Time to Tarry"
I Did Not Come to Bring Peace, But a Sword

This question was asked: What does it mean when The Lord says to stop judging His Word?

Thus says The Lord: Beloved, the time of testing this Word has passed, yet you test Me still. How is it you have yet to discern? For I have indeed opened My mouth to speak, and through My prophet I have spoken to this generation, for I shall surely set all these crooked paths straight. And behold, My every word convicts, bringing all who hear My words into subjection, for My every word is law. Thus it has also become your judge, testing the quality of your works, revealing the strength of your trust and that upon which you have built your faith.

Yet you sit still, pushing out the hand when My words oppose your will, holding fast when My commands shake up the status quo to which you have grown accustomed. I have already told you, that only those who fully embrace Me and obey My voice are given the right to be called children of God. And only those who receive the love of the Truth are set free. Yet you judge My Word and seek always to find fault with My prophet, that you might somehow be loosed from these bonds, as though the Way of The Lord was akin to shackles and chains.

Beloved ones, whoever commits sin is a slave of sin. And a slave does not abide in the house forever, but only the children abide forever. Therefore if The Son sets you free, you are free indeed, as it is written.

It is written also: *Do not speak evil of one another. For whoever speaks evil of a brother, or judges a brother, speaks evil of The Law and judges The Law. But if you judge The Law, you are not a doer of what The Law says, but a judge.* Thus in the same way, one who speaks evil of My messenger and judges My prophet speaks evil of Me and judges the Word. And one who judges the Word will by no means obey it, but have set themselves up as an authority, a judge, held captive by their own evil thoughts.

Again, one who refuses My messenger can by no means receive My message, and one who judges him has blinded themselves to the Truth. For there is none righteous, no, not one. Yet The One who sent the message is true. Thus the one who delivers My Word must also be its recipient, or how shall I send him? And all those who judge can do nothing and shall receive nothing; even that which they have shall be taken away. Therefore what I have written stays written, and what I have spoken stands.

For the time of choosing has come, all shall be sifted;
Even by this Word shall it be accomplished,
A great division!...

For as it is written:
I did not come to bring peace, but a sword...

Says The Lord.

1/5/10 **From YahuShua HaMashiach, Our Lord and Savior**
For Someone Who Claims the Apostle Paul Was False
And For All Those Who Have Ears to Hear
Discernment

Thus says The Holy One of Israel: Have I not spoken to the discernment of spirits and prophets already, saying, *"You will know them by their fruits"*? Is it not written: *Blessed is he who comes in the name of The Lord, and how beautiful are the feet of those who preach The Gospel of Peace, who bring glad tidings of good things*? Yet you have failed to see. For the scales removed from the eyes of My servant Sha'ul (also known as Paul) remain upon you.

How is it you do not recognize My servants? How is it you have failed to see past the doctrines of men within the churches? For they do always twist the Scriptures, misusing and abusing My Word to uphold their own way, forsaking The Holy Law by permission in MY name.

Thus you also lack understanding. For the shadow of the veil which covers them has fallen upon you. For those who know Me know those I send. And those in whom I dwell receive My words with gladness, whether spoken into the ears of My prophets or placed within the hearts of My apostles.

Thus I shall speak plainly, that you may know the folly of your speech: Sha'ul, My apostle and prophet, whom I appointed and sent, kept The Commandments of God and ceased not from proclaiming My name in truth. Even unto death, he did not cease from testifying to the truth of who I am.

For it is written: *The people of God are those who keep The Commandments and have the Testimony of YahuShua The Messiah. And their testimony is true.* Therefore, again I say to you, let not the churches of men deceive you, nor let any self-appointed teacher, pastor, preacher, minister or priest lead you astray. For they do greatly err.

Therefore thus says The Lord, to all who have eyes to see and ears to hear: Who among you has committed no murder, whether in heart or in action? Who among you has committed no adultery, whether in heart or in action? Who among you, O peoples of the earth, has committed no sin?! Behold, all have fallen short of the Glory of God, all have failed utterly in their attempts to gain righteousness; even the works of the most righteous among you are but filthy rags before Me. And for this reason did I come into the world, manifest in the flesh, to bear the full weight of the sin of this world - Immanu El.

Therefore get wisdom, get understanding,
And seek My face in sincerity and in truth...

Humble yourselves, that you may receive
True knowledge, that you may come
To know Me as I truly am...

Says The Lord.

1/7/10 **From YahuShua HaMashiach, Our Lord and Savior**
The Word of The Lord Spoken to Timothy
For All Those Who Have Ears to Hear
Choose Me

Thus says The Lord: Beloved ones, I am The Answer you search for, The Truth you seek - The Only Way, The Only Truth, The Only Life. Apart from Me there is nothing of any value; apart from Me there is no life. Therefore who you choose, not what you choose, is the answer. For who you choose defines what you do. And whosoever chooses another, and not Me in truth, has chosen themselves, and has done according to their own will.

Thus those who embrace My words
Have taken the first steps in the
Knowledge of how to truly abide in Me...

Indeed, those who have written
This wisdom upon their heart
Have already crossed the threshold...

I am The Lord.

2/4/10 **From YahuShua HaMashiach, Our Lord and Savior**
The Word of The Lord Spoken to Timothy
For The Lord's Little Flock
And For All Those Who Have Ears to Hear
Obey God

This question was asked of The Lord: Lord, by putting You first, and refusing to take part in the modern holidays of men, are we dishonoring our parents and family who say we should take part?

Thus says The Lord YahuShua: Beloved, a sincere desire to be free from the iniquity of this world is good and well-pleasing to The Lord. For one who truly loves Me seeks to please Me. And those in whom I dwell will run from these holidays of men, which I hate, despising them. Yet one who remains in disagreement with My Word in the Volumes can in no wise be gathered, for they have denied Me. And any who reject My Word, in favor of the doctrines and traditions of men, embrace that which runs contrary to Me.

For I tell you the truth, anyone who refuses, disagrees with, or speaks against My Letters or My prophet has rejected Me in favor of their own way. Pride has ensnared them, and arrogance has become their close friend. Behold, they have embraced the world and its evil ways, and seek not the approval of their Father in Heaven, but of men. And all who seek the approval of men must walk through the valley with them; and all who remain friends of the world have made themselves enemies of God, as it is written.

Therefore all lovers of the world shall surely be left in it; they shall not escape! For assuredly, I say to you, this world shall be shaken and the glory of men shall be broken down! And in like manner shall all those left in the world be humbled, severely abased - many broken and uplifted, and many more broken and condemned, says The Lord.

Therefore concerning these holidays
Of men, which I hate...

Let all those who have received
The love of the Truth depart from them;
Let the division be made clear...

And let those who say they know Me,
Yet make no effort to pick up their
Cross and follow Me, bear the weight
Of their burden in the Day of The Lord.

Therefore, concerning the question of breaking one Commandment in favor of another, the answer is this: I AM FIRST, of which The Commandments also testify. For those who truly love Me seek to obey My voice, and those who obey My voice have also fulfilled The Moral Law. For I am, and have always been the goal at which the Torah aims.

And all those in whose heart I am foremost serve Me without constraint, seeking always to place Me first, above all else. For these walk in My ways, doing those same things I did. They do not add to the Word which I have commanded them, nor do they take away from it.

Behold, they keep The Commandments of God, as He commanded them and as they are written, and not as the churches of men would have them be.

Thus those who say no to sin, and stay separate from that which is an abomination in the eyes of God, have broken no Commandment. So then to honor any parent who transgresses The Law, by taking part in these perverse holidays of men, is to transgress The Law. Yet by honoring Me in truth, obeying the Word of The Lord, one can by no means transgress The Law.

Therefore those who ask, *"Would you break one Commandment to obey another?"* speak without knowledge, having also failed to recognize the lie hidden within. For those who ask such questions have given heed to the subtle deceptions of the evil one, by which they are also led, seeing contradictions where none exist.

> *Again I say to you, who you*
> *Choose defines what you do;*
> *And whosoever chooses another*
> *And not Me in truth has chosen themselves,*
> *And has done according to their own will...*

> *Yet to disobey God is sin...*

> *Therefore call on My name and make*
> *Your repentance full, by departing*
> *From those things which are not lawful,*
> *Standing apart from those things I hate,*
> *And you shall surely be delivered...*

> *Says The Lord.*

2/4/10 **From YahuShua HaMashiach, Our Lord and Savior**
The Word of The Lord Spoken to Timothy
For The Lord's Little Flock
And For All Those Who Have Ears to Hear
Addendum to "Obey God"

Thus says The Lord: My sons and daughters, you have yet to understand My Word and My will, concerning these things which I hate. When a parent says to their child, *"Obey me,"* yet their request leads their child into sin, the child who has received knowledge of My ways must choose to walk in them. For by refusing to obey their parents in that which causes them to sin, they have not dishonored their parents, but have obeyed the Word of The Lord, doing that which is right and good in My eyes, revealing that which is most needful. Beloved, this is where you have erred. For you still listen to the whisperings of the evil one; listen not to his subtle and dark speeches!

[Timothy] Brothers and sisters, satan would have us believe that even while we are obeying God it is still possible to sin, and that placing God's will over our parent's will will cause us to break the Fifth Commandment! Do not be ensnared! Obey God!

Thus says The Lord: Beloved, awake! For I tell you the truth, you have yet to come into the full knowledge of who I truly am; nor do you understand My ways, neither are you willing to walk in them. Learn to see with new eyes and restored vision, and no longer be constrained by doubt, nor let fear hold you captive.

For knowledge of Me is understanding, and My spirit brings forth new awareness in those who have truly received, whereby satan's power is easily broken. Be fully awake, therefore, and no longer give heed to the corrupt teachings of men or the churches.

Beloved, by disobeying a parent in regards to these modern holidays of men, you have testified to them by your refusal. And by your actions you have shown them a better way, magnifying that which is first. Thus in righteousness you have blessed them by your example. Where then is the dishonor?

Again, I say to you, one who chooses Me and performs My will does not sin. Therefore, obey your parents and honor them in all things, save that which causes you to disobey the Word of God; honor NO request from one who chooses sin, asking you to be a partaker with them. For all who know and understand the origins of these holidays of men, and do not take a stand against them, have shown themselves to be in agreement with those who sin against Me. And all those who compromise or make concessions dishonor Me and have no love for God in their hearts.

Be My examples, therefore...

Come out from among them and be separate;
Do not touch what is unclean and I will
Receive you, as it is written...

Obey My voice and walk in My ways,
Revealing to every onlooker that
I am indeed first, the greatest of all loves.

2/10/10 **From The Lord, Our God and Savior**
The Word of The Lord Spoken to Timothy
For The Lord's Little Flock
And For All Those Who Have Ears to Hear
(Regarding the Feasts of The Lord)
Walking in the Footsteps of The Messiah's Passion

Thus says The Lord to those who believe, to those who have ears to hear, eyes to see, and a heart which longs to know Me as I truly am: Three are fulfilled, one is, and three are to come, coming quickly. Of the three fulfilled, you shall remember and honor them according to how I command you. The dates and times, the new moons and seasons, are not the focus; rather, YahuShua is the focus. For the significance of these Holy Days is found in their meaning and revealed by their order, even as all find their fulfillment in The Messiah and their completion in the coming of The Lord.

Thus you shall not keep My Holy Days as the world, nor as those held captive in the churches of men, nor shall you follow the futile traditions of the Jews. For those who deny The Son deny The Father also; their worship is in vain. For the Jews reject The Son of Salvation, and the churches of men pollute His name and corrupt His image without ceasing. For they do always follow the dictates of their own hearts, and in their stubbornness they hold fast to religion, embracing the commandments of men, walking in every perverse doctrine and tradition thereof, which I hate!

Therefore you shall set yourselves apart from them, and do all I command you: You shall honor the Passover a week before the time, beginning Tuesday at sundown. You shall walk in the footsteps of Messiah, and remember, blessing His name and giving thanks according to each day He fulfilled in His Passion. Four holy convocations, plus one, shall be kept.

As The Messiah kept The Passover,
So shall you in like manner keep The Passover...

As He was afflicted, you shall fast...

As He slept in the tomb, you shall mourn...

And as He rose from the grave,
You shall rejoice and sing praises...

Behold, you shall complete the week
With joy and feasting...

Then later shall you remember
The Bridegroom being taken from you,
And rejoice in the Blessed Hope of His soon return.

In this way will you begin to partake of the hidden manna, and your hearts shall be glad, causing you to see with greater eyes; your understanding of the Glory brightening as you enter into a more profound knowledge of the salvation of God, which is accomplished and fulfilled in The Son of Man.

For the Holy Days are revelation, revealing hidden things kept secret since the world began - signposts of things to come, a foretaste of The Kingdom, a glimpse into the Glory of God even as the Scriptures, unfolding and coming to light as the will of God is manifest.

And though you are counted as last partakers by the Jews, and scorned by those who dwell in the churches of men, I tell you, you shall be first partakers. For I have set you apart as an example, and by these things shall you bear witness of My comings and goings. For I am The Lord, and I shall surely follow the counsel of My own will.

For I do not receive counsel from men, nor shall I follow the line which they have stretched out for Me, that I might adhere to their rules or meet their expectations; rather I do that which is right and good in My own eyes. Therefore those who diligently seek to know The Father must abide in The Son, and obey His voice - living testaments to those without knowledge, an ensign to all nations, soon taken up, first partakers of the Glory.

Indeed, many who are counted as first will be last,
And many who are counted as last shall be first...

For those mocked and persecuted
For My name's sake must be first...

Even as those who are mocked and persecuted
Because of this Word shall be first also...

I AM THE LORD.

4/26/10 **From The Lord, Our God and Savior**
The Word of The Lord Spoken to Timothy
For All Those Who Have Ears to Hear
Wisdom

Thus says The Lord: True wisdom is not of man, nor is it found in the earth, but from above - heavenly, holy. For that created was created according to the wisdom of Him who created it and by whom all things consist, knowing their form from the beginning. Therefore the fear of The Lord is indeed the beginning of wisdom, and the knowledge of The Holy One is understanding, as it is written.
Yet in vain men continue to seek out wisdom, yet never find it; they search for knowledge, yet it remains just outside their reach. For apart from Me there is no knowledge, apart from Me all understanding passes away.

> *For I AM HE, The Only Fountain*
> *From which flows all wisdom and knowledge,*
> *The Source of all things...*

> *For I am He who spoke into the dark,*
> *Which was upon the face of the deep;*
> *Behold, I am He who divided*
> *The light from the darkness.*

Thus all things conform to the line which I have set. For My will is a rock which can never be moved, the confines in which all creation exists. And behold, the earth abides forever, and everything in it gives heed to the will of The Most High God, having come forth by the Word of My power. Thus that which has been corrupted shall be purified, and that which has become crooked shall once again be made straight, restored to the form in which I created it, according to that same wisdom by which it was made at the first - from Glory to Glory, by Grace of Grace, says The Lord.

So then all who receive of Me grow wise, receiving of that which is pure, learning to walk in that which is eternal... *As one being led along a mountain stream of living waters, filled with a fervent desire to seek out its source, drinking from it along the way, gaining strength in weakness, leaving all behind in their holy pursuit.*

Yet with the ungodly, it is not so. For the ungodly man proclaims the wisdom of the world, seeking always to lay hold on it, to make it his own. Thus he shall indeed gain the world, yet shall be left wanting, when all he has built up for the sake of his own glory comes crashing down. For all who remain married to this world shall surely share in its end. For the wisdom of man is like him - grass of the field, here today and tomorrow thrown into the fire.

And thus shall the wisdom and glory of man be destroyed together, along with that which had sprung up from beneath - lies, ever-growing deceptions, leading him away from The Truth and The Life. For like lost sheep all have gone astray; there are none who know, not one who truly understands.

They run to and fro in all the earth, neither seeing nor believing, grasping always at particles of dust blowing in the wind; worldly men sinking into the mire of their own ways, meet for death; a whole generation of dying children suffocating in the ever-shifting sands of religion, philosophy and science, falsely called truth and wisdom, built upon the corrupt knowledge of man, all of which shall be burned up in the Day.

Therefore here is wisdom, the only knowledge
Which endures forever, true understanding:

I AM...

And you are in life because of Me...

And all that is, even all these worlds
To every star you see in the heavens,
Was made according to the wisdom
Of The Father, brought forth and established
Through The Son, by whom all things consist...

For I AM, and have always been,
The Way and The Life, The Salvation of God,
The Only Truth from which all understanding flows...

YAHUSHUA-YAHUWAH.

5/15/10 **From YahuShua HaMashiach, Our Lord and Savior**
The Word of The Lord Spoken to Timothy
For Timothy's Wife, and For All Those Who Have Ears to Hear
Workers in the Field of The Lord's Harvest

Thus says The Lord: Behold, I have sent into My vineyard husbandmen, and one who is to be as a chief husbandman. And all those who are sent are of the same. Even all who seek Me in sincerity and in truth shall serve in like manner.

Behold, The Lord over the harvest has sent out a call to every tribe, tongue, people and nation, calling them out, that they might come and work in His field. Yet the laborers are few. For though many labor, few heed the call. They serve another master, seeking always after the praises of men. And behold, they have grown fat, they are swelled with pride; they have enlarged themselves and acquired much gain. Yet what they produce remains altogether wanting - bitter wine, fit for neither man nor beast, but only to be cast out. Thus they hate the smaller vineyards and the laborers thereof. For in the small vineyards the early and latter rains are abundant and are received in due season, the quality of the wine produced greater, its value beyond compare.

Beloved, you and your husband are of the small in number, the lowly vineyard, where the wine is superior and the latter rains abundant. For your husband has been appointed as a chief husbandman over this field and all its laborers. For he listens to Me, and delivers My commands; by him I make My plans known. And you transcribe what he receives, that it may be delivered in due season, to those who have drawn near and to those who remain afar off.

Therefore the one who The Master appoints, as both servant and chief husbandman, enters not the field, but stands outside relaying The Master's orders, with his helper beside him. And if the laborers hate the chief husbandman, have not evil thoughts entered their hearts, by which they have also judged falsely? For those who hate My messengers hate Me, for I have sent them.

Therefore all who harbor evil thoughts shall be sent away, and many shall be left desolate. Indeed all flocks shall be tested, every congregation sifted, no matter their number - whether great or small, bond or free, rich or poor. There shall be weeping and gnashing of teeth.

Again, I say to you,
The first harvest shall be lowly, of the lowly;
And the second plenteous, of the refined and penitent...

For many are called, yet few are chosen.

5/29/10 **From YahuShua HaMashiach, Our Lord and Savior**
The Word of The Lord Spoken to Timothy
For All Those Who Have Ears to Hear
Spoils of War

This question was asked of The Lord: Lord, what do You say regarding those who take it upon themselves to be "spiritual warriors," rebuking demons in the name of Jesus?

Thus says The Lord: YahuShua is My name. Therefore hear My words, O ignorant and vain generation, for you know nothing yet as you ought to know. For one who endeavors to gain advantage over that which they know nothing about shall surely be ensnared by it. Yet there are those who are chosen by The Father, in whom My spirit dwells, who may rebuke demons in My name, but only those to whom it is given. And this is not of their own authority, but My authority.

For as it is written: *No one can have anything unless God gives it, and apart from Me one can do nothing.* For I have already told you: *Those who seek to understand the dark will soon find themselves trapped in the midst of it, unable to break free. Yet those who seek The Light will find it, and I will show them The Way; in these darkness has no foothold.* For people who practice such offenses walk in pride, knowing neither Me nor My will. And any who seek to do battle with evil spirits, apart from Me, will fail and be severely harmed[1]. For I am The Only Lord of Hosts. I am Lord over Heaven and Earth, over good and evil; ALL are subject to My will, even to My every word. For where I am, there is no darkness at all.

278

What then is man? He is but flesh, his power of no use at all. And in his pride he seeks glory for himself, a false valor. And so he continually turns to his own devices, deceiving himself, thinking he stands though he has fallen. Foolhardy, he rushes into battle where he suffers injury after injury, ignoring his wounds, wounds which remain unhealed, infecting the whole of the body. Yet he continues on in his arrogance, his pride driving him forward, unable to see that he is cast down, saying within himself, *"Look at my accomplishments, look upon all I have done!"* And all the while satan laughs, saying, *"Behold my acolytes; see how these men of battle have become like me."*

Sons and daughters of men, you are no warriors...

You are casualties, spoils of a war
Which was won from the foundation
Of the world, of which I was also slain...

For I alone bear the scars of battle...

Lo, I bear them in My hands and My feet,
Upon My back and in My side, wounds which I
Received in the house of My friends, says The Lord.

---

1. Acts 19:13-16

6/5/10 **From YahuShua HaMashiach, Our Lord and Savior**
The Word of The Lord Spoken to Timothy
For a Sister in Christ
And For All Those Who Have Ears to Hear
Fasting

This question was asked of The Lord, for a sister in Christ: Lord, should we fast on the behalf of others?

[The Lord answered] Have not My servants fasted in your presence? Yet you have not discerned. For whatsoever one does with love, with compassion, with empathy, or with concern for their fellow man, is well and good in My eyes. Even to afflict one's soul on the behalf of another, in My name, is righteousness. For this is true love.

Therefore fast if you are so moved,
And do so according to your faith,
That it may be strengthened...

Yet do not take up a fast for
The dead, forsaking The Promise;
For this is contemptible in My sight
And bears only bitter fruit.

Neither shall you fast as a recompense for sin. For this is to deny The Holy Sacrifice, the forgiveness of sins. Therefore the one who fasts in remembrance of Me is wise, and the one who draws close to Me, placing Me above all else, will have peace.

For they have chosen to forsake their flesh, that they might be filled with grace and satisfied with truth.

Thus that which I had spoken in the
Wilderness is the very same by which
You shall live[1], as you seek to do the
Will of your Father in Heaven[2]...

Beloved children, I am enough!

I am The Only Bread which satisfies,
The Very Manna which came down from Heaven,
The One alone in whom is eternal life...

The Only Way, The Only Truth, The Only Life...

Says The Lord.

1. *Matthew 4:4*
2. *John 4:34*

6/5/10 **From YahuShua HaMashiach, Our Lord and Savior**
The Word of The Lord Spoken to Timothy
For a Brother in Christ
And For All Those Who Have Ears to Hear
The Ill-Favored of the Flock

This question was asked of The Lord, for a brother in Christ: Lord, how do I pray for those who blaspheme Your Word and persecute Your servants? How do I pray double for them? What does that mean?

Thus says The Lord: Where does a shepherd spend his time, and which of his sheep require the most attention? Therefore pray in like manner. For indeed the ill of the flock require the most attention, and the one in ninety-nine who has gone astray shall by no means be forsaken. And though there are many who stand inside locked gates, while you stand outside, do you not remain all of one fold? And when I have freed them, will you not all rejoice together?

Therefore treat them as such, and pray for them,
Even double, and it shall be well with you...

For those who arrive last shall be embraced
By those who had arrived first...

Therefore let your heart remember,
As you look to the day, says The Lord.

6/9/10 **From The Lord, Our God and Savior**
For a Sister and Brother in Christ
And For All Those Who Have Ears to Hear
(Regarding the doctrine of hell and eternal torment,
As taught in the churches of men)
That Which Is Not of Me Is Against Me,
And Comes From the Evil One, Says The Lord

Thus says The Lord, He who is holy, He who is true: Have I not made the matter known? Beloved ones, how is it you have yet to discern? Tell Me, in this doctrine of hell and eternal torment, as taught by those who call of themselves Christian, what fruit is displayed? - Love? Joy? Peace? Patience? Kindness? Gentleness? Goodness? Mercy?! So then if it bears no fruit, according to My own spirit, then from what spirit must this doctrine come, and upon what foundation is it built? For I have already told you, whosoever believes in The Son shall abide forever, and whosoever has not The Son shall perish and not see life. Therefore you do greatly err.

Behold, I shall speak plainly, so those who have ears to hear may hear and draw close, and so those who refuse to hear may forbear and depart: ANYONE who holds fast to the false doctrine of hell and eternal torment, as taught in the churches of men, DO NOT KNOW ME! Nor have they embraced Me in truth, nor does My spirit dwell within them; I DO NOT KNOW THEM! Thus refinement shall be their portion, and abasement their due reward, in the Great and Dreadful Day of The Lord! For by strong rebuke I must correct them, and with an outstretched hand shall I bring swift discipline upon them! For they have surely blasphemed My name, even on the highest order!

Therefore, beloved ones, hear My words and also understand: You must forsake this doctrine, for it is most perverse. You must withdraw yourself from all who teach this doctrine or seek to uphold it in any way. For it is written: *You can not drink the cup of The Lord and the cup of demons; you can not partake of The Lord's table and of the table of demons.*

Therefore come out from among them, and be separate...

Come to Me and embrace Me as I truly am,
And I also shall embrace you, setting you apart
From all these who have deceived you...

Then shall that which was brought forth
From a lie, as a veil of darkness to cover
The heads of My people, be destroyed in the light
Of pure understanding and undefiled wisdom,
Crushed beneath the weight of The Truth, which I am...

Says He who is faithful, He who is true.

6/10/10 **From YahuShua HaMashiach, Our Lord and Savior**
The Word of The Lord Spoken to Timothy
For All Those Who Have Ears to Hear
(Regarding unbelieving family members)
Be Instant In and Out of Season

My sons and daughters, what is trust with abandonment? What is obedience without expectation? Is not your reasonable service love without condition? Yet I tell you the truth, trust is more than letting go. For it remains standing that it must also be shown in your obedience and by your example, and by your willingness to never deny My name, no matter the time or the season.

Beloved, place your loved ones in My hands, as I have said, for at no time were they forsaken. For I am the gate for all My sheep, and they also will hear My voice in the day they are humbled, the day their hearts crack and their pride crumbles... *And oh what a cry shall be heard, oh what wailing shall come forth.*

Yet are you not also My hands and My feet, My voice, a testimony and a lamentation bearing witness of Me? Therefore, again I say to you, do not deny My name to please others or because of fear. Make no effort to keep the peace for their sakes. Rather as it is written: *Proclaim My words; be instant in and out of season. Reprove, rebuke and exhort, with all long-suffering, according to that which I have shown you.*

For one who truly loves Me speaks about Me, and remains faithful at all times and in every season. And one who places Me above all else has shown their loved ones who is first, and what faithfulness truly is. For there is no true love apart from Me; nor can one remain faithful unless they have received of Me.

Therefore to speak of Me in the
Company of others is to love them...

And to deny Me in the company
Of others is to hate them;
Whereby you have also revealed that
Your comfort is of more importance than
The Truth, and keeping the peace
More important than their lives...

Says The Lord.

6/21/10 **From The Lord, Our God and Savior**
The Word of The Lord Spoken to Timothy
For The Lord's Little Flock
And For All Those Who Have Ears to Hear
A Faithful Witness

Beloved, hear Me, says The Lord. Understand love and know mercy, then go and do justly as you walk humbly with your God, sharing all I have given you with everyone you meet. For again I say to you: *This Word, even every Volume to every Letter, is the Word of My glory which I have put forth once again; a testament of My love and sacrifice, the announcement of My coming, a proclamation of truth, revelation of who I really am - the Trumpet Call of God, so all those called and chosen may hear and come to Me in their proper time and season.*
And if they turn away or fight against you, pray for them. For they know not the valley in which they tread, nor do they understand they are walking into death; for they have yet to grasp the full weight of their error. Thus those who rebel against Me, and speak evil of you because of Me, shall surely receive of My strong rebuke - judgment at the time appointed. Therefore, warn them from Me. And in doing so shall you understand love and know mercy, and do justly. For this is to love your enemies, to bless those who curse you, and to do good to those who hate you.

My sons and daughters, it is time to love your neighbor as yourself. For only a wicked man would neglect his own people, only an evil man would fail to warn his neighbor, and only a sluggard would sleep while holding the trumpet... Only a man meet for death would fail to warn the people, when the sword is about to overtake the land, says The Lord.

7/19/10 **From The Lord, Our God and Savior**
The Word of The Lord Spoken to Timothy
For a Sister in Christ, and For All Those Who Have Ears to Hear
Foremost

The following was brought before The Lord, for a sister in Christ. She said, "I have been thinking of plastering the sides of my truck with something like, 'Adoption is the Loving Option'. I have not heard either 'Yes,' or 'No'. The reason I am asking you to ask The Lord is that I do not want to take away from what is already on the back tailgate of my truck (the TrumpetCallofGodOnline.com website sign)."

Thus says The Lord: Do not detract from it; let it stand alone. For My Word is fire, My every Letter purges the dross. Behold, by these Volumes shall I set all these crooked paths straight. For I am The Lord, and I do not change.

Therefore, let the Trumpet be blown loudly! Let the call to repentance go out and the announcement be made! For I have lifted up an ensign to all nations, I have set up a standard for this sleeping generation, a bright and shining lamppost for My people, a light, the glory of which shall not be diminished, but shall only increase by measure. For that which must be first is first, and that which I have spoken to this generation is set above all else, even above the atrocities of men. Behold, it shall surely crush them in the Day of The Lord's Anger.

Beloved, the little ones have always been Mine, and are with Me where I am. Therefore sound the Trumpet to those who are walking into death, to those who tread the wide path, for their destruction draws near.

For they have not turned aside from their evildoings, nor do they look back. Behold, they continue on, pressing forward by unjust gain, stepping upon the necks of the poor, breaking the backs of the needy, as they slaughter the innocent in droves. Thus My anger is aroused against the generation of My wrath, My fury is come forth like fire, and shall burn; behold, it shall not be quenched, until every form of wickedness is utterly consumed!

Therefore, again I say to you, trumpet My words
Loudly by all manner of speaking and devices;
Warn them from Me...

Says The Lord...

The One who sees, The One who knows.

VOLUME FIVE

8/5/10 **From The Lord, Our God and Savior**
The Word of The Lord Spoken to Timothy
For a Brother in Christ
And For All Those Who Have Ears to Hear
A Bruised Reed Swaying in the Wind

Thus says The Lord: One who sits upon the fence between two houses can not enter either one...

My son, I have spoken to you many times, and still you deny Me. Even now you rebel against Me, as you reject this Word spoken through My prophet. For I have indeed spoken it, yet I hear no "Amen". Behold, it is written in the Scriptures of Truth, and still you remain sitting upon the fence, with one foot planted securely in the pastures of men and the other dangling in the wind.
When you called to Me, did I not answer? And when you reached out to Me, did I not extend My hand? Yet you turn from Me, rejecting this Word, drawing back from My hand, refusing to be replanted. Thus between us a gulf widens on account of that from which you refuse to depart, on account of that which you hold on to so tightly.

Let go, My son! Let go!
There is no argument, no debate!
Obey NOT the commandments of men!...

For I tell you the truth, to choose the
Doctrines of men is to deny Me, and to uphold
Their traditions is to fight against Me!...

I AM THE LORD!

Thus before you I have placed an open door. Yet one may only pass through by coming to Me empty, free of the corrupt doctrines of men, standing apart from all their filthy traditions, which I hate.

My son, I shall speak plainly, for your sake, once again: NO ONE who upholds any part of the doctrine of hell and eternal torment, as taught in the churches of men, shall escape the Day of The Lord. For whether one holds to it in part or as a whole, they have surely blasphemed My name, even on the highest order.

Therefore I call you to repent, and to come out of the churches of men, to be separate. Only then will you begin to know Me, only then will you see Me as I truly am. Yet if you will not come out, nor be separate, most assuredly, I say to you, I shall leave you to refinement in the Great and Terrible Day of The Lord.

For as it is written:
I shall not lose one The Father has given Me...

Yet I shall surely refine them,
I must purge all who are left,
And by great tribulation shall they come into glory...

For I will turn My hand against them,
And thoroughly purge away their dross
And take away all their alloy...

Says The Lord.

8/5/10 **From YahuShua HaMashiach, Our Lord and Savior**
The Word of The Lord Spoken to Timothy
For The Lord's Little Flock
And For All Those Who Have Ears to Hear
In Spirit and In Truth

Thus says The Holy One of Israel: What is the knowledge of man? Is it not a stone of stumbling? And the pride of man, a rock of offense? How then shall the blind see or the deaf hear, unless I heal them? Or how shall one grab hold of the line, unless it is first placed within their reach?

Yet all those who call of themselves Christian seek out knowledge, only to proclaim their own glory before men. Indeed, they proclaim falsely that they know the Way, though they remain lost in their own deceptions. For as it is written: *My people are foolish and have no understanding; they are skilled at doing evil, but of doing good they have no knowledge; they refuse to obey the voice of The Living God, nor will they receive correction. Behold, truth has perished among them; it has altogether been cut off from their mouths!*
Yet My servants are wise. They fear The Lord, and wait upon Me with all patience and faith, doubting nothing, humble servants who study My Word, knowing I am The Author and The Finisher thereof. When they wake and when they lie down, I am there; I am their life, and they are My joy, says The Lord.
Therefore when My servants come to an impasse in My Word, according to their own understanding, what is their reaction? They continue on, without hindrance or doubt. For their relationship with The Author is intimate, their trust without reservation.

Thus they remain at peace, and wait upon The Lord for the light of understanding, knowing in their heart every word is true, ready to receive the spirit of the Word, stumbling not over its letter. And until My people are established firmly upon this premise, they will remain daunted, striving to see but never fully understanding, straining to hear but remaining dull of hearing.

Thus for My wise and faithful servants,
All barriers are removed...

For their peace is in the knowing,
I AM WHO I AM, though they yet
Stand at the beginning, unable to see the end...

An heir of all I will reveal to them
When the fullness of time has come in...

Says The Lord.

8/23/10 **From YahuShua HaMashiach, Our Lord and Savior**
The Word of The Lord Spoken to Timothy
For The Lord's Little Flock
And For All Those Who Have Ears to Hear
The Measuring Line

Beloved ones, you have sought Me; in this you have done well. Yet the fullness of My love you have yet to understand. For you have only tasted, having taken but a single sip from the cup of My glory. Indeed in your mind's eye you have seen, but only dimly, a passing glimpse of The Majesty from on high... *Therefore I ask you to take a leap! - A leap of understanding, a leap of faith, of steadfast trust! A wondrous leap wherein one lands solidly in My love, wherein peace flows beyond understanding and knowledge of The Holy One is made complete!*

Therefore hear My words, and have understanding: Those who sit at My table, also having one who speaks for Me in their midst, shall be tried by a greater line than their fellows - a measuring line over which many shall stumble and from which many shall flee; a plumb line which the churches hate and the world seeks to destroy, the line by which all is measured, by which right is separated from wrong; the line which I established from the beginning, unchanged, even from the foundation of the world.

Beloved ones, I tell you the truth, the people of this world do not know Me. Therefore I have come close, to unstop the ears of all who long to hear My voice and obey it; I have drawn near, to open the eyes of all who desire to look upon My face and partake of My glory; and behold, I have poured out My spirit to restore the hearts of the penitent, to breathe new life into all those who embrace My words and seek to remain in My love.

For I am come,
And have come already;
And behold, I shall also
Return and reveal My glory...

I have not departed from My people,
For My spirit dwells in My own...

Yet all must be broken...

Some broken before the time,
And many more after...

Says The Lord.

8/23/10 **From YahuShua HaMashiach, Our Lord and Savior**
The Word of The Lord Spoken to Timothy
For The Lord's Little Flock
And For All Those Who Have Ears to Hear
Breaking Through the Lines

Beloved ones, come to Me, and I shall give you rest. Be drawn to Me, that I may lift you up. For I tell you the truth, My wrath is coming. Behold, My anger is aroused, My fierce jealousy burns like a raging fire and is about to come to the full.

Yet do not waver, but understand. For My wrath is required, and the foundation of My anger rests solidly upon My jealousy, by which My unending sorrow is also revealed. For My wrath is born of sorrow, and My anger bursts forth as a husband jealous over his bride, My fury as a father protecting his children, as one mighty in battle breaking through the lines - recompense upon ALL who offend, upon ALL who have harmed My beloved! Vengeance upon ALL who have slain My little ones, upon ALL who took part in the murder of the innocent!

For the people have forsaken Me, and those within the churches of men refuse to accept Me as I am, nor do they seek to understand. And when I warn them of My wrath or speak of My anger, they do always turn to Me a deaf ear. For they can not bear to listen; indeed, they refuse to understand!

Behold, they hate the sound of My voice, and will not give heed to My correction, persecuting all those I send! Beloved, they no longer recognize Me, and want no part with Me as I truly am. Therefore My wrath shall come upon them on a day they did not look for, and My anger at an hour they did not expect. Behold, upon the whole world shall I pour out judgment on that day! Says The Lord.

8/28/10 **From The Lord, Our God and Savior**
The Word of The Lord Spoken to Timothy
For a Brother in Christ
And For All Those Who Have Ears To Hear
(Regarding the judgment of those who are raised
At the end of the thousand years)
Judgment and Mercy

Thus says The Lord: In the Consummation, all judged according to their works shall surely die. Yet in that day, if one calls upon the name of Salvation in true repentance, with sincere remorse in their heart, they will not be judged; behold, they shall pass from judgment into life. For I look upon the heart, I discern the thoughts and judge the innermost intentions; nothing is hidden before Me.

Therefore when the multitudes are judged, they will indeed be judged according to their works. For the books shall be opened and their works will be made known, even every idle word, and they shall be condemned. Yet again I say to you, those who call upon the name of The Holy One of Israel in sincerity and in truth, humbling themselves before Him, taking full responsibility for their works, confessing their sin, shall receive mercy. For YahuShua and *His* works now stand in their place, interceding on their behalf. For The Gift is never-ending, and all who come to Me will I in no wise turn away.

Therefore, My son, trust in My glory, and seek no more to understand My Word according to the letter, nor grab hold of it as though it can be fully grasped by any man. Rather seek to know Me as I am. For from this knowledge alone does all understanding flow into the hearts of My beloved, and they shall have peace, says The Lord.

9/16/10 **From YahuShua HaMashiach, Our Lord and Savior**
The Word of The Lord Spoken to Timothy
For a Brother in Christ
And For All Those Who Have Ears to Hear
Those Who Are Mine Shall Never Be Cast Off

Regarding Matthew 19:28: So YahuShua said to them, "Assuredly I say to you, that in the regeneration, when The Son of Man sits on the throne of His glory, you who have followed Me will also sit on twelve thrones, judging the twelve tribes of Israel"... A brother in Christ asked if Judas would be one of those twelve.

[YahuShua answered] My son, you consider things deeply, pondering that which others often overlook. Thus because of your zealousness you are called, should you choose to embrace your calling fully, receiving temperance unto peace according to the Spirit of Truth.

Yet what of another who has been called in like manner, who refuses to walk according to My will and purpose? Shall he continue in his office, though his heart testifies against him, with his actions bearing fruit of the same? My son, he shall not; his calling shall be given to another.

Therefore, hear and understand the loving mercies of God fulfilled in Me, even of those bitter tears which I have shed over all these who deny Me, over all these who betray Me by all they say and do: Beloved, in My anger I have indeed cast them out, appointing others to run in their stead. Yet I tell you the truth, though they now abide as one sitting along the wayside, they are in no wise broken off. For our bond is love, and any bond forged in My love can never be broken.

Behold, even amongst this little flock
Have I received many kisses after
The kind of My son, Judas...

Yet I tell you the truth,
I have never lost one who is Mine;
I am in love with My own...

And though their thoughts betray them,
Having given heed to many lies and
Deceptions from within and without,
I know My own, and I will never
Turn away anyone who returns to Me.

Therefore, again I say to you, Judas shall be with Me in paradise. For he repented in sincerity and in truth, with extreme remorse. And though the weight of sin can be very heavy, and remorse over betrayal can slay your heart, even to the point of death, My love is greater still.

Thus upon these twelve thrones, of which you have considered yet do not fully comprehend, will My twelve apostles sit, judging the twelve tribes of Israel. Yet Judas shall not be among them. Yet he shall indeed be there, even close at hand, and he shall be at peace, having spent many days wailing upon My bosom in the house of The Lord.

9/29/10 **From The Lord, Our God and Savior**
The Word of The Lord Spoken to Timothy
For All Those Who Have Ears to Hear
My Witnesses in the Day

Thus says The Lord: Look upon My witnesses, for they prepare My way before Me. And behold, the day is coming quickly when I shall also go before them, dwell within them, and be their rearguard. For as the angels which I had placed at the east of the Garden of Eden, and the flaming sword which turned in every direction to guard the way to the Tree of Life, so in like manner shall I guard My witnesses in the Day of Battle.

For I had sent My angels to block the way to the Tree of Life. Yet in the Day of The Lord, My servants shall eat from it freely, even as they shall also be its branches, partaking of its fullness, even the strength of the root. And if My servants partake of the Tree of Life, and the fullness of the tree dwells within them, then who shall be able to approach them, to do them harm by any means?

For I shall put My words in their mouths...

And set them over nations and over kingdoms,
To root out and to pull down,
To destroy and to throw down,
To build and to plant...

For I am The Lord, and I do not change.

10/11/10 **From The Lord, Our God and Savior**
The Word of The Lord Spoken to Timothy
For The Lord's Little Flock
And For All Those Who Have Ears to Hear
Death Unto Life

Beloved ones, there is indeed a death in which I am well pleased, and another which greatly pains My heart. For a great multitude shall be left in the Refiner's Fire, and all shall suffer the pains of death - for some, death unto life; and others, death into darkness.

And yet still others have been appointed to be taken through. These shall be for Me a remnant. Behold, I shall be their covering, hiding them from all who puff at them, a strong shield protecting them from all their enemies, a high wall which can not be broken down. They shall endure. For these are reserved for glory, to bring Me great glory in all the earth.

Yes, these are they who shall suffer as you must suffer, the same death of which you seek and shall surely be fulfilled, when I finish you - the shedding of the skin of this world, the crucifying of your old man with his sinful ways, the putting on of the new man who is renewed in the knowledge of The Truth, restored in the image of Him who created him.

For those who come into the world by way of water and blood were born from Life into life. Yet to return to My kingdom, one must be reborn from death unto Life. And though My will seems to be hidden from your eyes, it is not at all hidden. For I have proclaimed it openly from the beginning; I have not ceased from making My plans known. Yet from those who refuse Me, it is indeed hidden, though it passes before their eyes even now, says The Lord.

304

10/14/10 **From YahuShua HaMashiach, Our Lord and Savior**
The Word of The Lord Spoken to Timothy
For The Lord's Little Flock
And For All Those Who Have Ears to Hear
Pure and Undefiled Faith

Beloved ones, before you depart My table, consider this: Where did your faith come from, and by what means was it authored? Be not quick to answer, but consider. For I tell you the truth, I am not the author of your faith, nor did your faith begin with Me. For I did not come forth to increase the faith you already have, nor have I spoken through all these Letters to affirm that which you have already accepted; no, I have come to tear down and to supplant.

Beloved, I am calling you out of that to which you have grown accustomed, to be separate from that which has until now been the author of your faith. For some of you your faith began in the churches of men, and for others it was molded and shaped by the world, yet for most it was a combination of the two. Therefore I call you to see with greater eyes, with eyes like Mine. For I tell you the truth, your faith is against Me, even as the churches of men and this world are against Me, polluting My name and My glory without ceasing. For it is written: *Friendship with the world is enmity with God; whoever therefore wants to be a friend of the world makes himself an enemy of God.*

Therefore, I have poured out My spirit on all flesh in these last days, and by My prophet I have spoken; even by a multitude of words I have declared it. And thus I say it to you, once again: *I shall tear down, uproot and destroy, supplant, until I have set all these crooked paths straight.*

305

Thus I have called My people out, that they might
Come out from among them and be separate...

A people set apart for My name,
A people who keep The Commandments
And cease not from testifying to My glory,
A people of pure and undefiled faith...

A people joined unto ME...

Says The Lord.

10/19/10 **From YahuShua HaMashiach, Our Lord and Savior**
The Word of The Lord Spoken to Timothy
For All Those Who Have Ears to Hear
Women in Mourning

Thus says The Lord: I have stretched out My hands all day long to
a stubborn people, who walk in a way that is not good; a people
who do not obey My voice, nor will they incline the ear, but do
always follow the counsels and dictates of their own evil hearts; a
most rebellious generation who provoke Me to anger continually
to My face!

For they seek always a way to retain their corrupt riches, a way
to hide their shame, as they uplift themselves to new heights in
vanity - false glory! Yea they build great and lavish houses, setting
each one upon the shifting sands of man-made religion, perverse
tradition and the corrupt doctrines of men; behold, even their
steeples seek to pierce Heaven!

Woe, therefore, to this adulterous people! Woe to all these
women dressed in fine apparel! They are all as strangers to Me!
For they worship another god, and within their churches they
teach the people of another messiah, one which they themselves
have created! THESE ARE NOT OF MY BODY! THEY LOOK
NOTHING LIKE ME!

Behold, the churches have removed themselves far from Me! For
they have played the harlot, and cleave to the breast of another!
Tears, great anguish fills My heart! The stripes which I bore for
them remain, yet they continue to bruise Me and persecute My
body while mocking Me, spitting in My face on account of My
words, continuing in their unjust cause, that they might silence
My messengers and shut My mouth from speaking!

For the sake of envy they stone My Bride, and are quick to pass judgment upon the lowly, turning their backs on those who come seeking bread! Behold, they pollute the name of God without ceasing, even the name The Father gave Me (the name We share), refusing to embrace Me as I truly am!

Lo, even the least of their brethren are made to conform to their image, as they continue to heap up offenses one atop another throughout their generations! And those who depart their company, or bring forth a just complaint, are judged swiftly and very harshly, slandered and cast out. For they say within themselves, *"I answer to no one; I am free from The Law, and am in need of nothing. This is my house, and to IT am I married. I will follow the traditions of my fathers, and no one will turn me aside. For I am a bride-in-waiting, and will never be a widow!"*

Therefore I am coming down, and MY bride shall be taken,
My every treasure gone from this place...

And so it shall come to pass, the "bride-in-waiting"
Shall indeed become the widow;
For the husband which she had formed
In her own image shall die on that day...

And behold, only women in mourning shall remain...

Says The Lord.

10/28/10 From The Lord, Our God and Savior
The Word of The Lord Spoken to Timothy
During Men's Fellowship, For The Lord's Watchmen
And For All Those Who Have Ears to Hear
Trees of the Field

Thus says The Lord: My sons, what is a dry tree to he who holds the axe? Yet when the winds pass through and catch the man sleeping, is he not easily crushed by the weight of the tree?

Indeed, what is this forest full of tall trees before Me, standing so tall with roots deeply embedded in the world, blocking always the warmth of the sun at eventide, casting long shadows under which the wicked flock? Are they not soon left cold, standing in darkness? Are they not as those who seek shelter under a tree when the rains descend and the thunder crashes, who meet a quick end when lightning strikes?... *So is this people before Me, a most wicked and foolish generation, multitudes of slothful people seeking always the tall tree, taking shelter under branches which have grown far and wide, standing fast in the cold darkness of its shadow, oblivious to the setting of the sun upon this age of men!*

Therefore I am come to cut down every tree, which grows where I have not planted; behold, I shall level entire forests! For I have called forth My witnesses, men of promise, who I shall set over nations and over kingdoms, to root out and to pull down, to destroy and to throw down, to build and to plant, and no one shall be able to subdue them, by any means!

Yet you ask within yourselves, *"How can this be?"* My sons, My ways are not human ways, My thoughts not human thoughts. Here is wisdom: If a man can not be overcome by any means, what is he to other men?

And if a man can not be moved from his place, not one inch to the left nor to the right, what has he become compared with other men? And what of a man, My servant, who is one with The Messiah? Is he not an island which no one can reach, save I make it possible for them to do so?

Consider the squirrel and its ways. Does it not live among the trees, running up and down with ease, leaping from branch to branch with skill and grace, perfectly designed for its abode and purpose?

So shall My watchmen be in the Day of The Lord...

Prepared according to their task,
Established according to the Word of My mouth,
Filled according to their service,
Remade according to My purpose...

I AM THE LORD.

Therefore, again I say to you, all those who seek sanctuary under any tree which grows contrary to Me shall be struck down; indeed all who take refuge in these man-made houses, whose doctrines and traditions I hate, shall be crushed beneath the weight of their fallen riches. Yet all who seek sanctuary in The Messiah, all who sought refuge under the shadow of His healing wings, shall escape. Yet those plucked up and replanted shall be set as a high wall against the world, a strong tower standing firm in the midst of great and mighty men, fixed pillars which can not be moved nor broken down, men of valor in whom My spirit dwells like fire, says The Lord.

11/18/10 **From The Lord, Our God and Savior**
The Word of The Lord Spoken to Timothy
For The Lord's Little Flock
And For All Those Who Have Ears to Hear
Blessed by The Word of God

Who is a wise and faithful servant? Is he not one who receives the blessings of his Father without constraint, one who embraces My speech, whether soft or hard, even of that which I have spoken to another? A servant such as this is wise indeed. For he knows that every good gift and every perfect gift is from above, and comes down from The Father of Lights, with whom there is no variation or shadow of turning, as it is written.

Beloved ones, if I am He who reigns in your heart, The One of whom you testify is love and mercy, The One alone who knows all things, why do you resist My correction and seek only to embrace that which is soft? If I speak, and My words carry My spirit, put no difference between them.

For everything which comes from the mouth of The Lord your God is a blessing for all - a song for all those who have ears to hear, a vision to all who have eyes to see My splendor, painted by the Word of My glory, an overflowing fountain inside those whose hearts are wide open.

Beloved, it is time for you to truly believe without seeing, to obey My voice, whether soft or hard. It is time for you to follow your heart, and no more bow to the demands of your mind. It is time for you to embrace Me as I truly am, says The Lord.

11/30/10 **From YahuShua HaMashiach, Our Lord and Savior**
The Word of The Lord Spoken to Timothy
For All Those Who Have Ears to Hear
Mindful

Thus says The Lord: What is a son who is mindful of his father's ways, who pays close attention to his every word? Or a servant, who seeks only to serve his master? Or a faithful bride, who seeks always to please her husband in all her ways, whether he is near or far, in her presence or soon returning? Beloved ones, be mindful of these things and grow in wisdom, abide in trust and do not waver; be at peace. For I am indeed coming quickly, and My reward is with Me.

And behold, I am also coming to repay the nations, for all their forsaking of Me. Therefore sing for Me, beloved, stand up and blow the Trumpet. For the day is coming quickly, and is already here, when I shall place My voice within My servants, and together we shall speak as one. Therefore do not draw back, but lean forward, cup your ears and listen to the sound of My voice; be attentive and wide awake. For the time has come for Me to claim My own, to call them out and gather them together.

Therefore search your hearts and know Me, embrace Me as I truly am. Beloved, stop looking forward, as though I am afar off. Cease from looking backward, as though I am somehow beyond your reach - Look, here I am! See no more through the eyes of man, for flesh and blood deceive you. And by NO means am I that which men in authority have spoken concerning Me; the "Jesus" of the churches of men looks nothing like Me!

Beloved, wipe your eyes, and see!
Unstop your ears, and hear!
Open your hearts, and know, I AM HE!...

The Only Begotten of The Father,
The One True God and Savior, The Mashiach,
YAHUSHUA-YAHUWAH...

Immanu El!

12/7/10 **From The Lord, Our God and Savior**
The Word of The Lord Spoken to Timothy
For All Those Who Have Ears to Hear
Do Not Look Back; Escape to The Father's House

Thus says The Lord: Learn the lesson of Lot and his wife. It is simple, yet speaks to that which is to come and must be. For those who I have called out of a place shall in no wise return to it, nor shall they look back. They shall continue on toward safety, with their eyes fixed upon The Goal, walking always in line with the Spirit - praying without ceasing, giving heed to My leading, listening for My voice.

Yet there shall be many who will seek to flee the coming wrath, yet shall by no means escape it, for this world is condemned. Behold, many shall stop to look back, and their hearts shall fail them for fear, on account of that which is coming to pass before their eyes. For I have purposed and will not relent, I will not turn back - *CALAMITY upon the cities of men! Upon every city in every land, of every tribe, tongue, people and nation! CALAMITY upon the churches of men and every religion of man! Upon every denomination and religion in every land, of every tribe, tongue, people and nation! Not one polluted sanctuary shall stand before My face, anymore! For I am a jealous God, and I will not share My glory! Declares The Lord.*
For there is but One Sanctuary in which My people are to take refuge, One Shelter from the heat of the Day. Blessed, therefore, are all those who embrace Him fully and strive always to walk in His ways. They shall be hidden under the shadow of His healing wings, high and lifted up, says The Lord.

12/9/10 From The Lord, Our God and Savior
The Word of The Lord Spoken to Timothy
For Those in Men's Fellowship
And For All Those Who Have Ears to Hear
(Regarding the conflict which arises between those who keep
The holidays of men and those who obey the Word of The Lord)
Tear Down Every Whitewashed Wall of Abomination

Thus says The Lord: Purification of faith starts with the temple in which I dwell, and ends with the house in which My servants dwell. For the Day approaches quickly wherein My witnesses shall wield a staff and a sword; a staff to break, and a sword to cut and strike through. And wheresoever I send them, in where an idol is found, I shall cause a fire to well up within their hearts and they shall strike with ferocity, breaking every idol in pieces, cutting down every tree of abomination which stands against Me, piercing the heart of every man who upholds that which pollutes My name and My glory, whether he blasphemes in word or by deed. Behold, EVERY form of idolatry shall be utterly destroyed in that day! Says The Lord.
My sons, you fear a war which is waged already, a battle that has already come. And though I have said that I require peace in the houses of My servants, there can be no peace while abominations stand. Therefore, if peace is taken from a house in the name of righteousness, to rectify that which has polluted My name and My glory, this is acceptable with Me. For you have shown yourselves worthy of Me... Or have you forgotten the sword I bring?

Yet My words are only for those who believe, for those willing to set all these crooked paths straight, those who love Me more than these, says The Lord.

12/11/10 **From The Lord, Our God and Savior**
The Word of The Lord Spoken to Timothy
For a Sister in Christ
And For All Those Who Have Ears to Hear
Most Needful

A sister in Christ asked a question regarding the blood red moons of the past occurring on Holy Days and coinciding with significant events in Israel, and future blood red moons occurring on Holy Days, and what the connection might be.

Thus says The Lord: Beloved, why do you seek after signs and search elsewhere for proof? Since the creation of the world My invisible attributes, both My eternal power and My divine nature, have been clearly seen, readily perceived by those I have made, leaving them without excuse, as it is written. Even so, there will indeed be many signs. And those who have eyes to see will look upon them and acknowledge Me, and those who have received wisdom shall understand.

Yet I ask you, what is most needful and which is the greatest sign of all? And what of all these Letters I have put forth, are they not a sign in and of themselves? Or is your faith still in need of supports to prop it up, due to your lack of trust and a heart which remains unwilling?

For I have indeed lifted up My voice to this lost and dying generation, I have spoken plainly to My people, yet few have ears to hear, few stop and pay attention. Thus only those who seek that which is first, who fill themselves up with that which is most needful, will finish the day with strength enough to face tomorrow.

Therefore seek Me out at every opportunity,
Whether for a moment or for the hour,
That you may be renewed in My presence...

Looking always to The Blessed Hope,
Having tasted of it while in waiting...

Says The Lord.

12/15/10 **From The Lord, Our God and Savior**
The Word of The Lord Spoken to Timothy
For All Those Who Have Ears to Hear
(Regarding the holidays of men)
Deplorable Traditions

Thus says The Lord: All these things which these modern people do in My name, though they be called Christian or otherwise, I DO HATE! I loathe the sight of them! - Dead works! Abominations! Deplorable traditions, in where they have despised both Me and My Word!

Behold, even the churches of men pollute My name and My glory. Day after day, they twist the Scriptures and tread upon My Holy Law, in an effort to uphold their own way. Behold, from house to house they pollute the name of The Messiah, desecrating The Glory of My majesty, as they attempt to place the name of The Holy One upon their perverse traditions! Reason has altogether departed from them, the truth is cast down, and righteousness has perished! For not one is willing to embrace Me as I truly am!

Therefore, thus says The Lord to the churches of men: Your worship is in vain! Your offerings are not accepted! Behold, even your prayers are an abomination! For you do always turn your ear away from hearing The Holy Law, and have not ceased from practicing those things I hate! Modern Pharisees! Arrogant children!

Behold, you have made for yourselves a graven image, an intricately woven tapestry of man-made doctrine and idolatrous tradition, interlacing sin with sin, all in the name of your "Jesus," another messiah which you have created in your own image! Desecration! Blasphemy! YOU KNOW NEITHER ME, NOR MY WORD!

Thus I call all those who desire to serve Me
In truth and righteousness, to tear down
Every whitewashed wall of abomination!...

For this is not a light matter with Me,
But carries great weight, filling the cup of
My indignation throughout your generations!...

And behold, I shall surely pour out!...

Until My wrath is satisfied and My anger has abated,
Until the whole breadth of the whole earth
Is cleansed in the heat of My fury!...

Says The Lord.

12/21/10 **From The Lord, Our God and Savior**
The Word of The Lord Spoken to Timothy
For All Those Who Have Ears to Hear
As It Was in the Days of Noah,
  So Shall The Coming of The Son of Man Be

Thus says The Lord: The words of scoffers come forth from a hard and troubled heart, from a place void of understanding. Their words are like chaff, their every lofty assertion dust carried away by the wind. As a ship tossed about by rough seas, so is the plight of the ungodly; in a dark sea of confusion, they attempt to sail against every wind of doctrine which opposes them. Yet all their toil is in vain. For I am The Only Truth, I am God alone! And behold, all I have spoken is established and shall be; My Word yields to no man.

For I tell you the truth, the coming of The Lord is a terror to all who say they know Me, yet do not really know Me, a terror to all who deny Me and to all who offend. Therefore let the feet of the desolate stumble, and the ways of the ungodly return atop their own head - JUDGMENT for the rebellious! PUNISHMENT for the wicked! CALAMITY upon all nations who offend!

Therefore as it was in the days of My servant Noah, so shall it be with My faithful servants of this day also; and as it was then, so shall it be in the Day of The Lord's Anger - The door shall be shut! And upon the earth shall I rain down judgment, and bring up horrible calamity from beneath! The storehouses shall be opened and My wrath shall overflow, until I have covered the face of the whole earth in My vengeance, until I have wiped away all that offends, until I have utterly destroyed the kingdoms of men! Says The Lord Most High, He who comes with justice and recompense for all nations.

1/3/11 From The Lord, Our God and Savior
The Word of The Lord Spoken to Timothy
For All Those Who Have Ears to Hear
Treasuries of Wrath and Mercy

Behold, the time has come for wrath and recompense, for the anger of The Lord to be put on open display...

Therefore, thus says The Lord to His servants: Beloved ones, the time of ignorance has passed. Therefore blow this Trumpet, making use of every platform at your disposal; shout My words from the rooftops and cause an uproar, trumpet My wrath and reveal My anger; draw back from no man.
Indeed serve My words hot, and let their palates be set ablaze by My fierce rebuke. Show this most wicked generation no mercy in your speech, make no concessions, for My Word yields to no man. For My words are poured out like rain, and My voice shakes the house like thunder, My every word a hailstone released from the treasury of hail, which I have reserved for the Time of Trouble. Behold, My wrath is a consuming fire, a mighty earthquake, encompassing the breadth of the whole earth!

Yet I ask you, what is the treasury of My mercy reserved for those who repent? And what are the depths of My compassion for the little ones who suffer at the hands of men in this world? Does not My anger burn hot against all those who forsake or do harm to My little ones?! For as it is written: *It would be better for them if a millstone were hung around their neck, and they were drowned in the depths of the sea, than to suffer My wrath over these little ones!*

Thus in these words alone shall mercy be found,
In these words alone is there hope
And salvation for the penitent:

"REPENT! And turn from your evil ways"...

And all such similar words which I have
Spoken and shall continue to speak...

Says The Lord.

1/6/11 **From YahuShua HaMashiach, Our Lord and Savior**
The Word of The Lord Spoken to Timothy
For a Brother in Christ
And For All Those Who Have Ears to Hear
A Shout and a Trumpet

A brother in Christ asked: Is it OK to tell people The Lord is returning this year to gather, or is this date-setting?

[*The Lord answered*] Have I not spoken to this already?[1]

Therefore before I gather, say to them: "*Behold, The Bridegroom is coming! Go out to meet Him!*"

And after, say to them: "*I am a voice crying out in the midst of desolations and strong judgment, shouting the name of glory and pure righteousness, a trumpet of God until the end - MAKE WAY FOR THE COMING OF THE LORD!*"

---

1. *Matthew 24:36*

1/24/11 **From YahuShua HaMashiach, Our Lord and Savior**
The Word of The Lord Spoken to Timothy
For The Lord's Little Flock
And For All Those Who Have Ears to Hear
(Regarding modern reports of people being raised
From the dead and coming back from death)
False Miracles and Lies, Deceived and Ignorant People

Thus says The Lord: No man shall raise the dead, save I live in that man. And no account of one raising the dead in My name is true, save it was given them by Me to do so. Or have you never read this Scripture: *It is I who has done it?*

For I have indeed raised the dead through My servants in times past, and I shall do so again, yet this time is not yet. In that day My witnesses shall go out ahead of Me, preparing My way before Me, and by signs such as this shall My coming glory be revealed. For through them I shall indeed perform many signs and wonders, in the sight of many witnesses, to the glory of My name. Yet no man or woman in all the earth shall do these things, save those I send.

Therefore believe no report of one returning from death, speaking false tales. For as it is written: *The dead know nothing at all, for all their thoughts have perished with them.*

For satan shall indeed deceive many; and as it is written: *False messiahs and false prophets will rise and show great signs and wonders to deceive, if possible, even the elect.* Yet I tell you the truth, all is a lie, a very clever, well-planned deception. No miracle is found; only illusion and misdirection, accompanied by propaganda and dark sentences, great delusion to the darkness of many faces.

For there is but One in whom
The fullness of God dwells...

One alone who has the power to
Revive the dead and destroy the wicked...

One alone who holds all the keys,
Even over death and Sheol...

I AM HE!

1/28/11 **From The Lord, Our God and Savior**
The Word of The Lord Spoken to Timothy
For All Those Who Have Ears to Hear
(Regarding those who say The Volumes of Truth are
From the devil, who cite the Letters regarding Judas as proof)
Sons of the Devil

Thus says The Lord: That which glorifies Me can have only one source. And that which denies My sacrifice, as though it were not enough, steals from My glory, and this also has one source. For all who deny Me and steal from My sacrifice, to pollute it, have become sons of their father, the devil. And all who reject My words spoken to this generation reject Me, and shall by no means escape the Day of The Lord.

1/29/11 **From The Lord, Our God and Savior**
The Word of The Lord Spoken to Timothy
For All Those Who Have Ears to Hear
(Regarding modern false prophets)
Prophets Hananiah

Thus says The Lord: The false prophets gather, and the deceitful teachers increase in number like a plague; a great company who pollute My holy name in one accord, to the blaspheming of the Spirit; an ever-increasing multitude of self-appointed apostles, prophets and teachers, whose every word I despise in My zeal!

Behold the prophets Hananiah!...

And of his reward, they are fully worthy!...

Says The Lord.

2/4/11 **From The Lord, Our God and Savior**
The Word of The Lord Spoken to Timothy
For The Lord's Little Flock
And For All Those Who Have Ears to Hear
I AM COME

Thus says The Lord: My sons and daughters, have you not discerned? How is it you have yet to consider, to see with greater eyes? Beloved, let go of your preconceived notions and biased beliefs, put away all your self-serving expectations, and humble yourselves, that your understanding may be set free.

Therefore hear now, and consider these three words: I AM COME. Consider the whole of prophecy, and bow down; consider all My words, from the foundation of the world even to this day, and be greatly humbled; consider the vastness of My Glory and offer up perfect praise!
Beloved, as I AM, so also is My Word. And so I have spoken this one phrase in your hearing, even many times. Yet not one has truly discerned, not one among you has truly considered the scope of its meaning. For the whole of Scripture speaks to one end, the glory of The Holy One, He who is and was and is to come. And as the glory of The Messiah is fulfilled in this: One Way, One Truth and One Life, even the whole of The Scriptures in One, so in like manner have I revealed it to you, once again.

For the fulfillment of all things
Has come, and is revealed in this:

I AM COME...

The One who was has come;
The One who is, is come;
The One who is to come is coming
Quickly to fulfill and complete...

HISTORY HAS AN END...

And His name is The Great I AM,
The Holy One of Israel...

YAHUSHUA-YAHUWAH...

Immanu El!

2/8/11 **From The Lord, Our God and Savior**
The Word of The Lord Spoken to Timothy
For The Lord's Little Flock
And For All Those Who Have Ears to Hear
(Regarding a brother in Christ who fell away)
Pride Goes Before a Fall

Thus says The Lord: Why do you wane in the heat of persecution, little flock? And how is it you are taken aback, when one is led away from the Truth, while walking in disobedience? Has not the pride of man revealed such things? Where is your trust? Or have you forgotten the knowledge of The Holy, by which I have opened your understanding, and My glory which is put on open display?

Little flock, your brother remains My son, and I shall indeed go out after him, severely punishing all who lead My people astray, even with sickness and death. Did I not offer your brother his calling and give him much correction, as any good father should? Yet My sons are grown, and they must choose to obey.

And what shall I do when My sons choose to go their own way, running far from Me, squandering that which I had given them? Beloved, I shall surely let them go, I shall let them run far away; I shall let them do all they have purposed in their hearts to do, until they can run no further, until the bitterness of deceit wears them out and their pride weighs heavily upon them, and they fall hard upon the ground. Then shall they stop and consider, turning back to look, and there will I be, waiting.

Therefore hear and understand, beloved: The moment pride enters a man, the moment he stands in front of Me, to look elsewhere, is the same moment My hand is removed.

For I have shown you, My servants, what is good and that which I require: *That you should do justly, love mercy, and walk humbly with your God.*

Yet how can one behold My face while looking elsewhere, seeking glory for themselves? And how can one who has stepped in front of Me walk in My footsteps? Beloved, how shall one who runs away from Me, to tread another path, take My hand?

And so they must first be greatly humbled,
They must fall hard upon the ground...

Until the revelation of their error comes
Full circle, until they are truly ready
To give up their life for My sake...

Says The Lord.

2/9/11 **From YahuShua HaMashiach, Our Lord and Savior**
The Word of The Lord Spoken to Timothy
For The Lord's Little Flock
And For All Those Who Have Ears to Hear
Those Who Walk in My Ways Walk in The Light,
  Yet Those Who Forsake The Way of The Lord
  Abide in Darkness Already

A fellowship participant asked: Will you all pray for a sister in Christ? She is going through hard times, and is convinced that God is trying to kill her, or something along those lines.

Thus says The Lord: I know all My sheep. And though they wander and betray their own hearts, I do not punish them; they punish themselves. Therefore, woe to all who lay blame at the feet of The Lord! I do not stalk My sheep, as though they were prey! Yet I do go out after them, leaving the ninety-nine to seek out the one who has gone astray. And those who know My voice come running.

Therefore, let no one pollute My love anymore!
Nor let the remarks of the wayward enter in...

Turn to God, and seek to know My ways,
That you may walk in them...

For in doing so shall you come
To know Me as I truly am,
For The Father and The Son are One.

2/17/11 **From YahuShua HaMashiach, Our Lord and Savior**
The Word of The Lord Spoken to Timothy
For All Those Who Have Ears to Hear
I AM HE

My sons and daughters, from the beginning, I AM WHO I AM and shall be. Even to the end, I AM HE. From everlasting to everlasting, I AM. In this shall you find rest and know peace, says The Lord.

Therefore no longer bind yourselves to what you see, nor concern yourselves with the things of this world and its evil ways. Free yourselves by the knowledge I have given you, by the understanding that I AM WHO I AM, freedom in the knowing I AM HE. Beloved ones, I have defeated the world, I have overcome your sins; death is put to death because of Me. Behold, I am risen, death is turned backward - only life is and shall be.
Lo, I have defeated you also, if you would only surrender your life. For I gave up My life in place of yours, so you may receive of My life. Therefore, I ask you, how long will you withhold? How long will you wait before you let go? When will you fly? When will you believe? Believe, and you shall also know! For I have already told you, peace is in the knowing that I AM WHO I AM, and you are in life because of Me.

Beloved, you were made for Me, created for love's purpose;
I created you in My image, and gave you My breath, My life...

Therefore, this is life: I AM HE!...

Beloved, you worry, yet I AM HE. You weep, yet I AM HE. You stumble, yet I AM HE. Your hearts tear and break over all these sorrows, yet I AM HE. You struggle and are in turmoil, you feel lost, yet I AM HE. You grasp at the wind and have no understanding, yet I AM HE. You are persecuted by those you love, yet I AM HE. The world hates you, yet I AM HE. Everything you have is passing away, yet I AM HE. Death comes to take you into darkness, yet I AM HE! Do you not understand?! I AM ENOUGH! - The One who sees, The One who knows... No matter the time or the season, in every moment of your life, I AM HE! Says The Lord.

3/2/11 **From YahuShua HaMashiach, Our Lord and Savior**
The Word of The Lord Spoken to Timothy
For The Lord's Little Flock
And For All Those Who Have Ears to Hear
Brought to a Close

Beloved little flock, it is time for you to choose. It is time for your trust to be tried and your faith tested, to reveal of what sort it truly is.

Thus I am bringing this table to a close. For you did not seek My face when I called to you. And when I gave you correction, you turned to Me a deaf ear. And of My servants, these also you refused to hear. Therefore because you have refused Me, and because you have found fault with My servants, as you continually speak one against the other, wherein pride and judgment grabs hold and forgiveness flees away, this table is brought to a close.

And because some of you refuse to be separate from those who have hated both Me and My Word, who also speak evil of My servants, this table is brought to a close. And because some of you refuse to reach out the hand and give to those in need, and still others do so begrudgingly, this table is brought to a close.

Beloved, those seated at My table are given much, and ALL I have spoken is required of them. Thus some of you have treated My table with contempt, while still others have likened My table unto the churches of men, whose ways are an abhorrence to Me, whose doctrines and traditions I hate!

And worse still, some of you have built your faith upon My servants, using this table to prop up that which remains altogether lacking within you. I will not share My glory!

Nor is there any other stone upon which one shall be broken, nor any other foundation upon which one shall stand. Therefore, this table is brought to a close.

Beloved, it is time to choose, to make your decision...

It is time to bring your hearts forward, and be healed,
To make your repentance full;
Or to My bitter sadness, fall away,
And return to the world and its evil ways...

It is time to fall into Me unreservedly;
Or to depart, and walk through dry places...

Says The Lord.

3/7/11 **From The Lord, Our God and Savior**
The Word of The Lord Spoken to Timothy
For The Lord's Little Flock
And For All Those Who Have Ears to Hear
Treason

The kingdoms of men shall raise themselves up, though night has fallen; behold, out of deep darkness, the kingdoms of men shall rise and make themselves one by treason; by many deceits and false promises, by vanities and vain flatteries, by the heaping up of lies, shall they come together as one. They shall raise themselves up, boasting unity and peace and safety from the hand of The Almighty, until their loftiness flies high above all kingdoms, from those of ancient times even to this day...

YET THERE SHALL BE NO PEACE! Says The Lord. For I shall bring calamity in waves! Behold, the weight of My punishment shall increase by measure, bringing forth destruction without respite! Escape shall flee away, safety shall become a distant memory and no shelter shall be found, forcing the rebellious into the rocks, the mighty into the clefts of the rocks, and the kings of the earth into the caves of the mountains! From the least to the greatest, they shall all seek to hide themselves from the face of Him who sits on the throne and from the wrath of The Lamb!
Behold, the unity of the nations shall be eaten up, as the caterpillar devours the newly sprouted vine, as the worms beneath the ground eat up the roots! All shall wither, until the fire comes to set the whole field ablaze! By a spark and by a flame of fire, by a strike from roiling clouds, shall the fire be kindled by My own hand! Says The Lord.

VOLUME SIX

3/14/11 **From The Lord, Our God and Savior**
The Word of The Lord Spoken to Timothy
For All Those Who Have Ears to Hear
Pangs

What is the high branch of the palm tree to that of the weeping willow? For they know not each other's place. Each bears seed after its own kind, yet the ground beneath remains unyielding. And without the rain, the leaf fades and the seed flees back into the dust of the ground, unable to rise again. Therefore are they cut down as the cedars; they are broken and they are toppled when calamity comes to claim them, washed away. And who will mourn their passing or search out their seed, that they might be revived in another place?

Therefore hear the Word of The Lord, O peoples of the earth; stop and consider and be broken in pieces: For as I have spoken, so I speak; as I have done, so shall it be again. And though you make an uproar, and band together and make for yourselves a name, you shall surely be broken in pieces! Yes arm yourselves, prepare and come out, stand up and fight, yet you will surely be broken in pieces! For I am The Lord, and I do not change!...
Behold, a mournful cry is heard in the midst of every nation, bitter weeping comes forth from the coastlands, and the sound of gnashing teeth breaks out in every corner. For the Day of The Lord has come! For the peoples of the earth have forgotten Me, the nations have forsaken Me, and My own people hate the sound of My voice; indeed they refuse to walk in My ways, neither will they receive correction! Therefore the pangs must increase, the bearing down must come quickly, lest the seed be lost and the child fail to come forth. For if I do not bring forth, says The Lord, the child shall surely die before seeing the light of day... It is time.

3/25/11 **From The Lord, Our God and Savior**
The Word of The Lord Spoken to Timothy
For The Lord's Little Flock
And For All Those Who Have Ears to Hear
Reasonable Service

Thus says The Lord: Blessed is that servant of Mine who seeks out the poor, whose heart is eager to help the needy, for they know My ways and seek to please Me. Blessed also is My servant who gives out of the abundance they have received, for they walk in My ways. Yet most blessed is My servant who gives from their lack, for they do justly, love mercy, and walk humbly with their God; indeed, they have understood.

Yet woe to those who ignore the poor and draw back their hand from the needy, while they sit at ease in their abundance. For destitution is coming, and shall be born out of great desolation, in the day I take away their abundance and leave their houses desolate. Woe also to those who say they are My servants, yet refuse to help those in need, for only tears and sorrow await them. And woe to those who fail to give even the smallest amount, claiming they are in lack, for they have no trust, having learned nothing from the poor widow[1].

Little flock, have you learned nothing from My Word? Have you so quickly forgotten My Letters, in where I have taught you the way in which you should walk? Indeed, who you choose defines what you do, as I have already told you. And who are the poor and the needy? How have you treated them, while entreating Me? Do not lie to yourselves, beloved ones. Every one of you who sit at this table want for nothing.

Shall you mince words over a dollar, while others sit upon the ground seeking to draw water from a pit? Shall you covet five dollars or even ten as you drive about in your automobiles, while your brothers and sisters abroad willingly walk miles to preach My Word, with joy, even to their dying breath?

And still some of you sit at ease in your padded chairs, punching the keys, saying within yourselves, "*I am delivered.*" You are not delivered! From the power of sin, yes, My children, I have delivered you, yet some of you remain married to this world. And those who remain married to another, even to themselves, can by no means be joined unto Me, lest adultery be brought into the house of The Lord.

Beloved ones, you are My treasure. Yet some of you count yourselves as first, having loved another more than Me; therefore you must be last. For I search the hearts and minds. And that discipline reserved for the churches of men, is it not also for you, even to a greater degree? Or have you forgotten this Scripture: *For everyone to whom much is given, from him much will be required; and to whom much has been committed, of him they will ask the more?*

Therefore choose, make your decision...

It is time, says The Lord.

1. *Mark 12:41-44*

4/22/11 **From The Lord, Our God and Savior**
The Word of The Lord Spoken to Timothy
For All Those Who Have Ears to Hear
(Regarding Easter)
Join Not in the Error of the People

Thus says The Lord YahuShua: Those who knowingly celebrate Easter and its deplorable traditions hate My resurrection. Therefore, join not in the error of the people; have no part in their sin. For those who refuse My correction are foolish and must walk through dry places, and those who refuse to repent have secured their place in the valley of death. For the pride of man is a heavy stone, which increases by weight each day it remains unbroken.

Join NOT in the error of the people;
Have NO part in their sin!...

Says The One who sees, The One who knows.

344

4/29/11 **From The Lord, Our God and Savior**
The Word of The Lord Spoken to Timothy
For All Those Who Have Ears to Hear
(Regarding self-appointed apostles, prophets and teachers)
Subject to No Man

Thus says The Lord: Is My Word in need of confirmation by those who say they know Me, yet do not really know Me? Is the Word of My mouth subject to men, whose understanding remains altogether lacking, whose knowledge is corrupt and whose power is of no use at all? Shall My words be made subject to the approval of any self-appointed apostle, prophet or teacher? Shall flesh usurp the things of God? Can mortal man ascend above the throne of The Eternal? Shall the created rule over The Creator, or the corrupt sit as judge over The Holy? Shall any attempt to occupy My throne and not be cast down?!

For I tell you the truth, ALL flesh shall be humbled in the Day of The Lord; the whole world shall be bowed down! For all creation is subject to The Word of God, every living creature is put into subjection to The Almighty! Nothing in the earth beneath, or in the heavens above, shall usurp the will of The Most High!

Therefore, I ask you, do My servants seek glory for themselves? Have they so highly esteemed themselves, as to name themselves according to the gift? Are they so skilled in knowledge and cleverness of speech, that they may now appoint themselves to a certain office, without first being called? The gift is Mine! And I bestow it upon whomever I wish, whenever I choose!

For I call My servants out from among them, I appoint every office, and I Myself number their steps before them. For My gifts are given through the Spirit, and must also be received in Me. They are in no wise open to claim, nor shall anyone on earth assign them. For only those in union with The Messiah are able to walk in them.

Thus the highly esteemed shall be abandoned,
And the self-appointed severely abased...

Left to walk through the valley in the
Great and Terrible Day of The Lord,
Until death comes to claim them...

Declares The Lord.

5/6/11 **From The Lord, Our God and Savior**
The Word of The Lord Spoken to Timothy
For All Those Who Have Ears to Hear
A Blemish and a Stain

Thus says The Lord: Behold, the corrupt doctrines of the churches of men have crept into every corner; near and far, the doctrine of hell and eternal torment is embraced by the people.

Yet I tell you the truth, this doctrine is a loathsome spot on every garment worn in the name of truth! A detestable wrinkle within the tapestry of My glory! A horrible interwoven thread by which those who call of themselves Christian pollute My name and mar My image before the people, propagating that which came forth from the mouth of the dragon!

THIS DOCTRINE IS EVIL! And must be opposed by all who have received the love of the Truth. For I have indeed spoken to this generation, even as I have spoken in all times past. For I AM THE LORD, The Light in whom there is no darkness at all.

5/25/11 **From The Lord, Our God and Savior**
The Word of The Lord Spoken to Timothy
For All Those Who Have Ears to Hear
Gathered

The day has come, says The Lord, even as I had spoken it to My servant, that it should indeed come. For the heart of man is hard and unyielding, the state of man grievous. Injustice and atrocity increase, evil spreads forth across the land unimpeded. Lo, evil men in authority worship and serve the gods of the earth and bring harm upon My anointed; the outcry is very great. And because of this, the love of My servants is withheld and the hand of My elect is prevented from reaching out, locked doors at every turn.

Yet I tell you, rejoice! For the hand of The Lord is not prevented by any means, the arm of The Lord is in no way shortened! For the name of The Lord shall be exalted, the name of The Lord shall be spoken aloud, and all in the earth shall tremble!...

Behold, the Glory of God breaks through the clouds,
A mighty trumpet blast sounds in all the earth!...

From the heights of the mountains to the deepest depths,
Life bursts forth in the bodies of the dead!...

Behold, a loud voice is heard from Heaven:
"EARTH, GIVE UP YOUR DEAD!
BRIDE OF THE BLESSED, COME UP HERE!"

5/30/11 **From The Lord, Our God and Savior**
The Word of The Lord Spoken to Timothy
For The Lord's Little Flock
And For All Those Who Have Ears to Hear
Delight In the Ways of The Lord

Thus says The Lord: I have bestowed many gifts upon this generation, and lo, the small of My flock have received knowledge and revelation beyond compare. Yet I ask you, who has truly received? Who has been humbled by My words and given thanks? Who among all these scattered flocks has taken joy in My gifts? Beloved, who among this great multitude seeks out My will, to know it? And who, among all these so-called believers, takes pleasure in My Law, saying, *"I delight to do Your will, O God, for Your Law is written in my heart"?*

Yet My people remain foolish, and this little flock envious. For I tell you the truth: Unrighteous jealousy is the companion of fools. For those who envy also grab hold of jealousy, walking hand in hand with covetousness. Beloved, there is but One who sees, One who knows, only One who searches the hearts and minds - I AM HE. How is it then that My people sit in judgment, judging My Word and My will, resisting My ways as they look upon others with contempt? Shall you also seek to ascend above The Most High?! Shall *you* sit upon My throne?! For I tell you the truth, each time you sit in judgment and question My ways, you walk in satan's aspirations; you follow in his footsteps!

And when I bless another, why do you not take joy in it? And when I correct you, why do you resist and question My ways? Am I not The Lord? Do I not give to each according to their faith, according to that which I see in their heart?

Why do you in your arrogance set a line for Me to follow, or think within yourselves there must be a better way? And how is it you continually compare yourselves amongst yourselves, knowing this is unwise? Beloved, I have prepared a place for you!

Therefore offer up thanksgiving, and cease from your complaints. Forgive and bless, let go and obey, love one another and wash each other's feet. Take joy in all I do, especially in that which I bestow upon another. And when I feed you, eat from your own plate and give thanks.

Little flock, it is the last hour, yet many of you have stepped backward. Let it be known to you: One who treads the path, going up and down, stepping on and off at their convenience, treads not the path, but is like one who treads water. By no means shall they be able to keep their head above water, nor shall their strength deliver them in the Day of Troubles.

> *Therefore heed My words, and also do them;*
> *Be wise in your dealings with Me,*
> *Humble yourselves and remember...*
>
> *Blessed are those who run to Me,*
> *For they shall be blessed in My presence;*
> *Even more blessed are those who run to Me,*
> *Then obey My Word, for their blessing*
> *Is complete and they are at peace...*
> *Deliverance they shall surely know...*
>
> *Says The Lord.*

6/2/11 **From The Lord, Our God and Savior**
The Word of The Lord Spoken to Timothy
For All Those Who Have Ears to Hear
I Have Taken to Myself a Prophet

I am The Lord your God, and I have spoken by My servant, and behold, in him shall I increase. I shall be with him as I was with My servant, Moses. I shall speak with him face to face, and he shall go out and come in. I shall be with him like the pillar of the cloud by day, and as the pillar of fire by night. Behold, The Authority from on high shall dwell with men, and The Lord your God shall heed the voice of a man in that day.

Yet the people say, *"What man is this who exalts himself by his own words, and speaks with the authority of God?"* And thus they shall surely deny Me and persecute him. Hate shall well up within their hearts, and they shall seek to destroy him. Yet The Word of God shall speak, and the signs of The Almighty shall testify on his behalf. Behold, the cloud of The Almighty shall hide him, and fire shall fall from Heaven and consume his enemies round about, as in the days of old, says The Lord.

And though you yet resist My words, My Word shall speak and My judgments shall shout. For I have taken to Myself a prophet, and he shall go for Me. He shall prepare My way before Me, even as I have prepared his way before him. He is not holy, nor righteous; he is but a man, a man after My own heart. And though he stumbles as all men and fear grabs hold of him, for he is but flesh, I tell you the truth, I have surely purchased him from among men as part of the special offering[1]. I AM THE LORD.

Therefore, again I say to you, Timothy is My prophet, and through him have I made My plans known. For I do not change. Thus he shall go for Me, and a number like him, and they shall declare My judgments and warn the people. For the Day of The Lord is here, and the Great and Dreadful Day is about to begin, declares The Lord.

1. Also read: "All Have Been Purchased... Yet Few Have Accepted, Few Are Chosen" - Volume Two

6/6/11 **From YahuShua HaMashiach, Our Lord and Savior**
The Word of The Lord Spoken to Timothy
For The Lord's Little Flock
And For All Those Who Have Ears to Hear
Addendum to "Spiritual Famine"
Pentecost

Little flock, hear and understand the will and discipline of The Lord Most High. For I tell you the truth, Pentecost has been fulfilled; behold, it has passed them by unawares. Yet for some it remains, and shall also continue until the time. For many are called, yet few are chosen. Therefore have compassion and pray for them, beloved. For in the same way, you also looked to the time and waited for My words, yet they did not come. And some of you took it upon yourselves to run ahead, impatient, lacking trust, while still others waited patiently; yet all were unaware of My will, save one.

Beloved, here is wisdom: The penitent wait and bow down in thanksgiving. Yet the arrogant and false righteous stand up proudly, declaring their deliverance, a deliverance which has already passed and shall not come. For My hand is removed and My spirit taken. For only those in whom I see of Myself shall escape, and only those caught in My embrace shall fly away.
Thus as you were made to wait, so shall these within the churches of men wait. For they wait for a sound they no longer recognize, for a call to which they have shut their ears, for a shout from Him whom they have not known, a voice they have altogether rejected. For how can one who rejects My voice heed the call? And how can one who turns away from Me, embrace Me when the shout is made?

For they have surely joined themselves to another, they embrace another messiah, a false christ, who looks nothing like Me. Therefore they shall surely pass through the fire, for by no other means shall they be saved.

This then is what I command you, little flock:
Have compassion, and pray for your brothers and sisters
In the churches of men and for the unbelieving of Israel;
For they must endure much for the sake of My name...

And though the day has passed, lo it has ceased
For many, it has not altogether passed away...

For My spirit remains with the first election,
And shall be restored to the penitent after...

Says The Lord.

6/28/11 **From YahuShua HaMashiach, Our Lord and Savior**
The Word of The Lord Spoken to Timothy
For Timothy, and For All Those Who Have Ears to Hear
In The Bosom of The Father

Timothy, ask of Me any question, and I shall answer in accordance with your understanding. For that which can not be explained in human terms shall be shown you, and that which you do not understand shall be given you, and you shall understand. For there are languages which use no speech, and communication which comes by sight, even by touch, yet what I shall give you surpasses all of these...

For there is a place... A place beyond space and time, where eternity dwells and life has no end, where light takes its form and goodness is revealed, where the eyes of the redeemed may look upon the Glory of God and see His face... Where Heaven meets the earth and The Eternal dwells with men...

A place where Everlasting Love can be embraced and healing flows like a gentle stream, a place where time has no meaning and the stars flee away, where the brightness is excellent and the warmth thereof very soothing...

A place where joy comes by knowledge with pure understanding, where fulfillment comes by a strong embrace, and love's completion is met with great satisfaction through many tears flowing down the cheeks of the forever young; a place where understanding bursts forth in realization, revelation beyond words!...

A place where the hearts of the chosen are revealed, behold, they are uncovered, revealing their true form... The image in which I created them, restored... A simple quiet place, set apart, in the arms of The King.

7/1/11 **From The Lord, Our God and Savior**
The Word of The Lord Spoken to Timothy
For All Those Who Have Ears to Hear
The One Worthy of All Praise

Thus says The Lord God of Israel: The Days of Noah are here, the Day of The Lord has come in; and behold, the Great and Dreadful Day is very near!...

Therefore hear the Word of The Lord, O peoples of the earth, and gain wisdom: Are not the mountains risen up at the Word of My mouth? Do not the highest peaks break through the clouds at My command? Are not the depths carved out by My knowledge, and the seas filled according to My will? Who causes the clouds to gather together and bring forth rain? Who calls forth the wind from its place and stirs up the hurricane? Who speaks to the horrible mountain, causing it to burst forth, to spew its fervent heat? It is I who has done it, The One who formed it, The One who causes to be! My children, look upon the stars, upon the whole of the heavens, consider the vastness thereof, and know: *YAH has spoken it into being, YAHUWAH caused it to be!*
Behold, I have spread out life like a blanket, and caused it to multiply in all the earth; life fills every corner! And still mankind seeks out its beginnings and longs to know its source, asking in vain, *"Where did I come from, and why are we here? From what source did all this life come, and how did it get here? What is the beginning, and how will it end?"*

Blind and hard-hearted generation, deceived and ignorant peoples, foolish children, LIFE HAS A NAME! The Beginning and The End has walked among you! The Source and The Reason is here, and shall also come in great power and glory! From Him did you come forth, and to Him must you return, all you, His beloved. Behold, His names are many and wonderful! That which He is has no end, for as I AM so also is He! The Father and The Son are one, and our name, one - YAHUSHUA-YAHUWAH!

In the beginning was The Word, and The Word
Was with God, and The Word was God;
The same was in the beginning with God...

Through Him all things came into being,
And nothing in all creation was made apart from Him...

In Him was life, and The Life was the light of men;
The Light shines in the darkness,
And the darkness shall not overcome it...

And behold, The Word became flesh...

Immanu El!

7/25/11 **From The Lord, Our God and Savior**
The Word of The Lord Spoken to Timothy
For All Those Who Have Ears to Hear
Freedom Comes by Sacrifice

Thus says The Lord: I have called to the scoffer and to the wicked alike, that they might come forward and declare their evil thoughts, that they might come forth from their hiding places and walk openly in their rebellion. And thus they have answered, they have surely come out.

Yet of the Called, they have not come out. Indeed, few have rushed forward to embrace Me, few have come to Me without condition. Behold, I called to them, even to the great outpouring of My spirit; in page after page, I wrote to them, offering them many gifts; yea, with arms outstretched, I sought to uphold them and guide them. Yet they refused My voice and drew back the hand, turning to Me the back, for they want no part with Me as I truly am. And of My prophet, they have treated him as Micaiah. For the thoughts of their hearts do always betray them, and by their actions have they shown themselves to be in agreement with the insolent king[1].

My children have forsaken Me! Not one truly seeks to remain in My love! They have all become unprofitable servants; there is none who does good, no, not one! And when I send to them a prophet, they despise him on account of his words, which are not his own, treating My words as binding cords about their hands and their feet! For they do always dishonor Me, and within their hearts they cease not from their complaint!

Therefore that from which they seek
To be loosed shall bind them in the Day,
Until they willingly place themselves upon the altar...

Wherein freedom comes by sacrifice,
And true understanding by letting go...

Says The Lord.

1. *1 Kings 22*

7/28/11 **From The Lord, Our God and Savior**
The Word of The Lord Spoken to Timothy
For All Those Who Have Ears to Hear
God of the Living

Thus says The Lord: Who shall praise Me from the pit? What song is heard from the grave? Shall rotting flesh stand up and praise The God of Israel? Shall those turned to dust give Me glory?

Thus I tell you a mystery, behold, I speak to you a wonder: There is a people who sleep and a flesh which has no life in it, there are many who have been lost to the depths, a great multitude who have returned to the dust of the earth and can not be found, yet The Lord God knows their names and their dwelling places. Not one has passed from My sight, not one has been given up to the void. For I am God of the living, The One alone worthy of all praise!

I am not God of the dead, but of the living! For the dead have no ruler. There is no life in them; even all their thoughts have perished with them. No voice is heard from the grave; only complete and utter silence dwells there - darkness without time. For from the dust I created them, and to the dust they return. By My breath they were made alive, and without My breath they fall asleep. In the image of The Son were My beloved created, and in His likeness shall they be restored.

Behold, the day and hour is close at hand,
Yea it is very near, when the dead in Messiah
Shall arise and the sleepers shall awake,
When the rotting corpses are revived
And the dust gathers together once again...

From one end of the earth to the other,
Even from the deepest depths, shall My people
Rise up and give Me glory!...

Therefore let the children of Israel prepare,
Let everyone joined to Messiah step forward
And claim their inheritance...

For I have but to call out your name!...

Says The Holy One of Israel.

7/28/11 **From The Lord, Our God and Savior**
The Word of The Lord Spoken to Timothy
For The Lord's Little Flock
And For All Those Who Have Ears to Hear
Walking Through the Valley

My sons and daughters, hear now this parable, that you may gain wisdom and have understanding of that which I am about to do, of that which must be:

I have a great vineyard, with many grapes. I have provided both the early and latter rain and tended every vine, pruning them with sure hands and delicate fingers. Yet many wither, while others fail to produce, and still others are slow to ripen.

Beloved, I have waited patiently and tended My vineyard, doing all that was necessary to produce a fair crop, and now it is time for harvest. Yet I tell you plainly, it shall be a very lowly crop, a very small harvest, for few have ripened to maturity.

Thus they must be left to ripen in their season. And though the winds shall be harsh and the rains rare, behold, even all manner of plagues shall come, I must not gather them until their due season, says The Lord.

Thus I shall quiet My voice among you, little flock, and speak to you no more in this manner. For My prophet must be cut off from among you for a time. And though you endeavor to loosen these bonds, I will not forsake you utterly, I am with you still. Though I pull back My hand, I will not forsake you; and though you have yet to truly harken to My voice, I am with you still.

Behold, in your time of need, when calamity
And great devastation is on every side,
I will be there, I will not forsake you utterly...

For I have left a multitude of words to guide you,
And many husbandmen to point the way;
You will not be alone in the valley...

Trust in My ways therefore, embrace My correction,
And do not turn away from My discipline...

For as it is written:
As many as I love, I rebuke and chasten...

Says The Lord.

8/1/11 **From YahuShua HaMashiach, Our Lord and Savior**
The Word of The Lord Spoken to Timothy
For All Those Who Have Ears to Hear
The Harvest Is Separated, All Bundles Set in Their Places

Thus says The Lord: By My prophets have I made My plans known. Yet that which I am about to do is done already, and shall be. And that which I have spoken from the beginning, even to this day, is true. For the will of God can not be broken, even as The Scriptures. And if My every word is Scripture, then how shall even one word fail?

Yet My people fall away, and My little flock grows smaller still. For they seek to loosen these bonds in an attempt to flee this bundle. For the Way of The Lord is not known among them, and My words have ceased from being a blessing. And so they flee back into the world in an attempt to escape, as in all times past, for they have no root.

Yet I tell you the truth, none shall escape their bundle. For all bundles lie in the field already, each one tied securely and set in its place. Therefore as one attempts to flee this bundle, the truth of the matter is made plain. For they have not departed at all, but remain in the bundle in which I had placed them at the first. I AM THE LORD.

Beloved ones, I search the hearts and minds, even the innermost thoughts I know; even from the foundation of the world did I know each one of you, setting you in your place from the beginning. Yet some will say, *"What of free will and our right to choose?"* To these I say: You have chosen, and the will of your heart has spoken, and thus were you bundled and prepared. For I know My own.

Thus the Bride is chosen;
My blood runs through her veins,
My image is shown upon her face...

Behold, the light of My coming is reflected
In her eyes, for I have captured her gaze,
And she will by no means look away
Or seek after another...

Therefore some are plucked from
The world already, and shall also be taken;
They shall surely be gone from this place!...

Says The Lord.

8/20/11 **From The Lord, Our God and Savior**
The Word of The Lord Spoken to Timothy
For All Those Who Have Ears to Hear
A Just God and A Savior

Thus says The Lord God: My people do greatly err, for they believe that I have altogether become like them! Yet I am HOLY, and My words TRUE. For as it is written: *My thoughts are not your thoughts, neither are your ways My ways. For as the heavens are higher than the earth, so are My ways higher than your ways and My thoughts than your thoughts.* When I consider, all creation is before Me; from the most minute detail to the greatest, nothing is hidden from My eyes; behold, the whole universe abides within My understanding. For I am LORD and GOD, Creator of Heaven and Earth.

How is it then, I have become unjust in your eyes? Shall My ways be questioned by you?! Are you upset because I speak to the few in the same manner I spoke to My people, Israel, in the wilderness? And who is Israel? Is he a home-born slave in your eyes?! For I tell you the truth, those of My Olive Tree are free. Only those who have gone astray are slaves, and only those who seek to uphold their own way remain bound. For you can only serve one master. Or have you forgotten My words and the Way which was set before you?
Therefore I shall treat the one, who has knowledge of the Way and pollutes it, as the multitudes who forsake it. For those who have seen must now walk in that which I have revealed. And if they refuse, then by their own choice have they chosen to walk through the valley, until they are broken - atop or beneath, all shall be broken. For I am The Lord, and I do not change!

For I tell you the truth, all paths lead
To the foot of My throne, all must stand
Before the judgment seat of Mashiach...

For there is no other God besides Me;
A just God and a Savior,
There is none besides Me...

Thus those who receive of Me are made worthy,
And shall walk with Me forever;
And those who remain void and reject
My gifts shall cease, broken off forever...

Says The Lord.

8/29/11 **From YahuShua HaMashiach, Our Lord and Savior**
The Word of The Lord Spoken to Timothy
For All Those Who Have Ears to Hear
What Is Man?

Thus says The Lord: Beloved, upon what foundation does the love of God rest? With what thread is the Word of The Lord woven? Can any man know the mind of God? Can flesh touch The Holy? Tell Me, if you know.

And what is man, that he should be created in My image, the image of The Son of Man? For within man is My breath; I gave him life. He was made through Me and for Me; I caused him to be. It was My own blood which was shed for him, My own life which was poured out, even unto death. Therefore all those who come to Me and drink shall be made new; whether awake or sleeping, all My beloved shall arise and live. For I AM HE, The Resurrection and The Life.

Thus there is indeed a focal point of creation, of which I am always mindful, a reason I created the heavens and the earth and everything in them - *It is mankind.* Yet man does not yet understand what he is, nor can he comprehend what he shall be. For I have made man in My own image, that in the fullness of time he would come to dwell in Me and I in him, being at all times with Me where I am. In that day he will become like Me, for he shall see Me as I truly am.

Therefore prepare your hearts, beloved ones. Keep your eyes fixed upon Me, obey My voice, and heed the sound of this Trumpet. For the Day of The Lord has come; behold, ALL have entered in, says The Lord.

8/30/11 **From The Lord, Our God and Savior**
The Word of The Lord Spoken to Timothy
For All Those Who Have Ears to Hear
(Regarding the United States)
Desperation

Beloved, the time is short. And though your nation is in desperate need, it has yet to reveal its weakness for fear of its enemies. Yet it will not be able to hide the truth from the world much longer, for everything is about to change. And that which is held together by the weakest of threads shall break, and new alliances shall be formed out of desperation, and ALL shall fear, says The Lord.

10/25/11 **From The Lord, Our God and Savior**
The Word of The Lord Spoken to Timothy
For The Lord's Little Flock
And For All Those Who Have Ears to Hear
Narrow Vision

I called to you, yet not one truly heeds the call. I revealed a need, yet who has stepped forward to uphold My cause? Behold, I poured out My spirit, and still you remain unmoved.

Therefore this little flock is disbanded, even now you are dispersed, for in you I am sorely displeased. For I said that your faith was not to stand upon anything apart from Me, yet you fixed beams and set up supports, in an effort to uphold your own expectations. Behold, you built upon your own arrogant assumptions and private interpretations, and I knocked you down, breaking apart every pillar which you had erected falsely in My name.

And still you speak deceits within your hearts, saying, *"Where is the promise of His coming? The year draws to a close and no one is gathered"* - Faithless servants! Blind children! Not one word I have spoken shall by any means pass away, nor shall one word of My prophets fall to the ground! Indeed ALL shall serve My purpose, and come to pass according to MY will. For as it is written: *The vision is yet for the appointed time, it hastens, and in the end it will speak; behold, it shall testify loudly. And though it tarries, wait for it, for it shall surely come, it will not tarry.*

Beloved, stop looking upon My words with tainted eyes and narrow vision. Stop staring at My messengers; look past them and see with greater eyes. For I tell you the truth, your expectations shall never be met, your assumptions shall fall short, and your every private interpretation shall fail... *Yet I remain faithful, and My Word true, says The Lord.*

370

11/9/11 **From The Lord, Our God and Savior**
The Word of The Lord Spoken to Timothy
For All Those Who Have Ears to Hear
Full Circle

I have called the winds of heaven to blow upon the earth. I have stirred them up, that they may go forth and gnarl the branches, that they may blow hard against the multitudes and break down the walls - Let every tree topple and break the necks of the wicked! Let every wall come down with a great crash! Behold, the anger of The Lord shall increase by measure, until every foundation is broken up from beneath, until the face of the earth is once again without form, says The Lord.

Thus I have spoken, and who is able to restrain themselves from repeating My every word? Who will not prophesy, when the voice of The Almighty has entered his ear? For I tell you plainly, the day is coming and is already here, when I shall speak into the air and the voice of YAHUWAH shall thunder, reaching even to the ends of the earth.

Yet I ask you, how does a prophet hear and by what means is he revealed? Remember My words: *If there be a prophet among you, I, The Lord, shall make Myself known to him in a vision; I shall speak to him in a dream; even plainly I shall speak with him, not in mysterious sayings. For he has seen the form of The Lord and has sat in My presence, and knows that which is beyond words, and before him men shall fear.*

Therefore thus says The Lord, to all those who have ears to hear: Wait upon Me, with all trust and fear; stand steadfast and be patient. Accept My words, as I have spoken them and as they are written; do not add to My words, nor take from them. Neither form for yourselves any private interpretation; only give heed to My words and also do them, and prepare.

For My words are indeed that light
Which shines in a dark place,
A lamp and a beacon,
Preparing My way before Me...

Until the new day dawns and The Morning Star rises,
Filling the hearts of My chosen as they enter in...

Says The Lord.

11/19/11 **From YahuShua HaMashiach, Our Lord and Savior**
The Word of The Lord Spoken to Timothy
For All Those Who Have Ears to Hear
Blessed Hope

Thus says The Lord: There are many gathered together, of one heart and one mind; there are many scattered abroad, with faces turned by the wind, with chapped cheeks and red faces; there are many who have embraced him whose heel is lifted up against Me.

What are all these tears?! - Flowing streams without hope, torrents with no outlet, flooding sorrows drowning every hope and killing every good intention! What is this leaning upon God's people, oppressing them, crushing them?! Who are all these who spit in My eyes and lay stripes upon My back?! Are not My people delivered?! And still the voice of the multitude says, *"There is no hope in God."*
Dark counsel is increased! Concealed truth devastates the ignorant, while men in authority step upon the fingers of the innocent! How long shall dark counsel prevail?! Shall veiled intentions come upon My people, to do great harm in an instant?! Shall the nations lie down in death, for lack of remorse?! For I see no sincere repentance, nor has one truly turned about.
How long shall the multitudes swear by things made, and place their trust in the works of man?! For the desolate know not the things of God, nor is darkness able to understand; yea, the wicked gnash upon their teeth, the whole body convulses in the wake of mourning, for there is no rest.

Yet My hand caresses the cheeks of the hopeless,
As we watch the dawning of the day together...

For the strength of My arm uplifts the downtrodden,
My strong embrace heals the sorrowful,
Every beat of My heart revives the dead,
And the sound of My voice frees every captive...

Behold, the power of My love hides them away!...

Says The Lord.

2/19/12 **From The Lord, Our God and Savior**
For the Sons of Promise
And For All Those Who Have Ears to Hear
Mouthpieces of The Most High God

Thus says The Lord to His servants: To every prophet who went before was there a time of service, a time of great works done in the Spirit, according to My will. And thus shall it be for you also, if you remain faithful. For I have prepared the number, men of My choosing, a special offering who shall be set apart. Behold, I have drawn you out, separating you from amongst those who remain married to this world, even as I have done with every prophet and man of God who went before you, each at their appointed time, each in their due season.

Therefore let the Sons of Promise arise and take a stand, for the time has come! Let those chosen be established, the number fulfilled! For as it is written: *I shall dwell in My witnesses like a flame of fire, and well up in My servants like a boiling pool.* And they shall prophesy and declare My judgments against the churches and upon every religion of man, against the nations and upon all the cities of men.

Behold, My words shall increase by measure, and pass through the multitudes like fire! - Each word a flame which can not be quenched! Every diatribe a relentless fire breaking through the lines, surmounting every obstacle, crossing every border, inundating every land! And the pride of man shall be bowed down, and the arrogance of man utterly humiliated! Says The Lord.

3/25/12 **From The Lord, Our God and Savior**
The Word of The Lord Spoken to Timothy
For All Those Who Have Ears to Hear
Madness

Thus says The Lord: My people believe I have altogether gone silent, that I have shut My mouth from speaking through My prophets (for they are not My people). Behold, every false doctrine is strictly upheld, every filthy tradition fiercely defended, as the pride of the people escalates beyond reason; the lies do not cease!

Thus the churches of men provide My people with security in false hope, and put forth divinations of peace and safety, preaching prosperity in monologues of false praise and fake passion, abusing My name and misusing My Word, twisting it to uphold their own corrupt foundation, all in the name of unrighteous gain, as it is written.

Look how all these leaders in the churches assert their own authority, yet remain void of the Spirit! Look how they proclaim My name, yet fail to recognize Me! And look how all these unbelieving Jews and orthodox rabbis do the very same. Look how My words pass before the eyes of the ignorant Christian, and enter into the ears of the arrogant, self-proclaimed believer, who then turn and fight against Me!

Look how they in one accord persecute and slander those I send, and all this in the name of doing God a service! Look, how in one breath and in one moment, they recognize The Author of these Letters, and then turn and strike Me upon the mouth, blaspheming My words and desecrating My gifts!...

WHAT MADNESS IS THIS?! WHAT IS THIS WHICH FILLS MY PEOPLE?! Answer, if you know.

7/4/12 **From The Lord, Our God and Savior**
The Word of The Lord Spoken to Timothy
For All Those Who Have Ears to Hear
A Perverse Nation

This question was asked of The Lord: Is the U.S.A. still a "God-fearing" nation?

Thus says The Lord: Many yet fear Me, even the wicked deep within, yet very few have any love for God in their hearts. For this nation is most perverse, a nation which loves abomination and from righteousness is far removed - Thus I have spit them out! Behold, even the earth shall vomit them out! For they have greatly defiled the land, a multitude of dry branches, broken off, which shall by no means be grafted in again until they fall hard upon their faces, crying out, *"Blessed is He who comes in the name of The Lord!"*
Behold, this nation plants seeds of perversion without ceasing! They cultivate abominations and reap sin all day long, and into the night they revel in all their uncleanness! And when I look down upon this nation, I see Sodom bursting forth and Gomorrah overtaking the land! And when I peer deeper still, I see one nation in agreement, a people in love with themselves, a nation which loves its harlotries more than God! - An adulterous people! A most wicked generation! BEHOLD, A WHOLE NATION OF MURDERERS IS BEFORE MY EYES! Therefore I am come down to tread, until every wicked person is crushed beneath My feet and every evil man in authority dies a grievous death in this land!

Behold, I shall purge this
Great and awful vineyard;
I shall uproot and destroy!...

Until that which was lost is found,
And that which was hidden is
Brought into the open...

Until that which I have
Searched for is seen, once again...

Declares The Lord.

7/14/12 **From The Lord, Our God and Savior**
A Parable Given to Timothy
For All Those Who Have Ears to Hear
The Parable of The Aged Shepherd

There was a man, an old man full of years, who grew up tending sheep. And to this day he tends them still, arising early each day; even going out in the middle of the night when required, whether due to wolves or approaching bad weather. He tends his sheep, for he knows no other trade, and enjoys doing so. The shepherd has no family, nor children of his own. The sheep are his family, and he cares for them as such.

One day a man came to him while he was out in the field, and offered to buy all the sheep for a good price, and said, *"You are old and look very tired; let me take this flock off your hands. Then you can take the money and retire, and relax and enjoy life."* The aged shepherd paused and considered for a moment, and looked up at the man with a smile, and said with conviction, *"I am retired; I haven't had to work a day my whole life."*
The man was puzzled by this, and said, *"But you have been tending sheep your whole life, and caring for their lambs since you were a boy!"* As the aged shepherd's mind drifted back across the years, he sighed contentedly, and answered, *"Right. I have indeed been very blessed in my life."*

7/27/12 **From The Lord, Our God and Savior**
The Word of The Lord Spoken to Timothy
For All Those Who Have Ears to Hear
The Pomp of the Nations Shall Cease

This question was asked: What does The Lord think about the Olympics, and professional sports in general?

Thus says The Lord: It is an abhorrence to Me. For the athletes, who, for a pretense, give thanks in My name, do always offend. For they have surely taken the name of The Lord in vain. For what part do I have in their achievements? What part do I have in their vanity? In their sin?!

And look upon these monstrosities, which man has built for the sake of greed. Look upon the vanity and pomp of all these deceitful nations, and tell Me, what do you see? They enlarge themselves, while the needy are made to live in obscurity; behold they flaunt freedom, yet oppress their own people from birth to the grave! Not one does good - NOT ONE! All have gone the way of Sodom, every one of them follows in the way of Cain! And all, from the least to the greatest, have blasphemed My holy name!

Therefore as I have spoken, I declare it once again:

Let the glory of man be turned backward,
Let every countenance fall and every heart fail,
Until the pride of man is bowed down
And the arrogance of man is utterly humiliated!...

Declares The Lord.

10/16/12 **From The Lord, Our God and Savior**
The Word of The Lord Spoken to Timothy
For All Those Who Have Ears to Hear
A Heavy Stone, a Bitter Burden

Thus says The Lord: The walls of Jerusalem are fallen! The high walls crumble and are broken down! The people are given into the hands of their enemies, those who murder without cause! Blood fills the streets as the women wail over the dead, pouring out drink offerings upon the ground! My people are taken captive, and those who walk free are surrounded on every side, with no place to flee! By two and by three, the enemies enter in through the cracks; in droves they gather outside the city, that they might break down the gates!... *Jerusalem, O Jerusalem, why have you forsaken Me?!*
Even to this day, O Israel, you have not ceased from walking in the ways of your forefathers, stoning My prophets in word and by deed, seeking always to kill or imprison those sent to you. Have I not gathered you with a mighty hand from among the nations, restoring you to your own land, even granting you great increase? Yet you do not embrace Me, for you yet push out the hand against My Holy One; you refuse to drink from His cup.
How long shall you seek to murder your King?! How long will you deny The Way I have set before you?! How long shall you blaspheme The Truth, which I sent into the world to testify?! YOU HAVE FORSAKEN LIFE! You refuse the blood I poured out for you!... *O Jerusalem, Jerusalem, how long will you let His blood drip from your fingers?!*

WASH YOURSELVES! MAKE YOURSELVES CLEAN!
For I tell you the truth, the stain of your guilt remains,
As you pass it from one generation to the next!...

Thus YOU fulfill the curse by which
Your forefathers had cursed themselves!...

YOU freed the murderer and condemned The Innocent!
YOU murdered The Author of Life and
Hung your Salvation upon a tree,
Piercing His hands and His feet!

Behold, even those who dwell among you, who are called Christian, do pollute My name and crucify Me again and again in their hearts, by all they say and do; a very perverse people, a corrupt religion which looks nothing like Me; churches of men who worship themselves and their own ideals as they proclaim a christ, an idol, which they have formed in their own image, continually reshaping it to meet their own expectations, that they might uphold their own traditions, which I hate!... *Jerusalem, O Jerusalem, why have you forsaken Me?!*

Your enemies dwell at the gates and have entered the city! Behold, they dwell upon the mount desecrating the land, bowing down five times per day to their god, a false image, a very grave error, for he is no god; a religion built upon the works of the evil one, acolytes who walk in his footsteps, bearing fruit according to his likeness; multitudes of deceived peoples, a whole nation of evil workers practicing that which satan delights in!

382

O sons of perdition, you have no place in My Holy Mountain! For you shall be utterly destroyed, when it falls hard upon you! You shall be wiped from off the land, your every temple torn down and burned with fire! I shall bring upon you a great slaughter! From city to city death shall pursue you, and fire shall lick at your heels as you attempt to flee! Says The Lord God of Israel.

And when the day comes, yea it has come and is here, O house of Israel, when your enemies band together and come out to fight against you with numbers beyond compare, a great multitude; every man fitted with weapons of death and slaughter, an astounding company with many machines of war, a terrible army the likes of which has never been seen... *Jerusalem, O Jerusalem, shall I also forsake you, and leave you to the slaughter?! Shall I now turn My back on you, and leave you to annihilation?! O Israel, shall I let you burn in the fire?!*

Shall I leave Jacob to be plowed like a field? Have I gathered you together in one place, only to let you be overcome by your enemies round about? For you have indeed sinned against Me and you forsake Me still. Thus I tell you plainly, behold I speak it to you once again, though you have no ears to hear - I AM THE LORD. And I have dealt with you for My own name's sake, and not according to your wicked ways, nor according to your corrupt doings, O house of Israel.

Therefore, with the backward swipe of My hand shall I scatter those who have drawn near to destroy you, and with the blast of My nostrils shall all their wings be broken off! My footsteps shall shake the earth and bring destruction upon all their devices! The heat of My anger shall come up into My face, causing a terrible fire to consume them! My voice shall speak into the air, and many shall be driven mad!

Behold, in My jealousy and in the fire of My wrath I shall speak, and brother shall turn against brother, and nature shall rise up and fight against them! For is this not the day spoken of by My prophets of old? Is this not the day I declared from the beginning, that it would come? Is this not the day I rise up and defend My people Israel, and cause My name to resound in all the earth?

Go now and read what has been written, read what the mouth of The Living God has spoken concerning all these things, and now read also that which I have spoken through My prophet of this day, and tremble in fear.

For indeed, Jerusalem has become
A heavy stone upon the necks of all nations,
Even as it weighs heavily upon Mine also...

Thus as I have spoken it, so shall it be:
All who seek to cast off this stone
Shall surely be cut in pieces...

Says The Lord God of Hosts.

1/27/12 **From YahuShua HaMashiach, Our Lord and Savior**
The Word of The Lord Spoken to Timothy During
Men's Fellowship, For All Those Who Have Ears to Hear
Without Condition

My sons, listen closely as I speak to you this parable: There were three men who devoted their lives to God, three men who sought to serve The Lord their God in righteousness. The first went out feeding the poor and the hungry, doing all he could for the needy, as he was able. The second gave everything he had to those who asked, with no thought to himself, until the day came when he had nothing more to give and he too had to ask. Yet the third did not go out, nor did he give to all who asked, but bowed down each day seeking the will of God, wanting always to walk in the ways of The Lord.

Years passed by, and the three men continued in their walks, serving God each day as they were able. Then the day came when each was presented with a new choice, one which they had not faced before.

To the first, The Lord sent a prophet, saying, *"Thus says The Lord: Draw back now your hand from the needy, and no more go out to feed the poor and the hungry round about, but obey the Word of My mouth and sound the trumpet."* But he refused and went away in unbelief, appalled by the Word he had heard by the mouth of the prophet.

The second man was faced with a similar choice; to him God sent the Word of The Lord in a book. Yet because it was not found in his Bible, the man immediately rejected it and went his way in unbelief, appalled by the Word which had been given him in the name of The Lord.

And to the third, The Lord Himself said, *"My son, the time has come for you to give up all you hold most dear, to give up your life for My purpose, to serve without constraint... To be greatly hated and persecuted for My name's sake."* And with tears streaming, the servant said, *"Yes, Lord."*

Therefore, My sons, I ask you, of these three men, which one was truly devoted to Me, though all did good and fruitful works? For indeed many are called, yet few are chosen, few have ears to hear. Thus learning the lesson of obedience is far greater than witnessing a prophecy come to pass, or receiving healing by a miracle. For obedience is born of love. For those who have no trust seek after signs, and those who remain in unbelief wait for miracles. And those whose requests are met, while in unbelief, will soon demand them. And those who receive a sign, yet have no trust, will only expect the more.

Yet only those who love Me,
Without condition, will remain faithful...

And only those who truly know Me
Will endure in times of trouble...

Says The Lord.

12/27/12 **From The Lord, Our God and Savior**
The Word of The Lord Spoken to Timothy
For All Those Who Have Ears to Hear
Fulfilled

Thus says The Lord: Behold, the time has come. It is time for great things to be shown in the heavens above and upon the earth beneath, for the flood gates to be opened and the storehouses emptied, for all that is hidden to be uncovered and that which slumbers to be awakened.

For it is written: *It shall come to pass in the last days, says The Lord, that I will pour out My spirit on all flesh, and your sons and your daughters shall prophesy, your old men shall dream dreams, your young men shall see visions. Also on My menservants and on My maidservants, I will pour out My spirit in those days. And I will show wonders in the heavens above and in the earth beneath, blood and fire and pillars of smoke. The sun shall be turned into darkness and the moon into blood, at the coming of the Great and Terrible Day of The Lord. And it shall come to pass that whoever calls on the name of The Lord shall be saved. For in Mount Zion and in Jerusalem there shall be deliverance, among the remnant whom The Lord shall call.* I tell you the truth, this Scripture is fulfilled, even now, as you read these words, and is also to come.

Therefore, listen to the sound of My voice; give heed to My speech, embrace My Word spoken to this generation, and repent. Beloved ones, find solace in My words and have peace, whether brought to remembrance by My spirit or read upon the pages of My Book. For I am come.

1/31/13 **From The Lord, Our God and Savior**
The Word of The Lord Spoken to Timothy
For All Those Who Have Ears to Hear
Desolations

Thus says The Lord: Behold, the waves of the sea shall be risen up in the day of My anger, and they shall crash upon the shore and ravage the banks. The waters shall be very tumultuous, and with an awful noise they shall break down the barriers and pass through, reaching far and wide. For I shall strike the westernmost parts, causing the hidden foundations to rise up suddenly, and with great violence shall they be thrust upward from beneath. And the people shall be greatly astonished on account of the waters and due to the devastation.

Behold, the day is coming and is very near, when I shall utterly devastate the coastlands and bring forth judgment, even upon the whole of this great and mighty nation. For they have not ceased from upholding their abominations, nor have they turned back from their ever-increasing perversions, nor have they put a stop to the slaughter of the innocent.

Yes, they continue in their evil ways,
Passing laws and allowing even all things which
I said they shall not do, provoking Me to anger!...

Therefore I shall indeed stretch out My hand against them,
And bring upon them desolations of every kind,
Until My wrath is satisfied and My anger has abated!...

Says The Lord.

The following Volumes are available at
TheVolumesofTruth.com
TrumpetCallofGodOnline.com
And **TrumpetCallofGod.com**
As free downloadable PDFs:

THE VOLUMES OF TRUTH:
VOLUMES ONE THROUGH SEVEN

A TESTAMENT AGAINST THE WORLD:
THE LORD'S REBUKE

WORDS TO LIVE BY AND THE BLESSED

FROM THE VOLUMES OF TRUTH:
A RETURN TO THE GARDEN

For printed copies, please visit:
lulu.com/spotlight/trumpetcallofgod

Be a Part of The Trumpet Call

THEVOLUMESOFTRUTH.COM

ANSWERSONLYGODCANGIVE.COM

TRUMPETCALLOFGODONLINE.COM

God calls us to spread His Word by all manner of speaking and devices. Therefore, trumpet this Word loudly. Trumpeting materials are available as a free downloadable PDF at: **trumpetcallofgod. com/pdfs/be_part.pdf**

If you accept The Volumes of Truth as the spoken Word of God, please share this gift with others. And to all those who help spread The Word, THANK YOU! Your contribution of time and effort is greatly appreciated.

Beloved, I delight in that which one gives to Another in My name, and by the works of their Own hands and feet in all righteousness; This is the tithe in which I delight most...

Says The Lord YahuShua.

Made in the USA
Coppell, TX
05 January 2023

10440175R00243